Diaspora without H

Diaspora without Homeland
Being Korean in Japan

EDITED BY SONIA RYANG AND JOHN LIE

Global, Area, and International Archive
University of California Press
BERKELEY   LOS ANGELES   LONDON

The Global, Area, and International Archive (GAIA) is an initiative of International and Area Studies, University of California, Berkeley, in partnership with the University of California Press, the California Digital Library, and international research programs across the UC system. GAIA volumes, which are published in both print and open-access digital editions, represent the best traditions of regional studies, reconfigured through fresh global, transnational, and thematic perspectives.

University of California Press, one of the most distinguished university presses in the United States, enriches lives around the world by advancing scholarship in the humanities, social sciences, and natural sciences. Its activities are supported by the UC Press Foundation and by philanthropic contributions from individuals and institutions. For more information, visit www.ucpress.edu.

University of California Press
Berkeley and Los Angeles, California

University of California Press, Ltd.
London, England

© 2009 by The Regents of the University of California

Library of Congress Cataloging-in-Publication Data

   Diaspora without homeland : being Korean in Japan / edited by Sonia Ryang and John Lie.
      p.   cm. (Global, area, and international archive ; 8)
   Includes bibliographical references and index.
   ISBN: 978-0-520-09863-3
   1. Koreans—Japan—Social conditions.   2. Japan—Ethnic relations.   3. Marginality, Social—Japan.   I. Ryang, Sonia.   II. Lie, John.
DS832.7.K6D53 2009
305.895'7052—dc22   2008045210

Manufactured in the United States of America

19 17 16 15 14 13 12 11 10 09
10 9 8 7 6 5 4 3 2 1

The paper used in this publication meets the minimum requirements of ANSI/NISO Z39.48–1992 (R 1997) *(Permanence of Paper).*

Contents

INTRODUCTION. BETWEEN THE NATIONS:
DIASPORA AND KOREANS IN JAPAN   1
Sonia Ryang

1. OCCUPATIONS OF KOREA AND JAPAN AND THE ORIGINS
   OF THE KOREAN DIASPORA IN JAPAN   21
   Mark E. Caprio and Yu Jia

2. FREEDOM AND HOMECOMING:
   NARRATIVES OF MIGRATION IN THE REPATRIATION
   OF *ZAINICHI* KOREANS TO NORTH KOREA   39
   Tessa Morris-Suzuki

3. VISIBLE AND VULNERABLE:
   THE PREDICAMENT OF KOREANS IN JAPAN   62
   Sonia Ryang

4. REINVENTING KOREAN ROOTS AND *ZAINICHI* ROUTES:
   THE INVISIBLE DIASPORA AMONG NATURALIZED
   JAPANESE OF KOREAN DESCENT   81
   Youngmi Lim

5. *PACCHIGI!* AND *GO*: REPRESENTING *ZAINICHI*
   IN RECENT CINEMA   107
   Ichiro Kuraishi

6. THE FOREIGNER CATEGORY FOR KOREANS IN JAPAN:
   OPPORTUNITIES AND CONSTRAINTS   121
   Chikako Kashiwazaki

7. THE POLITICS OF CONTINGENT CITIZENSHIP:
KOREAN POLITICAL ENGAGEMENT IN JAPAN
AND THE UNITED STATES 147
Erin Aeran Chung

8. THE END OF THE ROAD?
THE POST-*ZAINICHI* GENERATION 168
John Lie

Notes 181

References 199

Contributors 219

Index 221

Introduction: Between the Nations
Diaspora and Koreans in Japan
Sonia Ryang

How many Koreans are there in the world today? Answering this question would appear to be a relatively simple endeavor, considering that Korea is a small nation. Yet it quickly becomes complicated, involving the calculus not only of demography but of political allegiance, social affiliation, and cultural identity. Divided among North and South, the population of the Koreas today amounts to seventy-two million, or so the readily available statistics say. However, millions more Koreans live outside the Korean peninsula. According to one set of data, as of 1995 there were 4,938,345 Koreans residing permanently overseas, with 1,661,034 in the United States and 659,323 in Japan; other significant areas of concentration were China (two million) and the former Soviet Union, notably Kazakhstan (about 490,000). The 2004 U.S. census recorded 1,251,092 Koreans, while the 2004 statistics from Japan's Ministry of Justice documented 607,419 Koreans registered as aliens (Yau 2004, United States Bureau of the Census 2007, Japan Ministry of Justice 2004). Such figures shift fast, reflecting temporary or permanent repatriation, migration, immigration, naturalization, acquisition of residence, and other residential arrangements. Depending on the legal practices and demographic methods of the host nation, "Korean" in this context could mean either Korean ethnicity (while claiming citizenship of the host country) or actual Korean nationality (while being denationalized and stateless in one's country of birth).

The demographic map of Koreans residing outside of their homeland reveals the cartographic traces of colonialism, World War II, the Korean War, and the Cold War. Koreans in Japan in particular are marked as reminders of Japan's colonial rule of Korea and the ensuing wars that shaped the global Korean diaspora. Despite its global extent and visibility, however, the Korean diaspora in general (and in Japan in particular) is not a familiar subject of diaspora studies. Rather, Western scholarship on Koreans in Japan has dealt with them as Japan's foreign minority, as if to concur with the Japanese nation-state's official stance of monoethnicity. This volume fills the existing gap between Korean studies and diaspora studies by locating Koreans in Japan in current Western discourses of diaspora.[1]

By stating the above, however, I do not mean to conjure a crystal citadel of diaspora studies and beg for "Korea" to be included. Discourses of diaspora are themselves unstable, heterogeneous, and (I might even say) promiscuous, in continual intellectual intercourse with multiple partners. The tendency for discourses of diaspora to gravitate toward strong emotion on the one hand and objective theory on the other, to obsess over the past while envisioning a utopian future, to slide into hopeless pessimism and then to surface with euphoric optimism—these attest to their capacity for incorrigibly multiple engagements.

1

Existing models of diaspora, when set in extremes, can be divided into the "classical" and "cultural studies" models. The classical model, exemplified by the Jewish Diaspora, is premised upon original ethnic persecution as the cause of dispersal and loss of homeland. It is accompanied by a strong sense of connection to home (or homeland), the loss of which is suffered collectively by the dispersed population. This may manifest as collective memory, myth, nostalgia, desire to return, organized action or commitment to homecoming, efforts to preserve one's original culture and mythical heritage, insistence on difference from the hostland population, and so on. As such, classical diasporas often take a politicized, collective form. Ongoing ethnic persecution becomes an ontological precondition for diasporic community formation.[2]

The second model is concerned with life's insecurity and an ongoing crisis of identity, which, although generally associated with modernity and the rise of the reflexive self, in this case is specifically related to the loss of an original homeland (real or imaginary), which may be perceived either as part of the past or of contemporary experience. In this model, one's diasporic self-consciousness and self-appointment as a homeless, displaced, and dislocated subject are critical in identifying a diasporic form of life. As such, the cultural-studies model takes as the most decisive criterion for identifying diaspora to be an irreducible diasporic consciousness or state of mind.

If the first model emphasizes the phylogeny (or collective genesis) of diaspora, the second stresses ontogeny (or individual genesis). But the two models are not as far apart as they first might appear to be—they both reside on a conceptual base of home and home*land*. There are people in diaspora for whom original exodus is no longer significant. There are those who are still deeply injured by recent exile and banishment. Some diasporas are unable to trace their origins to one country, since they originate from various parts of an entire continent that is now divided into many nations. Other diasporas are the result of recent civil wars among newly formed nations. Yet others may be able to trace the routes of ancestral dispersion across various parts of the world, due to multiple persecutions and displacement. Refugees in camps may eventually form diasporic populations. Wars of invasion and conquest may make original inhabitants homeless in their own land. What all of these examples hold in common is that their tie to the homeland is cut off—with more or less pain, more or less violence.

Numbering a little fewer than 600,000 in total, multiple generations of Koreans with diverse legal and residential categories live in Japan today. The majority (about 460,000) holds the special permanent residence status available only to colonial immigrants and their descendants. The rest, it would appear, consist of recent immigrants from South Korea, who arrived in Japan following the South Korean government's lifting of regulations on overseas travels in 1988.[3] When we think about the first generation of Koreans in Japan, the generation that was uprooted from its homeland and displaced to the colonial metropolis, it would seem that we are talking precisely about a classical diaspora—especially when we remember that colonial-era Koreans reached not only Japan but also Manchuria, Russia, North and South America, and the Pacific Islands and Southeast Asia during the war, and that after the war their homeland was artificially partitioned, thereby further complicating any return. After this first generation, the picture becomes more complex. There are Japan-born generations whose home was nonexistent from the outset: they were born as strangers in a foreign land, a land that may have become their cultural and practical home, but was not their home*land*. The difference in diasporic ethos between different generations is prominent, although neither has ultimately recovered homeland even to this day. In other words, if the first generation set the phylogenetic mold for the Korean diaspora in Japan, the Japan-born generations were confronted with the *ontogeny* of diaspora. In both cases, the whereabouts of the homeland is an important, unanswered aspect of life.

This does not mean that I identify the origin of the Korean diaspora in the colonial period under the Japanese (1910–45). During this period Koreans frequently (more frequently than in the postcolonial period) traveled between Japan and Korea, looking for better job opportunities. It was after World War II and, more decisively, the Korean War (1950–53) that the Korean diaspora in Japan was firmly formed: with the partitioning of the Korean peninsula into two mutually antagonistic and noncommunicating regimes amid the intensifying tension of the Cold War, a major portion of the Korean diaspora was effectively incarcerated inside the Japanese archipelago. Indeed, I do not attempt to establish any clear-cut point of genesis for the Korean diaspora in Japan, since the question of diaspora is not simply about when people began leaving their homeland—it is also about how people begin to form a diasporic consciousness, a matter that does not easily allow for precise dating.

2

Let me be more concrete and start by asking, Who are these Koreans in Japan who appear under such diverse names as *zainichi* Koreans, Korean Japanese, or resident Koreans? When we turn to Japanese-language literature, their names multiply even further: *zainichi chōsenjin, zainichi kankokujin, zainichi kankoku chōsenjin, zainichi korian,* or simply *zainichi* or *korian* or, more recently, *ōrudo kamā* ("old-comers," i.e., old-timers, denoting former colonial immigrants and their descendants) and *nyū kamā* ("newcomers," denoting those who have arrived from South Korea since 1988). These names are not given innocently; each reflect attempts at escaping stereotypes and denying ethnic labels, while at the same time being trapped in the vicious circle of reinforced stereotypes and ethnic segregation. What does this multiplicity of names tell us? It is here that I would like to begin my inquiry into the historical background of the Korean diaspora in Japan.

Korea was placed formally under Japanese rule via the Government-General of Korea from 1910 to 1945. During the colonial period, the Japanese used various terms for Koreans, none very flattering. In late-nineteenth- and early-twentieth-century Japanese literature, Koreans often appear as *yobo. Yobo* comes from a Korean term of address that may be translated as "you"; in context, however, it unmistakably embodies an image of inferiority and impoverishment, recalling the Japanese onomatopoeia *yoboyobo* (old and shabby). Korea at the time of its colonial annexation was represented in Japanese public discourse in general and travel literature in particular as a deteriorated, dwindling, and corrupt kingdom, which could be saved only by the divine intervention of the Japanese emperor (Ryang 1997a).

Officially, Koreans entered Japanese documentation as *senjin*. Abbreviated from *chōsenjin,* with *chōsen* meaning "Korea" and *jin* meaning "person" or "people," *senjin* became an epitome of Japanese disdain for and belittlement of Korea and Koreans. Korean dissidents were referred to as *futeisenjin,* meaning "rebellious and incorrigible Koreans." A folk legend among Koreans has it that the Chinese ideograph *chō* of *chōsen* takes a character denoting morning and royal reign, among other things, and it is believed that because of this connotation of royalty (i.e., of the emperor), the Japanese authorities deliberately deleted *chō* from *chōsenjin*. Even the term itself was often censored in print, as if to denote the unlocatability of Koreans inside Japan's colonial empire, which was itself evolving in complex directions.[4]

Japanese colonial rule of Korea (as with any colonial relationship) did not involve simply the oppression and exclusion of Koreans. The situation of Koreans who had come to reside in Japan was much more ambiguous. For example, in 1925, when universal male suffrage was implemented in Japan, Korean men residing in Japan received the same privilege as Japanese men, as long as they were officially registered in local municipalities in Japan as residents (Matsuda 1995). The residential registry, or *kiryūbo* in the language of the day, was distinct from the household registry, or *koseki;* the latter stayed permanently in the place of origin—in the case of a Korean man, in his hometown in Korea—while the former had to be made at the actual location of residence—for a Korean man residing in Japan, in his residential town in Japan.

In 1939, as the military situation in China and the Pacific intensified, the Japanese authorities in Korea introduced household registry reform, which was designed to make Korean household registry identical with registry in Japan proper. The cosmological significance of this seemingly bureaucratic reform can be understood when we remember that since the Meiji Restoration (1868), *koseki* bore a double meaning: it was both an administrative means for head-counting to facilitate taxation and conscription, among other things, and a moral and ideological certification of the emperor's rule over an extended, countrywide household. The household head was assigned the task of ensuring and policing household members' loyalty to the emperor. Any transgression against emperor-focused moral, ethical, and political codes of conduct was supposed to be punished by the household head in the name of the emperor.

The Korean household registry, which had existed before the colonial takeover of Korea by Japan, carried an entirely different meaning and function: it was a record of homage to one's own lineage and clan. The clan ancestor, therefore, was at the apex of each Korean household registry. Unlike in Japan, Koreans did not have a concept of family-state with the sovereign as their national ancestor. On the contrary, Koreans worshipped clan ancestors and lineage origin [*pongwan*] and followed strict incest taboo prohibiting endogamy within the same clan, preserving the wife's maiden name after marriage as a proof of exogamy in the book of clan genealogy [*jokpo*]. Hence, in a Korean household registry, it was the norm to find two or three family names: the name of the household head, that of his wife, and in cases where the household head was the eldest son and living with his mother, the family name of the household head's mother.[5]

In the Japanese household registry, by contrast, each family name embodied one unit within the emperor's extended family and hence only one family name [*uji*], that of the household head, was entered; the wife took her husband's name. (In cases of son-in-law adoption, the heiress's last name would be the only name.) Accordingly, under the reform all Korean household registries were unified under one name, that of the household head. This reform, referred to in Japanese as *sōshikaimei* (creating the last name and reforming the first name), became decisive in changing the subject-position of Koreans in the empire, for this made them eligible to be enlisted in the emperor's army and to serve as civilian subordinates and sex slaves for the military (as did hundreds of women).[6] The reform, which became law in 1941, encouraged (but ultimately did not force) Koreans to adopt Japanese or Japanese-sounding names. Thus, under colonialism, Koreans came to experience double identity, manifested in the split between one's original Korean name (for the ancestor) and a newly created Japanese name (for the emperor).

3

The end of World War II found more than two million Koreans in Japan. As Mark Caprio and Yu Jia show in chapter 1, within a couple of years the number of Koreans remaining in Japan was drastically reduced; by 1948 only 600,000 or so Koreans were in Japan—they were to form the core of the diasporic Korean population in postwar Japan.[7]

With the end of the war, the nomenclature for Koreans was rearranged. Reflecting the first generation's contemporary assumption that all Koreans in Japan would be repatriated, Koreans called themselves *zairyū chōsenjin,* "Koreans remaining in Japan." This name contains a strong sense of temporary sojourn in Japan and was equally preferred by the U.S. Occupation and Japanese authorities, as they, too, assumed that all Koreans would disappear from reborn postwar Japan. *Senjin* was abolished; instead, the full enunciation of *chōsenjin* became common. And although the term *chōsenjin* semantically means "Korean," the name was by no means value-free. Its use in Japan for a long time (and in some ways even today) evoked strong insult, denigration, and dehumanization.

The postwar process by which Koreans were positioned in Japanese society was shockingly efficient—efficient in terms of total exclusion. (Although, as Kashiwazaki argues in chapter 6, this exclusion also entailed self-exclusion on the part of Koreans.) In 1947, all non-Japanese residents in Japan came to be subjected to alien registration (as opposed to residential registration). Koreans lost their residential registration and their records were transferred to the alien registration. One day before the proclamation of the new Japanese Constitution in 1947, the last decree of the emperor of Showa, *chokurei,* ruled that all Koreans in Japan were to lose their national affiliation to Japan. In 1949, in the first postwar application of the Prevention of Destruction Law, a Korean expatriate organization, the League of Koreans (Joryeon), was suppressed and its properties and cash savings confiscated. The League had been formed in October 1945 and rapidly veered toward support for North Korea; its major goals were the repatriation of all Koreans and teaching Korean to Korean children in Japan as part of their preparation for repatriation. (The Republic of Korea, or ROK, and the Democratic People's Republic of Korea, or DPRK, were both founded in 1948.) The League's numerous Korean schools were closed down under martial law in 1948, and it was suppressed the following year. In 1950, the Korean War broke out, splitting the Korean population in Japan into committed supporters of South Korea and North Korea, respectively. Finally 1952 came. With the signing of the San Francisco Peace Treaty, the *koseki* was used to rule who was Japanese and who was not; anyone whose *koseki* was found outside Japan proper [*naichi*] was deemed non-Japanese (see Pak 1989 for details).

Upon the signing of the San Francisco Peace Treaty, all of Japan's former colonies were freed from the colonial yoke, thereby freeing Japan itself from the burden of compensating Koreans and other former colonial subjects remaining in Japan and guaranteeing their human rights. As of 1952, neither the DPRK nor the ROK was recognized by Japan. This meant that Koreans in Japan had no home government as long as they lived in Japan. With the end of the Occupation and the return of sovereign power to the Japanese nation, former colonial subjects whose homeland was not recognized by Japan as a legitimate nation-state (this category included Korea and Taiwan) were rendered completely stateless. The Japanese government's immigration bureau is on record stating that neither *kankoku* (South Korea) nor *chōsen* (Korea, but commonly associated with North Korea)—terms that appear on the alien registration cards of Koreans in Japan—meant a nationality or the name of a state, since Japan did not recognize either (Ryang 1997b: 122).

At the same time, due to the continuing pronatalist population policy that had originally started in 1940 under the national eugenics law, Japan's population grew strongly until the late 1960s and early 1970s, obviating any need for immigrant workers. And as a defeated party in World War II, Japan did not face an influx of refugees. As a result, former colonial subjects—the majority of whom were Korean—were the only stateless persons in Japan until recently.

4

Koreans—as with any diasporic people—are divided, and their internal division has been a sharp, irreconcilable one, reflecting both the artificial partition of their homeland and the fratricidal civil war that impressed a finality on the expatriate community's split loyalties. With the emergence of the two antagonistic regimes, the very names of Koreans in Japan came to bear an unambiguous political identification. Divided between *chōsen* and *kankoku*, the former denoting simply "Korea" (not the name of any existing state) and the latter denoting the Republic of Korea (a state name), the terms of identification on the alien registration certificate became a fierce battleground for expatriate politics during the Cold War. Nevertheless, despite their sharp political and ideological divisions both expatriate groups stood on a firm assumption that Koreans in Japan were Japan's foreign minority, not a domestic minority, and whose home existed in Korea—the question was which regime they took to represent home.

For a long time and perhaps to some extent even today, North Korea regarded South Korea as a puppet regime of the United States and therefore "inauthentic," and vice versa. In official publications, each used brackets when denoting the other state's name, to demonstrate that the other was an impostor. Similarly, each had its own name to refer to the other, North Korea calling the south *konghwaguk nambanbu*, the "southern half of the DPRK," South Korea calling the north *pukhan*, the "northern ROK." In this sense, naming was closely tied to authenticity, with each state insisting on its exclusive truthfulness and legitimacy as the national home for all Koreans, while denying the other's existence as illusory and illegitimate.

Seen from the Japanese government's point of view, however, it did not matter either way. Because Japan had no formal diplomatic relations with either Korean government until 1965, whether a Korean person was *chōsenjin* or *kankokujin* made no difference: both names embodied, from the Japanese authorities' point of view, the same degree of statelessness, disenfranchisement, and unstable residential status.[8]

The situation changed dramatically in 1965. With the signing of the Japan-ROK treaty that year, South Korean nationality became an official national identification under Japanese law; furthermore, whoever opted for this nationality also gained permanent residence in Japan. Thus, the Cold War division now translated into a real difference between those Koreans in Japan supporting North Korea and those supporting the South, with the latter having access to residential stability, diplomatic protection, and overseas travel documents, and the former having no such things. So whereas *kankokujin* now denoted a real nationality, *chōsenjin* still simply stated that a person's ancestry existed on the Korean peninsula.[9]

After the 1965 treaty, the name *chōsen* came to denote North Korea somewhat exclusively. Even today, a widespread misunderstanding in Japan (and beyond) is that those who do not have South Korean nationality among Koreans in Japan have North Korean nationality, even though this could not possibly be the case, since North Korea does not grant its nationality to overseas Koreans except for cases such as North Korean diplomats. Technically speaking, there can be no North Koreans in Japan, for the Japanese government makes no diplomatic acknowledgment of North Korea. No office at any governmental level in North Korea possesses documentation or registration of any sort on Koreans in Japan, while no Korean living in Japan, regardless of political sympathy, exercises voting rights or any other form of civil and political participation in North Korean society.[10]

The self-referential nomenclature of the North Korea-supporting expatriates, *konghwaguk haewoe kongmin* (DPRK's overseas nationals), is not based on a legal foundation but is an ideological enunciation. As such, it is a typical example of self-image constructed in coordination with North Korea's official naming of overseas Koreans and in rejection of any association with the South Korean state. This itself is diaspora's unexpected twist, since more than 98 percent of first-generation Koreans in Japan came originally from the southern provinces.[11] It is only because of Korea's postwar partition, which was widely seen as merely temporary, that the majority of original southerners sided with the northern regime. The desire to recover an "authentic" homeland in this case translated into the choice of the North, as its leadership, embodied in the renowned thirty-two-year-old guerrilla fighter Kim Il Sung, was seen right after the war as genuinely anti-Japanese, as opposed to the southern regime under Syngman Rhee, an elderly returnee from the United States who was married to a foreign woman and possessed a Princeton Ph.D. But it also needs to be emphasized that as far as older generations were concerned, the strong belief in the temporary nature of Korea's partition lingered on; amid Cold War tension, their politically driven desire to be identified with homeland considerably clouded their self-understanding as a diasporic people (Lie 2000).

5

The polarization of the Cold War was destined eventually to weaken, not simply with the fall of the Eastern bloc at the end of the 1980s but also because of changing international relations between Japan and the two Koreas, as well as between the two Koreas themselves. At the same time, by the 1980s Koreans in Japan were no longer dominated by the first generation's homeland orientation. Demographically, the Japan-born generations became the majority, and the realization subsequently became widespread in the community that a Korean homeland was no longer readily attainable: Japan, like it or not, was their home. This was felt in diverse branches of everyday life. For example, marriage statistics show that from the mid-1970s on, Koreans became more likely to marry Japanese than other Koreans (Kim 1996: 179).

Today the predominant majority of Koreans in Japan marry Japanese. Most Korean children attend Japanese school, learning and speaking no Korean. Faith in either Korean regime has seriously declined. While the legal and civil disenfranchisement of Koreans in Japan remains unchanged, culturally Koreans in Japan are fully familiar with and fluent in Japanese social norms and conventions. One added factor since the late 1980s is a continuous, large-scale flow of South Koreans as migrant workers, overseas students, immigrants, and settlers. Compared to those "newcomers," preexisting Koreans in Japan stand culturally remote from today's South Korea.[12]

Already during the 1980s, with the increasing erosion of the North-South division among Koreans in Japan, the changing generational composition of the Korean population, and the increasingly likely prospect that Koreans would continue to live in Japan, talk of a "third way" began to be heard. Variously deployed and interpreted, this "third way" has different meanings, but typically it refers to an orientation that diverts focus from the homeland toward the conscious awareness of long-term Korean existence in Japan.[13]

More recently, as the association with either North or South has waned, the term *zainichi*, meaning "existing in Japan," has become common currency for representing Koreans in Japan. This name does not come without problems, in my view. To begin with, the term is parodic; it inverts the reality of the treatment of Koreans by the Japanese state. In this system, Koreans are treated as outsiders and their exclusion is justified on the basis that they do not have Japanese nationality. By calling them *zainichi*, as if they merely "exist" inside Japan, the name obscures their clear disenfranchisement. Although calling oneself *zainichi chōsenjin* or *zainichi kankokujin* no longer denotes exclusive association with either the northern or southern regime, the contours of *zainichi* life are becoming more complex and volatile. The parody name *zainichi* condenses this complexity: in spite of the diversity of names for Koreans in Japan, not one captures them properly. This in turn is implicated in the way the Korean diaspora in Japan is perpetuated in terms of its uncertainty and insecurity.[14]

In 1992, all Koreans in Japan who were legitimately able to trace their residential origin in Japan to the colonial period, and their descendants who were born and residing in Japan, were made special permanent residents, or *tokubetsu eijūsha*. This change was accompanied by diverse improvements in residential status, including lenient stipulations for deportation in felony cases. It should be emphasized that unlike U.S. permanent residency, which is seen as a bridge between foreign status and citizenship, special permanent residence in Japan has no such potential. It is a permanent fixture of life and under no circumstances is Japanese citizenship granted on its basis.

In the meantime, the ambiguity of national affiliation continues intact. Although those with South Korean nationality may have a South Korean passport, they do not have the resident registration number, the 13-digit ID, initiated about four decades ago, combining birth date, gender, the first registration region, and registration order (Kim T. 2005). This ID number is computerized and is required for everyday routines such as Internet registration. Unless one has a number that can be identified in the South Korean Information and Security Agency database, one is in practical terms not a South Korean national. Koreans in Japan who have South Korean nationality do not bear such a number and do not appear in the database. For this reason, if the South Korean passport carried by a Korean traveler from Japan expires abroad, a South Korean embassy in the given country cannot renew or reissue it.[15] Those with South Korean nationality in Japan are also exempt from military service and taxation; in exchange, they are ineligible to vote or stand for election. In other words, their South Korean "nationality" is, to say the least, incomplete.

In contrast, the minority of Koreans in Japan (roughly 5,000 today) who do not have South Korean nationality are stateless.[16] Rather than being recognized as stateless, however, in lay terms they are often regarded as "North Koreans." There is no North Korean nationality recognized at any level of Japan's legal and juridical establishment, as I have mentioned. Yet the Cold War ideology by which "not South Korean" automatically equals "North Korean" lingers on, especially in the current global climate of U.S.-led demonization of North Korea. In Japan, this climate has triggered anti–North Korean abuse and violence against those who lack South Korean nationality and/or who are affiliated with the North Korea–supporting expatriate organization, the General Association of Korean Residents in Japan, or Chongryun in its Korean abbreviation (see Ryang 1997b on Chongryun). As my own chapter 3 in this volume shows, after the September 17, 2002, revelation that North Korean agents had secretly kidnapped a total of thirteen innocent Japanese from Japan's shores during the 1970s and 1980s, Koreans in this category were made extremely vulnerable.

6

One of the influential works of Fukuoka Yasunori, a pioneer scholar among Japanese sociologists of Koreans in Japan, is entitled *Hontō no watashi o motomete*, which may be translated as "in search of the true self" (Fukuoka and Tsujiyama 1994; see Fukuoka 2000 also). The assumption here is that Koreans' true self can only be expressed through a "real name," or *honmyō*—that is, a Korean name. The issue of *honmyō* has served as a stage for one of the fiercest debates on the identity politics of Koreans in Japan. Even today, a great degree of scholarly attention in Japan is placed on the role names play in personal identification and the assertion of ethnicity.[17]

Against *honmyō* there is one's *tsūmei*, or "passing" (or Japanese) name. Normally, *tsūmei* was inherited from the colonial legacy of *sōshikaimei* (described above). Often Korean students who attend Japanese school use *tsūmei* at school, which successfully buries their Korean identity, because— among many other factors—phenotypically, Koreans and Japanese are identical. In the 1970s and 1980s, left-leaning Japanese teachers, motivated by desire to help Korean children in Japanese schools come to terms with their ethnic heritage, began encouraging young children to take up their *honmyō*. Often marked by a ceremonial declaration in front of the entire class, called *honmyōsengen* (declaration of one's true name), children participated in a dramatic "coming out" ritual that was intended to enable them to be true to themselves.

This well-intentioned intervention did not come without repercussions, however. Particularly with younger children, whose primary motivation might well have been to please a teacher they adored, the controversy is obvious. Furthermore, the Korean name the child declared to be hers or his was often foreign and completely new to her or him. More seriously, the burden of ethnic identity, the vulnerability of revelation, and the discomfort of rebirth were borne solely by the child (Hamamoto 1995). Children who went through *honmyōsengen* were suddenly told that the culture, language, and environment that they thought they were entitled to by birthright were not theirs, that they were strangers and guests in the place they were born in and grew up believing to be their home, and that they had to find their homeland someplace else. Certainly it made children enormously vulnerable and in some measure traumatized them. The issue of *honmyōsengen* calls our attention to the conditions that surround the act of diasporic identification. Unless the environment guarantees at a minimum the security of the person who is identifying him- or herself as a member of the marginalized, ostracized, and depreciated group, the act itself risks endangering and victimizing the identifying person. After all, what *is* the true self of a diasporic subject? Is there such a thing? Is the use of *honmyō*—the name under which one is registered in the alien registration, the apparatus with which the Japanese state controls Koreans—an identification of one's true self (as implied by Fukuoka and many other Japanese researchers), or is it in effect a submission to state authority?

Regardless, the use of *honmyō*, or indeed in this case the recovery of *honmyō*, became crucial for naturalized individuals with Korean heritage in Japan. But according to Chikako Kashiwazaki, who interacted with naturalized Koreans belonging to two different groups, *Minzokumei o torimodosu kai* (Association for Reclaiming Ethnic Names) and *Paramu no kai* (Wind Society), even within these groups there were differences about which name was most truthful and authentic in its expression of ethnic and personal identity (Kashiwazaki 2000b). Nevertheless, as Youngmi Lim argues in chapter 4, the issue of naming continues to bear significance especially among ethnic Koreans who were naturalized as Japanese.

Until roughly the 1980s, Japanese immigration officers would demand that the applicant for naturalization adopt a Japanese-sounding or Japanese-style name as opposed to a Korean name. It was reminiscent of colonial household registration reform and played an effective role in augmenting the negative connotation associated with naturalization (Kashiwazaki 2000a). Moreover, it would be more than simplistic to unproblematically group naturalized (former) Korean persons as Koreans in Japan, when their citizenship is truly Japanese. Nonetheless, it is undoubtedly true that they are placed in an ambiguous position with respect to both the Japanese mainstream and Korean communities due to the Japanese state's fundamental philosophy of equating the nation with a singular ethnicity. By the same token, and I think it is important to reiterate this, the South Korean nationality possessed by the majority of Koreans in Japan does not extend full rights of South Korean citizenship. And, needless to say, those Koreans in Japan that do not have South Korean nationality are more precarious still.

It is all very well to condemn passing names as the legacy of colonialism. But as long as there exists strong discrimination against Koreans in Japan—whose mark is most clearly discerned by name rather than skin color or accent, for example—the use of a name is no simple matter. When a subject prefers a particular name—no matter how compromising such a deployment may be in the eyes of the nationalist orthodoxy—how can others (ethnic community leaders, teachers, parents, or even the nation-state or history) force them to use another name? Whether a Korean name is *honmyō* for an individual is not a given, since otherwise it would be tantamount to assuming that one's alien registration name has to be one's real name. After all, who decides which name is true to the person? The law? the community? parents? teachers? or the person herself? Rather than assuming that the "true self" exists in "true Korean names," we should withhold conclusions about the authenticity of names. There is no one-to-one correspondence between one's Korean name and one's ethnic identity, precisely because of the double (or multiple) agency inherent in the ontology of diaspora: diaspora is an ongoing search for self and as such, the journey of self-creation knows no end.

7

What does the foregoing tell us about the Korean diaspora in Japan? It has been documented abundantly—and not only in the present context—that diasporic peoples end up having more than one name, speaking more than one language, imitating different accents, and acting "native" in more than one culture. They are forced to do so in order to acclimate to host environments or to raise children in many strange lands. If this is the basic form of life for a diasporic people, where can we possibly find authenticity? Is there, again, such a thing as an authentic diasporic subject? The quest has gone on forever and will continue to go on, precisely because of the nature of diaspora as a form of life—as one endless search for authenticity. The unresolved saga of *tsūmei* and *honmyō* is telling in this sense. In other words, diasporic authenticity can exist only in the plural. But what does this do to diasporic individuals?

In a way, (singular) authenticity is a luxury that only people with a secure homeland can afford (see Radhakrishnan 1994). Born in one's own homeland, the land where one's parents, grandparents, great-grandparents, and ancestors were born, raised as an unequivocal member of the community, fully franchised and entitled, with rights so validated and solid that their existence is not even consciously blessed—people who have a homeland can afford to have one and only one name, one personhood, which they can deem true. Their travels are safe and secure and never one-way, for they have a home to come back to. They can remain themselves no matter where they go. No departure is definitive, no loss permanent, no parting forever, no death strayed, for they know they have a secure home in this life or the next.

People without homeland by contrast are forever in exile, wandering, in search of home, land, and security. Death is near, or at least so it feels, for they do not know who they are and where to live and die—by using this name or another, by speaking more than one language depending on the need, they exist as sojourners, foreigners, outsiders, outlanders, and therefore intruders, polluters, unwanted guests, unrecorded populations, people without papers, people who do not belong in the dominant political order. During the colonial era, the poet Cho Ki-Cheon sang of Koreans leaving their hometowns for northeastern China: "*Salaseo kalkot eopko, jugeoseo mutchilkot eomneun . . . muleopoja tongpoyeo, muleopoja tongpoyeo . . .* " (Let me ask you, my fellow countrymen, let me ask you. Where would you go live in this world? Where would you be buried when dead?).

National belonging is usually the prerequisite for being human in today's world, divided along nation-state borders: it is a life's national status that matters. When an international flight crashes, nations rush to find out which of their own were on the casualty list, as if it doesn't matter whether anyone else lives or dies. From another perspective, the recent debate in the United States on eavesdropping by the National Security

Agency was clearly marked along domestic-national and international lines, as if to say as long as phone-tapping involved international lines, no human rights were violated.[18]

The history of Koreans in Japan testifies to the tight linkage of rights and citizenship. Only when they were given an option for a (South Korean) nationality did they win basic human rights (such as residency) in Japan (in 1965); when they were located outside the national-imperial order (in 1948 and 1949) they suffered persecution under martial law. When they were seen as part of the imperial mother nation, their treatment generated a complex yet logical rationale: for example, they gained the right to vote (in 1925) and equal "entitlement" to fight, serve (including sexual service), and die for the emperor (during World War II). When their tie with Japan as a nation was severed, their basic human rights were eliminated.

Many researchers on Koreans in Japan, especially those with a political conscience and passion for justice, argue that Koreans in Japan are treated like subhumans, like second-class citizens, and are discriminated against inside Japanese society. On the basis of the foregoing, however, I suggest that they are not in fact discriminated against *inside* Japanese society, since they are actually *outside* Japanese society. They are not subhuman but merely and nakedly human, lacking the protections that full national incorporation provides. Furthermore, to argue that they are treated like second-class citizens would be missing the point, since they are not citizens of Japan in any capacity whatsoever.

8

Where do the preceding inquiries lead us? The contributors to this volume open up multiple windows for debate and discussion. Their chapters show that, despite (or perhaps because of) the unsettling proximity of diaspora to death, there are many ways to *live* diaspora meaningfully and strenuously.

Mark Caprio and Yu Jia and Tessa Morris-Suzuki, in their respective essays, consider two significant moments of return for Koreans in Japan. Caprio and Jia's chapter is a reminder that the Korean diaspora in Japan was created by tumultuous international politics in postwar East Asia, involving not only U.S. occupations of both Japan and South Korea, but also prejudice held by the Japanese toward Koreans and by peninsular Koreans toward Korean returnees. Koreans in Japan were not simply a forgotten people within the scope of postwar U.S. policies in Asia, but also a population unwelcomed by fellow Koreans in Korea itself, due in part to the postcolonial eruption of anti-Japanese sentiment that regarded returnees with suspicion of having been tainted by the Japanese. The lack of preparedness on the part of the U.S. Occupation forces in both Japan and Korea also played no small part in creating the postwar Korean diaspora. In this way, the authors argue, the Korean diaspora in Japan is as much a product of colonialism as (if not more) a creation of postwar international politics.

Morris-Suzuki's chapter, which is a tour de force of both archival research and historiographical interpretation, reveals the role played by the Japanese government and the International Committee for the Red Cross in the 1959 opening of the repatriation of Koreans from Japan to North Korea. The repatriation of Koreans from Japan to North Korea itself is an anomalous event, considering, as we have seen, that most first-generation Koreans in Japan came originally from the southern part of the peninsula. In a political stunt to outdo South Korea, which was continuously having difficulty reaching an agreement over postwar settlement with Japan, North Korea opened the repatriation route for Koreans in Japan. It was for a long time understood as North Korea's conspiracy to recruit cheap labor from Japan in the aftermath of the devastating Korean War, glossed over with overheated rhetoric and propaganda. Morris-Suzuki sheds a completely different light on the repatriation by using hitherto classified documents and incorporating interviews with individuals whose lives were directly implicated in this process (including one person who made a difficult U-turn from North Korea back to Japan), clarifying the role played by other parties, including the Japanese government and the ICRC. At the same time, she humanizes those Koreans who took the option of moving to North Korea, not necessarily or primarily because of their ideological commitment to the socialist regime, but because of other, more "close-to-home" factors such as poverty, unemployment, and worries about their children's future.[19]

Youngmi Lim, Ichiro Kuraishi, and I turn toward the introspective investigation of Korean diasporic lives in Japan. I inquire into the recent transformation inside a North Korea–supporting faction of Koreans in Japan, following revelations that Japanese citizens were kidnapped by North Korean agents during the 1970s and 1980s. This community has been made hypervisible and, accordingly and paradoxically, extremely vulnerable after North Korea confessed to its past vices, and there have been numerous assaults on female students attending North Korea–sympathetic schools. I address persistent anti-Korean elements in Japan's public decision-making echelons, which are intolerant of difference beyond the pale of their brand of multiculturalism. As such, in Japan's rhetoric of self-victimization since the revelation of the kidnappings, an undeclared political war against Koreans in Japan has already started. My chapter is thus as much about Koreans, their cultural representations, and identifications, as it is about Japanese society itself as a receptacle for diasporic community.

Youngmi Lim, taking up a different kind of visibility, the "colorless color line" among *zainichi* Koreans as well as Japanese, explores everyday identity politics as practiced by Korean individuals who have taken Japanese nationality. Whereas existing studies of Koreans in Japan have relied heavily on the organized structure and network of pro-North, pro-South, or some other ideology, Lim focuses on the intricacies of naturalized Koreans' personal lives, whose basis is firmly rooted in Japan and necessitates no particular political commitment, yet requires daily micro-level decisions to come to terms with a complex existence. This focus is not only illuminating but also highly effective in furthering our understanding of the rapidly shifting contours of Korean diaspora in Japan. Lim shows that diaspora is not simply an organized political movement but can exist among individuals, atomized and mutually isolated, even though scholars of diaspora have not yet captured this middle ground. This problem emerges acutely with the Korean diaspora in Japan, because, as we have seen, Koreans who became naturalized as Japanese have no possibility of adopting a hyphenated identity (as would be possible in the United States), either legally or socially. Thus, Lim's chapter enables us to think about a form of citizenship that is not easily separated from ethnicity or race, and its implications for a diasporic community, especially when diasporic persons do not "belong" to that community politically, actively, or self-consciously.

Kuraishi presents recent examples of self-representation and self-projection by Koreans in Japan from film. By unfolding the excess of exoticism and stereotyping of Korea, the unknown, as captured by both Japanese and Korean producers of successful and popular films in contemporary Japan, *Pacchigi!* (Head-butt) and *Go,* Kuraishi explores the interrelation between Japanese popular culture and the commercialization of ethnic politics. We are made to wonder how a diasporic minority can (or cannot) take control of its own destiny, cultural image, and reality, amid the high waves of capitalist modernity and materialistic desires to render almost any aspect of human life into exchangeable currency.

Chikako Kashiwazaki's chapter lays bare the recent structural changes in Japan regarding the treatment and positionality of Koreans in Japan, while tracing how foreignness has been strategically deployed by resident Koreans in Japan in the 1940s and in more recent decades. In addition to giving a statistical update on the internal constitution of Japan's ethnic minority population, she highlights the activities of grassroots organizations of Koreans in Japan along with their Japanese supporters, who demand recognition for their social and political participation in Japanese society as the rights of foreign residents, or *teijū gaikokujin*. Kashiwazaki explicates the complex workings of local politics and the projection of ethnic identity with conscious reference to globalization.

Erin Chung's chapter, with its wealth of data and information, is a rare and valuable contribution not only to this volume but also to studies of the Korean diaspora across the world: Chung compares Korean communities in Japan and the United States, an endeavor that has not been taken up by scholars of diaspora. Attending to the striking difference between these communities' origin, history, political organizations, and homeland orientation, Chung asks how the notion of citizenship has constituted and been appropriated and deployed by these communities in varying, yet closely comparable ways. This pioneering act of comparison delivers an extremely complex picture of two different yet parallel diasporic communities. Both Kashiwazaki's and Chung's chapters form powerful pillars to support and supplement the historical insights of Caprio and Jia and Morris-Suzuki, which can be in turn read against the ethnographic and cultural analyses presented in Lim's, Kuraishi's, and my own chapters.

Concluding the volume, John Lie writes of the recent debate—a fierce debate—among *zainichi* intellectuals revolving around concepts of identity and diaspora, with a focus on the work of Kang Sang-jung and Tei Taikin. Lie also alludes to the uncertain future of the Korean diaspora in Japan, appropriate for a closing of a book like this one, which is necessarily left open.

No doubt, studies of the Korean diaspora in Japan and elsewhere will continue, expand, and be strengthened because of their relevance within a global modernity subtended by the shadows of diasporic realities. I simply hope this volume will at least set the stage in part for such studies. By no means should it be read as presenting a unified vision of what diaspora is and means. Far from it: the contributors here respectfully disagree on such concepts as citizenship, identity, and diaspora itself. As with any scholarship that aspires for discursive openness and candor of exchange, this volume refrains from artificially forcing unity upon the concepts, views, and positions taken by its authors. As such, the volume's strongest intervention, I hope, would be to open up a broader dialogue on the Korean diaspora.

We do not know when or whether diaspora will ever be resolved, either historically or contemporaneously speaking, as a form of life. One intuitively expects that the dispersion and displacement of people from their original homes will continue as long as the world is built upon its segmentation along national borders. The Korean diaspora in Japan is a witness to the predicament of the world's current congregation of nation-states, for diasporic people's peculiar statelessness, the bareness of their lives, keep the fundamental questions of the rights of humanity unanswered.

1. Occupations of Korea and Japan and the Origins of the Korean Diaspora in Japan

Mark E. Caprio and Yu Jia

The announcement on August 15, 1945, by the Japanese emperor declaring Japan's intention to accept the Allied forces' terms of unconditional surrender sent Koreans throughout the empire into the streets in celebration. For the first time in decades they could freely associate with their fellow countrymen, communicate in their language, and wave their national flag [*taegeukgi*] as Koreans without fear of punishment.[1] The United States estimated that three to four million Koreans resided overseas at this time. Korean communities could be found throughout the eastern part of the Asian continent (including the Russian Far East), as well as in other parts of the Japanese Empire including the Dutch East Indies, Hong Kong, the Philippines, the South Pacific, and Taiwan. The island of Sakhalin also hosted a significant number of Koreans, as did Australia and Hawai'i. The majority of overseas Koreans resided in Japan and Manchuria: the U.S. Joint Intelligence Study estimated that there existed 1.45 million Koreans in Japan and 1.475 in Manchuria (United States Joint Intelligence Study Publishing Board 1992: 271).[2]

Liberation encouraged many overseas Koreans to return to their ancestral homeland. Within a year after the war's end the population of southern Korea increased by an estimated 22 percent, or slightly fewer than 3.5 million, a figure that included repatriated Koreans, 510,000 refugees from the North, and 700,000 births over this period ("Report on the Occupation Area" 1992: 488). Not all Koreans returned. Postwar political and economic circumstances discouraged an estimated 600,000 Koreans in Japan from repatriating. An indeterminable number of Koreans smuggled their way back into Japan after returning to Korea. The task of this chapter is to examine the factors that influenced the creation of a Korean diaspora in Japan during the postwar occupations of Japan (1945–52) and southern Korea (1945–48) by the United States.[3]

PREPARATIONS FOR KOREAN REPATRIATION

The Che family did not wait for liberation to repatriate. As the battles ravaging East Asia approached the Japanese archipelago, municipal agencies began advising urbanites to vacate to rural environments. Authorities also urged residents from the colonies to return to their homelands. Sunny Che's father, a medical doctor with a private practice in Nagoya, decided to heed this advice and moved his family to Korea in March 1944, exactly one year before the United States began firebombing Japan's major cities. Dr. Che's foresight benefited his family in a number of ways. First, it allowed the Ches to return with most of their belongings. They were able to send to Korea those belongings that they could not carry with them—enough to occupy three workers with three weeks of packing. The family also did not have to compete with other Korean returnees for housing and other basic necessities. Prior to their arrival, relatives secured for them a large house—the biggest in the neighborhood—that recently had been abandoned by a Japanese family (Che 2000: chap.18).

These advantages were not available to others who repatriated after liberation. Koreans remaining in Japan, entangled in postwar confusion, found it challenging to secure basic essentials such as food, housing, and employment. Added complications arose from the ill-prepared Occupation forces that arrived in both Japan and southern Korea. Repatriated Koreans discovered a situation in Korea even more troubling than what they left in Japan. Despite its inhospitable environment, Japan at least offered the option of continuing a semblance of the lives they had built since crossing over. Many of those who returned to the Korean peninsula arrived with little, if any, economic, social, or even cultural foundation upon which to start new lives.

The Allied powers formally addressed the issue of Korean independence for the first time in December 1943 in Cairo, where the United States, Great Britain, and China signed a communiqué. The three signatories, and later the Soviet Union, recognized that Japan would forfeit its control over the Korean peninsula. They also agreed to delay Korean independence by adding the often-quoted phrase, "in due course Korea shall become free and independent." The declaration that Japan would eventually lose possession of the Korean peninsula marked an important clarification by the Allied forces on the issue of Korea's postwar status. Debate over whether Japan would be allowed to retain its colonies continued until the end of the war. Both during and after the U.S. Occupation of Japan, some American and Japanese officials believed it was a mistake to separate Japan and Korea.

By delaying Korean independence and dividing the peninsula geographically and then politically, the Allies seriously complicated overseas Korean repatriation in the postliberation period. Their failure to rectify this injustice solidified the Korean diaspora in Japan. Specifically, those Japan-based Koreans suspected of even remote connections with the communist North risked imprisonment, torture, and possible death if they attempted to return to southern Korea, the ancestral home for the vast majority of this population (98 percent of first-generation Koreans in Japan; Ryang 2005a: xvi).

The U.S. government began to prepare for Korea's postwar occupation even before it met with the British and Chinese in Cairo. One of the first preparatory reports to be compiled, the "Survey of Korea," offered a broad sketch of the Korean people and the Korean peninsula. This June 1943 report distinguished Korean ethnicity as separate from that of other Asian peoples: "The Korean is racially distinct from both the Japanese and the Chinese, although he has some ancestry in common with both. In both physical and psychological characteristics he is much closer to the white peoples than either of his neighbors, and some anthropologists believe that the prehistoric Korean racial strain was very largely Caucasian, and probably Tajik in origin" (United States Military Intelligence Service 1992: 25).

One page of this study arranged pictures of Asian eyes to help officials distinguish Koreans from Japanese, as well as from Filipinos and other Asian peoples (United States Military Intelligence Service 1992: 27). One purpose for drawing these racialized distinctions (as erroneous as they are) might have been connected to U.S. interest in using Koreans in the war effort against the Japanese. One year later the U.S. State, War, and Navy departments collaborated to compile a joint report that reviewed efforts made to exploit this potential, with suggestions ranging from employing Korean independence groups for espionage or sabotage missions to organizing Korean POWs into a battalion under the Korean flag (McCarthy, Richardson, and Cox 1992). These attempts failed and the postwar image of Koreans remained that of a people against whom the Allies had battled, rather than an ally.[4]

Korean POWs who had fought in the Japanese army and other undisclosed informants provided the United States with information for policy reports designed to facilitate the postwar administration of the Korean peninsula. Interrogators primarily focused on two points: finding out about the Japanese-Korean relationship and determining Korea's postwar leaders. Questions were raised: Should the Occupation administration in Korea quarantine Korea-based Japanese to protect them from revenge-seeking Koreans? Who might the Korean people support as future leaders of their country? Interrogators also attempted to test Korean loyalties. Korean responses helped U.S. officials determine whether these POWs could be used in its war efforts, but a more important issue was whether they should regard the Korean people as friend or foe. The answers to this question also enlightened U.S. officials on how the Korean peninsula could be administered, as well as how Japan-based Koreans might be treated following Korea's liberation.

Kim Chengnei, a POW who was described as "very intelligent and cooperative," provided his interrogator from the Office of Strategic Services with important information on Japanese-Korean relations on the peninsula. Kim explained that he was "forced to 'volunteer'" for the Japanese military just before his scheduled graduation from Joseon Christian College (now Yonsei University). When asked for his impressions of Korean attitudes toward the Japanese, he responded that Koreans working for the Japanese police were hated by nearly all Koreans; other Koreans employed by the Japanese bureaucracy were "just making a living so other Koreans do not think ill of them." Kim separated pro- from anti-Japanese Koreans by their level of intelligence: he believed that Japanese propaganda had a greater effect on those with less education (Yi 1992: 318–322).

Interrogators were also concerned about the safety of Korea-based Japanese. Would the Korean people seek revenge after liberation? Underlying their questions were two possible scenarios: the quick repatriation of Japanese after the war to protect them from Koreans, or delaying the repatriation of key technicians and officials to help train their Korean replacements. Not surprisingly, interrogated Koreans expressed hatred toward the Japanese and the belief that this sentiment was shared by a majority of their fellow Koreans. Most did not predict revenge attacks on Japanese expatriates. One unnamed informant, however, believed that Koreans would seek retribution through violence: "Nearly all Koreans would take the first chance to massacre Japanese civilians. So many Koreans have been killed by the Japanese that the population would be eager for revenge" (Yi 1992: 174–179).[5]

A second line of questioning addressed the role of overseas Koreans in the future administration of the Korean peninsula. Would, for example, any of the exiled members of the Korean Provisional Government, established in Shanghai in 1919, gain support among the Korean people? One informant correctly predicted that while "inside [domestic] Koreans" were familiar with the Provisional Government, it was "unlikely [that] Koreans in Korea would either welcome or cooperate with" members of this body, even if it were to gain United Nations support. This informant expressed "indifference" toward the "outside [international] Koreans": The Korean people feel that they "left their country not for patriotic reasons but in order to get an easier living, to get sympathy, admiration and financial support from the people of the United States" (Yi 1992: 191).

Kim Chengnei separated those Koreans who left Korea before 1937 from those who left after simply to seek fortune. He considered the overseas Koreans inappropriate for leadership positions owing to their insufficient knowledge of Korea's present conditions. Thus, Koreans repatriating from either the Soviet Union or the United States should not assume a central role in postliberation administration or economic development (Yi 1992: 326). This belief was echoed by the anonymous informant cited above: "the very training of most of the Outside Koreans . . . would make them unfit for leading positions." Korea's postliberation leaders, he added, should be "men on the spot, who are well known to and have the confidence of the inside Koreans" (Yi 1992: 191–193).

The POW Fukuyama Masakichi, a Korean national referred to by his Japanized name, commented generally on repatriation, remarking that "all exiled Koreans would be gladly welcomed by the Koreans." The Korean people, he added, held the exiled leaders in high esteem, as there was a dearth of people in Korea with great leadership ability. Fukuyama predicted that he would favor the outside Korean over the inside Korean should all else prove equal. The exception was the Japan-based Korean. While most Koreans would accept them, he felt that they should not be offered positions of high responsibility (Yi 1992: 316).

Loyalty was also central to Kim Chengnei's distinction (which we have already mentioned) between educated and less-educated Koreans repatriated from Japan. In evaluating their usefulness to postliberation Korea, Kim stated that "Koreans who lived in Japan for a number of years as laborers or business men are most likely to be imbued with the Japanese ideas." Educated Koreans, by contrast, were not so likely to be inculcated and thus would be less pro-Japanese. He also cited individuals' activities in Japan as an important determinant of how they would be received upon their return. Those who acted without suspicion would more likely be accepted by Koreans (Yi 1992: 328).

Interview data were cited in a number of reports compiled by U.S. officials before the war's end. The first, "Korea's Capacity for Independence, Historical Background," was drafted in late January 1945. The question assumed in the report's title was critical, as the duration of the Korean Occupation had yet to be determined, with one estimate projecting it to last as long as that endured by the Filipino people—half a century. This report recognized the Korean capacity for self-government, declaring that "self-government is a matter of opportunity and experience, and there is no valid reason to suppose that the Koreans would be less capable than other Asiatic people if they were once provided with the proper environment." The compiler's conclusions on the role of the Korean Provisional Government reflected those offered by the informants: it could not be recognized unless there existed evidence of popular support. This report makes no mention of the part to be played by repatriated Koreans in rebuilding postliberation Korea (Research Department, U.S. Foreign Office 1992: 213–216).

Informants also forewarned the U.S. occupiers of the dire living conditions that Koreans faced. One Korean deserter from the Japanese military reported that people aged 20–40 years received a monthly ration of mixed rice, beans, and millet of only 2 *go* 3 *shaku* (roughly 14 ounces; 1 *go* = 0.381 pints, 1 *shaku* = 0.038 pints), a concoction sufficient to last but 15–20 days. People of other age groups received less. Fish was rationed when available; vegetables were "scarce." Many farmers preferred to exchange their harvest for clothing and other essentials on the black market—which paid up to ten times the market price—over selling it at established markets (Yi 1992: 235). Were these conditions to continue into a postliberation occupation, the United States could hardly expect their efforts to yield success. One informant stated: "Without assurance of food supplies, employment, and a reasonable standard of public health, the most attractive and conscientiously planned system of democratic government would be an empty shell. The Koreans would be disillusioned and would lose faith in the United Nations" (Yi 1992: 193). This warning proved to be prophetic; from the outset the U.S. Military Government in South Korea faced the predicament of improving Koreans' standard of living, and it continued to fail at this challenge throughout the Occupation.

A second report, "Aliens in Japan," prepared by the Office of Strategic Services (later the CIA), represented the most complete assessment of Japan's foreign population and the first serious attempt to coordinate postwar Occupation policy and foreigners' future political status. Issued in late June 1945, this comprehensive report traced the history of migration by Koreans to Japan, described their living conditions, and proposed policy to direct their repatriation or future status should they remain in Japan (United States Office of Strategic Services 1945: 14). Understandably, it devoted far more attention to the Korean population, which comprised the majority (90 percent) of Japan's total foreign population, than it did to other non-Japanese populations.

The report did note that Koreans had been crossing between peninsula and archipelago since the beginning of Japanese rule. Most traveled to Japan with the idea of returning eventually. Between 1917 and 1940 the total number of Koreans returning to Korea was 75 percent greater than those going to Japan. It further suggested that many Koreans entered Japan illegally, a problem to which Japanese officials responded by establishing a campaign, "Stop Smuggling Week," complete with posters and advertisements. It estimated that by 1940, about 200,000 Koreans had illegally entered Japan. Strapped for labor by wartime conditions, in March 1945 the Japanese government lifted all restraints on Korean immigration, causing a sharp rise in the Japan-based Korean population, which soon grew to more than two million people.

"Aliens in Japan" painted the Korean-Japanese relationship in rather negative terms. The Korean people lived apart from the Japanese and were unwilling to assimilate. It listed two reasons for this situation: first, the Japanese discouraged Korean assimilation, and second, the Japan-based Korean, "in the main, very poor, uneducated, and unskilled, even by low Korean standards," was vastly inferior to the Japanese. The report mimicked many of the negative stereotypes used by the Japanese to justify their country's 1910 annexation of Korea as well as their continued administration of the Korean peninsula: the Korean people "do not possess the Japanese fever for hard work"; they appeared to be "slow moving and lazy," and they were "not as conscious of cleanliness as the Japanese." On the positive side, the report applauded Japan-based Koreans for their remittance of a "high percentage of earnings" to their families in Korea (United States Office of Strategic Services 1945: 7–15).

The report noted recent trends that showed Korean residents opting for extended, if not permanent, stays in Japan. This was evidenced by increases in Korean families (as opposed to individuals) in Japanese-Korean marriages, and in Korean births in Japan. More Koreans in Japan now realized the importance of acquiring Japanese language proficiency to escape from economic hardship. The outbreak of the Pacific War also expedited Korean assimilation, but, rather than their "conviction of . . . [Japanese-Korean] equality," it was the wartime situation that drove these efforts. The report seemed to question whether their ambition to assimilate would persist once the wartime catalyst disappeared (United States Office of Strategic Services 1945: 19).

The final section of "Aliens in Japan" offered suggestions for handling the estimated two million non-Japanese in need of "liberation, protection, or segregation from the Japanese." The report foresaw that a small number might "constitute a menace to Allied military operations" and would have to be incarcerated. Many others might prove useful to occupation efforts. It categorized Japan's foreign residents into four groups: Allied POWS, members of the diplomatic corps, imprisoned Allied citizens, and other foreigners. These groupings eventually were used to determine ration levels and order of repatriation during the Occupation. The Japan-based Korean population was placed in the "other foreigner" group, along with other "Asiatics"—members of countries neutral to Japan, White Russians, and people from other Axis states (Italians and Germans). The report advised authorities to handle members of all groups as individuals, as it was impossible to establish a uniform policy for any of the groups. Members of the "Asiatic" group provided a case in point: they "may be either friendly or enemy"; even those who had become citizens might be either pro- or anti-Allies; others might have collaborated with the Japanese (United States Office of Strategic Services 1945: 34–35).

The report further advised authorities to assume that collaborators and enemy agents could be found in "almost every conquered country of Asia," as these peoples assisted the Japanese in conjunction with their revolutionary activities against the British, Dutch, and French colonial governments. Policy toward these peoples, it advised, should be determined by an international agreement with the country involved. Regarding repatriation, the report acknowledged that not all "Asiatics" would opt to return home. Two factors would determine this decision: the repatriates' financial and cultural assets and the postwar condition of their ethnic homelands. Indeed, these two factors proved to be critical determinants in individual Koreans' decisions regarding repatriation (United States Office of Strategic Services 1945: 37).

OCCUPATION POLICY AND CONDITIONS IN JAPAN

Choe Seog-Ui was eighteen when the Japanese surrendered; at age nineteen he accompanied his mother back to Korea. He recalls that upon hearing the emperor's surrender announcement, his first thought was that unless there were extraordinary circumstances (such as pro-Japanese sentiment), "all Japanese-based [Korean] brethren [zainichi dōhō] would return to their home country [hongoku]. Hardly any Korean would wish to remain in Japan (Choe 2004: 40). Choe did return to Korea, only to find himself back in Japan six months later, joining an estimated 600,000 Koreans who chose to forgo repatriation.

Despite prior warnings from informants and prior knowledge gleaned from the reports cited above, the U.S. occupations in both Korea and Japan proved incapable in many respects of coordinating a smooth postsurrender Korean repatriation. Many Koreans like Choe would soon discover that both postwar Japan and postliberation Korea erected a number of social, political, and economic obstacles that complicated Japan-based Koreans' decision to repatriate. While the policy in Japan pledged to assist those wishing to return to their homeland, in effect it charged the Japanese government with the responsibility for both financing their trip and guaranteeing their safe return. Due to the lack of liaison between the occupations, repatriation procedures were heavily compromised and implementation was a disaster. Some Koreans, apparently unaware of Japan's responsibilities, admitted that their inability to pay for transportation to Shimonoseki—a primary return port—kept them in Japan (J. Kim 2005: 57, 149). In addition, the dire circumstances that Korean families faced in meeting basic living needs—a roof over their heads, food to eat, and a job—prevented their return.

The recommendations in "Aliens in Japan" forecast one obstacle: the U.S. inability to define Korea as friend or foe. The State, War, and Navy departments' joint directive to Supreme Commander General Douglas MacArthur regarding Japan's minority populations—issued in October 1945—only confused matters further. After declaring Chinese, Taiwanese, and Korean residents to be "liberated peoples"—that is, peoples "not included in the term 'Japanese'"—the report quickly muddied that statement by acknowledging that these peoples "have been Japanese subjects." Thus, if necessary, they "may be treated . . . as enemy nationals" (United States Joint Chiefs of Staff 1945). The ramifications of this inconsistency were felt by Koreans in both Japan and Korea.

Such confusion reflects the generally complicated relationship between colonized and colonizer. Many Koreans unequivocally demonstrated their anti-Japanese sentiments by physically battling the Japanese or refusing to cooperate with them, infractions for which they served time in prison, were tortured, and even sacrificed their lives. Other Koreans clearly benefited from the Japanese presence. The success of Korean entrepreneurs depended on their willingness to cooperate with the Japanese administration (Eckert 1991). Koreans who "volunteered" to participate in Japanese institutions presented a different set of problems. Did the inductee into the Japanese military volunteer for this position or was he coerced to join?[6] Did the Koreans who migrated to the Japanese archipelago do so of their own volition, or were they coerced into going by Japanese or even Korean agents?

Policies introduced by the U.S. Military Government in Korea to accept Japan's surrender and guide the new Korean state to sovereignty suggest further questions regarding the status of Koreans as ally or enemy. One question left unanswered was why the United States and the Soviet Union divided the Korean peninsula rather than the Japanese archipelago—as in Europe where Germany (and its colony) was divided. Peninsular Koreans aggressively asked why the U.S. Military Government appeared to favor the Japanese over Koreans, an allegation that the administration acknowledged. Within weeks of the arrival of the United States, Political Adviser H. Merrell Benninghoff sent the following message to the U.S. Secretary of State: "The removal of Japanese officials is desirable from the public opinion standpoint but difficult to bring about for some time. They can be relieved in name but must be made to continue work. There are no qualified Koreans for other than the low-ranking positions, either in government or in public utilities and communications" (Benninghoff 1945: 1049). In other words, the Japanese authorities would maintain their positions until further notice. Public pressure eventually forced the United States to change this policy. But periodically Koreans complained that the Americans favored their erstwhile enemy over the Korean people they had come to liberate.[7]

Japan-based Koreans, along with Taiwanese residents, did not help their cause when they made headlines for illegal activities such as black marketeering. Richard L. G. Deverall, the Supreme Commander for the Allied Powers (SCAP) Chief of Labor Education, claimed that all Koreans in Japan were "a bunch of black marketers" (Deverall 1952: 256). Other illegal activities were politically motivated, such as the Korean uprisings in the Kobe and Osaka areas against Korean school closures. Koreans arrested for their participation in these activities faced indictment and trial in Japanese courts, in keeping with Occupation policy for those who failed to qualify as Allied nationals or United Nations citizens (see Inokuchi 2000 and Koshiro 1999).

Korean ties with leftist organizations in Japan proved to be the most imposing barrier to repatriation, particularly after 1947 when SCAP ordered the Japanese government to purge communists from professions of influence, including education, politics, and the arts. Japan-based Koreans had begun organizing soon after Japan's surrender. On October 15, 1945, they formed the League of Koreans in Japan (Jaeil joseonin ryeonmaeng or Joryeon). Two months later the League petitioned the Occupation administration for permission to form a "People's Republic" in Japan (Lee 1981: 65–66). Occupation and Japanese authorities seemed to attribute any problem that concerned Koreans to alleged communist ties.

Concerns over Japan-based Koreans' susceptibility to communist ideology matched U.S. beliefs that the southern half of the Korean peninsula (reflecting the Korean people in general) was "extremely fertile ground for the establishment of Communism" should it be granted independence (Cumings 1997: 198). This raised concern that communist agents were entering Japan "in the guise of [Korean] refugees" ("Report on the Occupation Area" 1992: 489). The August 16, 1948, "Staff Study Concerning Koreans in Japan" claimed that these Koreans served as "the link between Japanese communists and those of the continent of Asia—Korean, Chinese, and Russian" (United States Department of State Diplomatic Section GHQ SCAP 1948).

Beginning in 1948, the administration of Syngman Rhee in the newly formed Republic of Korea (ROK) instituted staunchly anticommunist policies that essentially prohibited repatriation for most Japan-based Koreans suspected of having joined left-wing organizations. Those who returned to the ROK—they could not yet repatriate to the Democratic People's Republic of Korea (DPRK)—faced interrogation, imprisonment, and possible execution. Douglas MacArthur, disagreeing with Japanese Prime Minister Yoshida Shigeru's 1949 suggestion that all Koreans unable to "contribute to [Japan's] reconstruction" be forcefully repatriated, remarked that since they were "mostly North Koreans" they "would [all] have their heads cut off" by the ROK government (Finn 1992: 238). The characterization "mostly North Korean" was untrue in the literal sense, given that most Japan-based Koreans came from southern Korean towns. As a reference to ideological disposition it was equally problematic: many claimed membership in both the leftist Joryeon and the conservative Association for Korean Residents (Jaeilbon joseon keoryu mindan or Mindan).[8] Indeed, clearly identifying Koreans ideologically proved to be a problem. One definition provided in August 1948 by Mindan President Pak Yeol labeled as communist "anyone who does not support the present [South] Korean government" (United States Army, XXIV Corps 1948: 573–574).

Pak's policy recommendations both encouraged and discouraged Korean repatriation. He reported that in discussions with the newly elected President Syngman Rhee, both had come to the conclusion that all Korean communists in Japan should be deported to the ROK. In addition to deporting Korean communists, Pak recommended that skilled Korean laborers be induced to return, and that the National Traitor Law (then under consideration in the South Korean National Assembly) be used to arrest all those who refused to return. Pak acknowledged that Korean representation in Japan would be necessary to assist those who chose to remain in Japan.

He volunteered Mindan's services to act as the Korean government's sole agent until official representation could be established. His recommendation that Korean children be educated in Japanese schools (with elective Korean language courses offered) coincided with U.S. Occupation policy that ordered Korean schools closed, but conflicted with the needs of Koreans hoping to eventually repatriate. U.S. officials identified a weak sense of ethnic identity among Koreans in Japan as one of the most critical obstacles that prevented their successful resettlement in Korea (United States Army, XXIV Corps 1948: 573–574). They based this conclusion on the fact that many Koreans who had been raised in Japan had limited knowledge of their ancestral culture and limited facility in speaking the Korean language.

Policies formed and supported by the Occupation administration in Japan also negatively influenced repatriation decisions. Even if Japan-based Koreans refrained from participating in black market or communist activity, and even if they maintained a strong sense of Korean identity, limitations imposed by the Occupation authorities on the material possessions they could carry with them outside of Japan forced many Koreans in Japan to either repatriate by dangerous, unauthorized routes or simply remain in Japan. Like Japanese repatriates from the colonies, Koreans were allowed to carry only 1,000 yen per person. One report issued from U.S. Army Headquarters in South Kyeongsang Province in Korea argued that this amount would allow its bearer to "exist for [little] more than a few days, and [was] . . . extremely inadequate to enable [the Korean] to begin life anew" ("Critical Refugee Situation" 1996: 370–373). Anything in excess of this amount was confiscated. Although the Occupation authorities issued a receipt for the confiscated funds, they gave insufficient information on how to use it to claim the money. These restrictions discouraged the more industrious Koreans eager to transfer their business skills to Korea but "unable to exchange this hard-earned money, their whole life's savings, [to establish] any new enterprise."[9] Koreans who arrived at a port without exchange facilities, or at night after they were closed, found themselves unable to exchange even the 1,000 yen to which they were entitled, and thus without valid currency ("Critical Refugee Situation" 1996: 370–373).

During an interview with Caprio in Tokyo on July 11, 2005, Choe Seog-Ui revealed that some creative Koreans, particularly those who repatriated early, were able to circumvent these restrictions. He admitted to repatriating with much more than 1,000 yen and was able to exchange his extra money with people returning to Japan. His family also brought with them thirty boxes of belongings, ten of which were stolen by Koreans (rather than confiscated by U.S. military police) after his arrival. It is not clear just how prevalent these practices were, and Choe recalled that it became much harder to carry this much back in later years. His case apparently was not exceptional, however. Letters sent from Korea to Japan but intercepted by Occupation authorities detailed ways that repatriating Koreans could smuggle money.[10]

SCAP completed its first major review of this policy in May 1948, when its Diplomatic Section submitted the aforementioned report, the "Staff Study Concerning Koreans in Japan." This report came on the heels of the first general election in the ROK, which brought the Rhee administration to power in August. The election affected Japan-based Koreans in different ways. The establishment of a legitimate government on the peninsula cleared one of the hurdles that had complicated Korean repatriation—the lack of a sovereign Korean state to return to. The conservative (anticommunist) stance adopted by the Rhee administration prevented Koreans affiliated with the pro-North Joryeon group from returning. The "Staff Study" considered a variety of ways to reduce other obstacles to return, and it recommended policy for handling those Koreans who chose to remain.

The report evidences the same negative images found in previous reports: Koreans were intent on establishing political autonomy in Japan rather than returning to Korea; they sought links with mainland communist groups; and they participated in illegal black market transactions that escaped the "control or tax authority of Japanese Government." In addition, the Korean people did not easily assimilate into Japanese society: they had endured the "long-standing prejudice of the [Japanese] and [were] uneducated and generally [carried an] underprivileged character." The report noted that the Japanese "would be only too happy to see all Koreans leave Japan" (Diplomatic Section GHQ SCAP 1948: 2–3).

The report's recommendations were controversial. One required Japan-based Koreans to register as nationals of the newly established ROK as a first step toward repatriation. This demonstrated either an insensitivity toward Korean ideological predicaments or simply a desire to quickly rid the Occupation of the Korean nuisance. It surely did not consider the consequences that the majority of Koreans would face should they cooperate, nor did it consider more appropriate repatriation routes, such as to Soviet-occupied northern Korea. The report's recommendation that those who refused to register be made to "retain" their "Japanese nationality [as determined by] Japanese law" ignored the fact that Japanese law had never recognized this population as Japanese "nationals" [kokumin], not even under colonial occupation.[11]

William J. Sebald, Political Adviser to SCAP, responded to the Staff Study in February 1949. He criticized its call for forced Korean registration, arguing that it would trigger an opposite effect by removing their incentive to return to Korea. This would deprive Korea of the "industrial and commercial skill it so eagerly desires," as well as increase friction between Japanese and Koreans. Another long-term recommendation gained general acceptance: that the United States wash its hands of the matter and leave it to the Koreans and Japanese to decide after both states reestablished sovereignty (United States Political Adviser for Japan 1949).

The Korean and Japanese governments were able to reach agreement on the fate of Japan-based Koreans just before the United States ended its occupation of Japan in 1952. Syngman Rhee—who had demonstrated little interest in this issue—used the negotiations to further other issues such as territory disputes and reparations. The two sides readily agreed that Japan would offer permanent residency to qualified (i.e., noncommunist) Korean residents, and could arrange deportation for "undesirable" Koreans.

What the two sides did not discuss was the conditions under which Koreans in Japan could apply for citizenship (Cheong 1991: 106–107). The Japanese began to construct a concentration center in Kyushu to house unruly Koreans waiting to be deported, and they actually succeeded in deporting to South Korea 285 Koreans charged with illegal entry into Japan. The Korean government rejected another 125 Koreans on grounds that their illegal entry was prior to the September 1945 cutoff date (Cheong 1991: 126–127).

Cheong Sung-Hwa notes that the division between desirable (or qualified) and undesirable (or communist) Koreans coincided with the general views held by both Japan and the ROK. The United States, which envisioned the future of Japan-based Koreans as "Japanese nationals," appeared most interested in framing this problem in citizenship terms. The South Korean and Japanese governments, which envisioned this population as "allied nationals" and "foreign nationals" respectively, both agreed that citizenship should not be considered an option (Cheong 1991: 66–67).

THE KOREAN PENINSULA AND REPATRIATION

Absent from the discussion on the Japan side, in both the Staff Study and Sebald's commentary, was substantial discussion of the conditions on the Korean peninsula that complicated repatriation. Both reports considered in depth the conditions that Koreans faced in Japan, but neglected to address this important question that confronted anyone contemplating repatriation, although both suggested that the SCAP raise the amount of money that Koreans could bring with them to 100,000 yen. This constituted a serious oversight, considering the large number of Koreans who decided to return to Japan even after successfully repatriating (Morris-Suzuki 2004).

Choe Seog-Ui is succinct in his recollections of the situation that greeted him upon his homecoming soon after liberation. His family decided that his father and grandparents would return ahead of the others—in November 1945—to make living arrangements for the family. The following April, Choe crossed over with his mother, carrying with him "the aspiration to contribute to Korea's reconstruction." But his aspirations soon faded: "I returned to my hometown [to find] no home in which to live, no job at which to work—a truly wretched situation [*santantaru jōkyō*]." He then lists a third problem that gravely affected the reception that peninsular Koreans gave returnees from Japan. "My inability to speak Korean as I wished truly broke me up. In the end, distressed, I decided to temporarily return to Japan to study before once again returning to Korea to make a fresh start" (Choe 2004: 42). As the eldest son, his decision was not easy and drew his father's protests. Ultimately Choe would not return to visit the ROK until 1980, after his father had died.

The confused situation wrought by Japan's defeat brought hardship to those who had maintained residency on the peninsula; the addition of two million returnees only exacerbated an already difficult situation. As Choe recalled during his interview in 2005, although people in the homeland welcomed their return, they were hardly in a position to lend a helping hand. The most immediate problem that repatriated Koreans faced was securing basic living essentials—housing, food, and employment. The U.S. Military Government in Korea organized temporary shelters for returnees but could not guarantee them housing when they were forced to vacate these facilities. One Korean articulated this concern in a letter dated July 10, 1947, to the U.S. Enemy Property Central Office in South Kyeongsang Province, the first stop for most of the returning Koreans. The author, who provided an address but no name, first expressed gratitude to the U.S. military for defeating Japan, and to the U.S. Military Government for providing repatriated Koreans with housing. Eighty families who had returned from Japan and Manchuria shared his apartment complex. But problems, he lamented, appeared to be just around the corner, as they would soon have to vacate: "And now in the very difficult condition of the house problem, we cannot find another house . . . as soon as [we] lose our house, we must [start] wandering about on the street" (Anonymous 1996: 318).

A report issued five days later by Jack Snow, a civilian adviser for the General Relief Bureau of the U.S. Military Government in Korea, outlined the extent of the housing problem. As no appropriate structures were available for "refugees" returning from abroad, the "cattle breeding station . . . was the only suitable vacant building where the several hundred families could be moved in this emergency." The emergency was triggered by hundreds of families housed in dock warehouses facing eviction to make room for Port Authority facilities (Snow 1996: 396–401).

News of the dire situation on the peninsula reached Koreans in Japan quite early. On December 17, 1946, Dai Suyung, Chief of the Pusan Branch of the Seoul Committee Meeting, Korean Association in Japan, petitioned the Military Governor of South Kyeongsang Province to "make great[er] efforts . . . for [the] welfare of our provincial people and for [the] stability of refugees' living [conditions]." His primary concerns were housing and jobs: ". . . there were no firm equipment [homes?] to secure their living. So they have to wander about the streets, because they couldn't get any houses to live in, and they have to starve to death, because they couldn't get any job[s] to support their living." The solution that Dai proposed required the U.S. military government to make available to repatriated Koreans hotels, restaurants, prostitution houses, barracks, and even temples that had once belonged to the Japanese (Dai 1996: 406–407).

Koreans returning from abroad also found it difficult to procure food. This complaint was one voiced by almost all residents of the Korean peninsula, including the U.S. military.[12] U.S. Commanding General John R. Hodge of the Military Government and Dai Suyung agreed separately that Koreans needed three *hop* (1 *hop* = 525 calories) to meet the daily minimum food requirements, yet on average the Korean diet averaged but two *hop*. Inadequate nutrition was partly a result of disrupted food distribution mechanisms in the aftermath of Japan's defeat. But as in Japan, the military government also faced the problem of insufficient production. In December 1946 an incomplete report estimated that the provinces managed to contribute but 28.23 percent of their allotted quota (United States Military Government in Korea 1996: 81). By the following October farmers approached their quota (97.1 percent), although it appears that quotas had been decreased drastically—from 4,358,000 to 706,500 *seok* (1 *seok* [Japanese *koku*] = 5.119 bushels) (South Korean Interim Government 1996: 172).

A report issued in late August 1946 offered one important reason for the quota deficits experienced that year: price controls. The U.S. Military

Government, to control inflation, set the price of rice artificially low. Farmers, upon discovering that selling rice at this official price prevented them from purchasing other basic commodities, "withheld most of [their] rice from the official market and created a black market for [their] surplus." This maneuver caused both prices and wages to rise dramatically (Kermode 1946: 111).

Even if the Military Government had been able to correct southern Korea's housing and food problems, there still remained one more critical subsistence shortage: paid work. In our interview in July 2005, Choe Seog-Ui admitted this to be the primary factor that forced his return to Japan. On September 13, 1945, soon after arriving in Korea, General Hodge attributed the problem partly to the Korean people's lack of industry.

> Almost all Koreans have been on a prolonged holiday since surrender on 15 August. It is apparent that their idea of independence is freedom of all cares of work and that the world will support them. Since arrival of American troops here there has been no show of industry in the Jinsen-Keijo [Incheon-Seoul] area and but little interest in returning to any normal pursuits. (Hodge 1995: 3)

Further in the report, however, he gave other reasons for unemployment, which included

> hundreds of thousands of Koreans out of work because of the collapse of war industries. Manufacturing of all types is now at a standstill for a lack of raw materials and there is no possibility of immediate correction through turning war industries into peaceful manufacturers. This, combined with the release of Koreans from Japanese Army control, amounts to a tremendous problem particularly with winter approaching. (Hodge 1995: 5)

A report circulated later that year described a situation similar to what repatriated Koreans had experienced in Japan—a lack of legitimate job opportunities resulting in illegal means of subsistence such as the black market. This development, it observed, "has resulted in a great increase in crime and has thrown a heavy burden on the civilian and military police" ("Critical Refugee Situation" 1996: 371). Repatriated Koreans also faced cultural barriers that complicated their efforts to resettle in Korea. Many, like Choe Seog-Ui, who had been raised in Japan, could neither speak Korean nor follow Korean customs and mannerisms adequately. In short, thanks to the cultural and racial biases held by the U.S. Military Government, a lack of basic security and livelihood, political turmoil, and the ill-coordinated liaison between the Japanese Occupation and the

Korean Occupation, a substantial number of Koreans found themselves stranded in postwar Japan.

Despite the difficulties outlined here, it must be remembered that roughly two-thirds (1.4 million) of Koreans returned to southern Korea from Japan within two years following liberation (Seo 1999: 95). In addition, Koreans entered southern Korea from other parts of the Japanese empire, including northern Korea, Manchuria, the South Pacific, and even Australia and the United States. The U.S. Military Government in Korea proved incapable of handling this diversity. Word circulated to those who remained outside the peninsula of the dire situation that awaited them should they decide to repatriate. Their decision not to return to Korea left an estimated 600,000 Japan-based Koreans—as in the past the majority resided in Osaka, but large populations remained in Tokyo and Aichi and Hyogo prefectures (Nishinarita 1998: 43; United States Office of Strategic Services 1945: 14; De Vos and Chung 1981: 226)—in a state of ethnic limbo: self-images of racial and cultural homogeneity held by both Koreans and Japanese complicated their membership in either society. Never Japanese enough to pass for Japanese, they faced discrimination in schools, in employment, and in society. For example, in 1950, 79 percent of Japan-based Koreans were either unemployed or working as day laborers (Pak C. 1999: 108). At the same time their long residence in Japan tainted their Korean-ness as evident by their less-than-native ability to speak the Korean language and observe Korean custom. Those affiliated with leftist organizations found their political beliefs a barrier to repatriation, at least until the late 1950s (see chapter 2 in this volume).

Occupation administrations, despite intentions to the contrary, frustrated repatriation. In Japan, the limitations placed upon Koreans wishing to return prevented them from doing so with their total estate. Those who did repatriate encountered a situation that greatly inhibited their capacity to begin a new life in what was for many an unfamiliar home. Alien registration laws adopted in the 1950s—adapted from legislation enacted to control the U.S. communist population—further segregated the Japan-based Korean population and complicated their capacity to assimilate into Japanese society. SCAP washed its hands of the problem after the 1948 "Staff Study" failed to provide practical answers to the problem of repatriation. In sum, the legacy of the U.S. occupations in both Japan and Korea set in motion the decade-long process that established Japan-based Koreans as a diasporic population in Japan.

2. Freedom and Homecoming

Narratives of Migration in the Repatriation of Zainichi *Koreans to North Korea*

Tessa Morris-Suzuki

In the nonfiction essay that concludes *War and Peace,* Leo Tolstoy wrestled with a problem that haunts all history writing. When we look at the "infinitesimal" histories of individual lives, each person appears as a free human being, determining the course of his or her actions. But when we look at the "ocean of history," with its vast movements of peoples, revolutions and wars, each person seems caught up in a tide of events beyond individual control (Tolstoy 1978: 1339).

This age-old conundrum of freedom versus determinism lies at the core of many historical and political narratives, but nowhere is it more central than in narratives of migration. The distinction between "free" and "forced" cross-border movement is fundamental to contemporary academic discourse, media debate, and international law. To historians, this distinction is often superimposed on the division between "free labor" and "slavery"—a topic about which there has been long and heated controversy. There is widespread acknowledgment that most migrations throughout history have been "forced at some level" by social or ecological pressures. Yet many scholars still accept Theodore Schultz's insistence that it is useful to differentiate between "those compelled to migrate against their own perceived self-interest" (for example, victims of the trans-Atlantic slave trade) and "those who are able to exercise choice over the decision" (quoted in Eltis 2002: 5–6).

In the world of contemporary border politics, similar language is used, but the dividing line is drawn somewhat differently. Here the issue is not normally the distinction between the movement of free labor and the slave trade, but rather between those who are forced by persecution to flee across frontiers, and those who migrate for economic or other reasons. In the mass media, this distinction is often assumed to equate to a divide between the good "genuine refugee," who deserves sympathy and protection, and the bad "queue jumper," "illegal entrant," or "bogus refugee," who supposedly abuses the goodwill of the public in a selfish search for economic gain (Ager 1999: 2).

The history of the repatriation of some 90,000 Koreans from Japan to North Korea in the years 1959 to 1984 raises two particularly profound problems for our understanding of migration and diasporas.[1] The first concerns the distinction between "forced" and "free" movement across national boundaries. The repatriation was unusual in that it was one of the few mass migrations in history where the "free will" of each migrant was meticulously checked and recorded by an impartial, humanitarian body—the Geneva-based International Committee of the Red Cross (ICRC). In a formal sense, then, it was the most indisputably voluntary of migrations. It was also, however, an extraordinary process, shaped (as we shall see) by complex and covert Cold War maneuvers.

The second and related problem concerns the notion of "returning home," for this, of course, was not a "diaspora"—a dispersion—but rather a "return," a "homecoming." And at the heart of all myths of diaspora lies the dream of home. The voluntary character of the return movement was, on the face of it, all the more obvious for this reason. What could be more natural than for an exile to wish to return home? In fact, however, the repatriation story complicates both narratives of freedom and narratives of homeland. The great majority of the returnees—who left Japan for North Korea at the very time when the Japanese economy was entering its phase of "miraculous" economic growth—came from the southern half of the Korean peninsula. In one sense, many were undoubtedly "returning" to the dream of a future reunited homeland; in another, most were going to a place they had never seen before and to which they had no ancestral ties.

Although the repatriation story has many unique features, I believe it is an important focus for reconsidering some assumptions about the nature of cross-border movement in the modern world. In this reexamination of the repatriation story, my central aim is to question the casual ease with which we use those two small but irresistible words: "free" and "home."

Research on "free migration" is shaped by two contrasting approaches. On the one hand, there are those who emphasize the individual choice of each migrant; on the other, there are "structural" approaches which stress that these choices are pushed and pulled by a host of factors beyond the migrant's knowledge or control: transportation routes, global labor markets, the social networks forged from the experience of colonization, and so on. Recent economic theories of migration have tried to borrow a little from each approach, suggesting that "migration decisions are not made by isolated individual actors, but by larger units of related people—typically families or households, but sometimes communities, in which people act collectively not only to maximize expected income, but also to minimize risk and loosen constraints associated with various kinds of market failure" (Massey et al. 1998: 21). The choice of this language for speaking about cross-border movement seems to me to raise great problems. It too easily obscures the power relations at work within those "collective decisions"; it too readily treats the "free choice" to migrate across national boundaries as though this were analogous to the choice between (say) buying a new car or taking a holiday in the Caribbean.

Christopher Davis has observed that much theorizing about migration is written "as though that movement were itself without friction, or problematic only from the point of view of history and identity, without reference to basic obstacles or practicalities." Part of the reason for this bland academic view of migration, he suggests, may be that it reflects the way in which most academics themselves experience international travel (Davis 1999: 60). For the majority of frontier-crossers, however, the borderland they traverse is not the level playing field of liberal economic theory but a minefield littered with unexploded fragments of history and politics: citizenship restrictions, national security laws, ethnic prejudices. When considering journeys across these landscapes, in other words, it needs to be remembered that choices that are in some sense "free" may still be burdened with suffering, fear, and uncertainty. They are also often irreversible choices, whose consequences have drastic effects on lives, not only of those who make the decisions but on family and friends, even on the yet unborn. And all this is true of the choice to stay still as well as of the choice to move.

The story I tell here seeks to complicate the comforting narrative of "voluntary return," which has been widely accepted in Japanese society and elsewhere for the past forty years. But at the same time I believe that it is important not to go to the opposite extreme and present the Koreans who "returned" from Japan to North Korea simply as hapless pawns of cynical international power games.

Along with the sheer scale of the human suffering which it ultimately entailed, one element that makes the repatriation particularly historically significant and particularly painful to confront is precisely its ambivalence. In one sense, those who "returned" to North Korea were pushed and pulled, not just by the deep-flowing currents of the turbulent ocean called the Cold War, but also by a very deliberately created web of lies, conspiracies, and propaganda. But in another sense, many of those who chose to "return" from Japan to North Korea did indeed exercise a choice, and many exercised it shrewdly, with an awareness of the limited options open to them and a determination to make the most of those options. Above all, their stories are as diverse as their personalities and backgrounds, and in attempting to reassess the meaning of the repatriation it is essential not to lose sight of that diversity. Here are just a few of those stories.

THREE STORIES ABOUT VOLUNTARY REPATRIATION

First Story

On August 11, 1959, the ICRC announced its decision to provide assistance to the Japanese Red Cross "with a view to preparing for the repatriation of those Koreans living in Japan who express a desire to return to the place of their choice in their country of origin." The announcement evoked the "principle of free choice," which the ICRC interpreted as meaning the choice of Koreans in Japan to remain where they were, or to be repatriated to either North or South Korea.[2] In practice, however, while North Korea had offered free transport, jobs, and housing to "returnees" from Japan, the South Korean government showed a clear reluctance to receive repatriates. The actual choice, therefore, was between remaining in Japan or going to North Korea.

The ICRC's assistance to the repatriation project involved sending a twenty-two-person mission whose task was to ensure that the repatriation was truly voluntary. All returnees were expected to have a face-to-face meeting with an ICRC official, at which they were asked to confirm that they were indeed leaving of their own free will. Over the two years following the departure of the first repatriation ship in December 1959, some 70,000 people embarked on the one-way voyage to the North Korean port of Cheongjin, and all (apart from some small children) participated in this "confirmation of free will."

One of those 70,000 was a woman whom I shall call Ms. Choi.[3] She arrived in Niigata (the port of departure for North Korea) in summer 1960 with her six children. When asked by the ICRC official on duty about her decision to go to North Korea, Ms. Choi explained that she came from South Korea, where her parents still lived, but that her husband had been arrested for handling stolen goods and sentenced to two-and-a-half years' imprisonment. He had also been fined 120,000 yen—a sum which he had only be able to pay by selling the family's house. Ms. Choi herself had been arrested as an accomplice and given a ten-month sentence, but "she had promised the police to repatriate . . . , whereupon they had let her go free." As she put it to the ICRC representative, "there is no other means but to repatriate, although she would do anything to remain in Japan. She was a Catholic and did not want to go to a country where they have no religion."

Concerned at Ms. Choi's evident lack of enthusiasm for a future in the Democratic People's Republic (North Korea), the official suggested that, instead of boarding the ship for North Korea immediately, she should remain in Niigata for a week to reconsider her decision. The Japan Red Cross officials who ran the repatriation center in the port city agreed to look after her during that time. Later the same day, however, the ICRC representative received a call from the Japan Red Cross, telling him that Ms. Choi wished to speak to him again, as she had now made up her mind to leave right away.

On this second meeting Ms. Choi explained that she had discussed the matter with her eldest son over lunch and was determined to depart for North Korea. Elaborating on this decision, she said (according to the ICRC memo on the matter) that she "had no place to live even if she could stay in Japan, as none of the apartment house owners would care to rent a room to a family with six children. She could not support the children and pay for a house; she would never earn enough for seven persons if she worked honestly and was afraid that she would offend the law again. If she asked to be supported by the government it would prevent her fifteen-year-old son from attending high school, and yet she wished her children to be well educated. The North Korean government offered to educate the children gratis, which would be a great help to her. The Koreans in Japan have no chance to obtain a good future, and she would gladly sacrifice herself for the children's sake, thinking of their future."

She also added that "no matter where she was, she and her children will remain good Christians. Although going to North Korea was like going to prison for her, she will sacrifice herself in order to make her children happy—they are eager to go."[4] On the basis of this free choice, it seems that the ICRC approved Ms. Choi's and her children's departure. What happened to them after they arrived in North Korea is unknown.

Second Story

I have known Ms. Pak for about two years. She is a young professional who lives in Tokyo—soft-spoken but articulate and very politically aware. She understands the complexities of the return movement both from books and from personal experience.

Ms. Pak's grandfather came to Japan in the colonial period from a small village in southern Korea. He traveled around Japan from one workplace to another, and eventually he and his wife and three children settled in Japan, where Ms. Pak's father was born. The eldest son became an enthusiastic member of the Japan Communist Party, and in the 1960s he joined the mass repatriation to North Korea out of ideological conviction. As in the case of many returnees, his departure created deep rifts within the family. "If he'd taken his Communist Party card with him," says Ms. Pak, "he could have become a member of the North Korean Workers' Party, and then his life would have been easier. But he left the Party Card behind, and his relatives, who were ashamed of having a 'Red' in the family, burnt it." He was sent to a rural area but later moved to the city, working in various factory jobs. Now he is an old man, living in North Korea with children and grandchildren of his own.

Ms. Pak visited the family in North Korea twice during her student days. On one occasion she spent several months in Pyongyang, and she has happy memories of this second visit. The Korean students from Japan stayed together in a dormitory, but in their free time they could go around the city unsupervised and were also allowed to visit and stay with relatives. She deliberately bobbed her hair and wore local clothes. "I could pass for a local if I didn't have to have a long conversation," she says.

Her uncle has had an extremely hard life, but even if he were able to speak the truth, Ms. Pak doubts whether he would complain. He is a very "serious" [*majime*] person, and has chosen his path in life out of genuine belief. It is his children who feel the costs of his choice most keenly, and she senses that they are distressed at the sufferings that their father has been through. The third generation is different again: they have only known life in the Republic and seem to take things for granted.

Third Story

Rika Hiroshi (as he was then called) was eight years old when, one day, his parents sat him down for a serious conversation. They told him that he was not, as he had always naturally and unthinkingly assumed, Japanese but Korean; and his real name was not Rika Hiroshi but Yi Yang-Su. "I felt," he says, "as though my whole being had been negated. I didn't speak Korean. I'd never been to Korea. At that stage I didn't even really understand the difference between North and South Korea."[5]

Yi Yang-Su's father had come to Japan with his family as a small child in the 1920s. He had an enthusiasm for learning, had taught himself to write poetry, and held a job in the local government of the town of Toyohashi when he met and married Miyo, a Japanese woman from the same town. They met through their shared membership in the local *tanka* poetry society, but their marriage was deeply opposed by both families.

On April 19, 1952, on the very day when the San Francisco Peace Treaty came into force, the Japanese government unilaterally revoked the Japanese nationality of all former colonial subjects—an act arguably in contravention of the 1948 UN Universal Declaration of Human Rights, which states that "no one shall be arbitrarily deprived of his nationality nor denied the right to change his nationality." Since Japanese nationality law was patriarchal, Japanese women married to Koreans, like Yi Yang-Su's mother, lost their Japanese nationality at the same time.

Yi Yang-Su's parents' marriage was not a happy one. His father was prone to violent attacks of temper, and by the time Yi was nine or ten years old, his mother had decided to leave her husband. But in Japan during the 1960s, the life prospects of a divorced mother with a small child, both of whom were foreigners, were not good. Yi's parents were left-wing, and his father was a member of the Communist Party. Just at this time, the repatriation movement to North Korea was getting under way. Yi remembers the glowing account of North Korean society contained in the book *North of the Thirty-Eighth Parallel* [*Sanjūhachidosen no kita*], which was serialized in the *Asahi shinbun*, and he recalls the pictures of abundance and prosperity that he saw in the North Korean illustrated monthly magazine *Korea* [*Chōsengahō*]. His mother and he decided to join the repatriation to North Korea in search of a new life.

They packed up and dispatched their belongings in big wooden cases, traveling on the repatriation train to Niigata. Three months before they were due to leave, Yi Yang-Su had moved from his Japanese school to a Korean school run by the North Korean–affiliated General Association of Korean Residents in Japan (Chongryun), where he began to learn Korean. But the day before they were due to board the ship for North Korea, they were told that they would not be allowed to make the journey. North Korea was accepting Japanese women married to Koreans if they were traveling with their husbands, but would not accept a Japanese woman unaccompanied by a Korean spouse. Yi and his mother returned to Toyohashi, where they struggled to cope on their own in an impoverished district mostly inhabited by *zainichi* Koreans. Yi attended *chōsengakkō* (Korean schools) and when he was in high school once more attempted to repatriate to North Korea. However, he was again told that his mother would not be allowed to accompany him, and he refused to leave her behind.

In adulthood, Yi became a passionate campaigner for the rights of *zain-*

ichi Koreans and a harsh critic of Chongryun. In the 1980s, he took part in the campaign to resist the fingerprinting of foreigners by the Japanese government, became Secretary General of the Society to Help Returnees to North Korea, and participated in the founding of the North Korean Refugee Relief Fund. He is deeply critical of the fact that many Chongryun leaders encouraged others to go to North Korea while remaining in Japan themselves, and he has worked to highlight the plight of the large but unknown number of returnees who fell victim to political purges, particularly in the 1970s, disappearing into North Korean labor camps from which many never returned.

ANOTHER STORY:
REPATRIATION IN THE POLITICS OF THE COLD WAR

These three very different personal stories open up some of the complexities concealed by the notion of "voluntary return." There is also a fourth story, which greatly adds to those complexities. It goes like this.

The Origins of Mass Repatriation to North Korea

The first moves toward the mass repatriation of *zainichi* Koreans to the Democratic People's Republic of Korea (DPRK, i.e., North Korea) occurred in the second half of 1955, on the initiative of the Japanese government and Japanese Red Cross Society (JRC). However, most aspects of this initiative were veiled in deep secrecy until 2004, when the archives on the subject held by the ICRC in Geneva were opened to the public. (For further details, see also Morris-Suzuki 2005, 2007.)

In September 1955, the JRC's newly appointed director of foreign affairs, Inoue Masutarō, began to raise with the ICRC the possibility of its becoming involved in assisting a repatriation of Koreans from Japan to North Korea. In December, the JRC followed up by forwarding to the ICRC a request for repatriation by an unspecified number of "North Koreans"—a request that had apparently reached it via Chongryun. With the approval of the Japanese Foreign Ministry and Ministry of Justice, the JRC asked the ICRC to supervise a mass return of *zainichi* Koreans to North Korea.[6] This seems to have been part of a well-coordinated political strategy. On January 16, 1956, the Foreign Affairs Committee [*gaikō chōsa iinkai*] of Japan's ruling Liberal Democratic Party (LDP) discussed "the rapid repatriation of North Koreans who wish to return to their homeland," and the issue was placed in the hands of former Foreign Minister Okazaki

Katsuo—a leading LDP power broker who had been active in developing an unsuccessful proposal to deport "subversive Koreans" during the Korean War (Ashida 1992: 68).[7]

As the declassified documents indicate, a group of politicians and officials including Okazaki, former Prime Minister Ashida Hitoshi, and others had come up with an innovative idea: by using the international Red Cross movement (with which Okazaki had helped to negotiate the repatriation of Japanese from China and elsewhere), it might be possible to assist the "voluntary return" of a large number of *zainichi* Koreans to North Korea. If this "voluntary return" were overseen by the ICRC, the Japanese government would be able to remain at arm's length from the scheme, avoiding the political odium that a policy of mass deportation otherwise would attract—particularly deportation to a communist country in the middle of the Cold War. Indeed, the whole project could become a praiseworthy act of humanitarianism.

The main intermediary in pursuing the project was Inoue, a retired diplomat who had been Okazaki's junior colleague in the prewar Ministry of Foreign Affairs. He had served as an analyst of East Asian communism within the ministry, and his younger brother (also a diplomat) was to be a key figure in crucial negotiations with South Korea, held not long before the start of the repatriation.[8] Close contact between the Japanese government and the Red Cross was nothing new. The JRC had long-standing associations with the political elite and the imperial family, and its Foreign Affairs Section was half-jokingly referred to in the media as the "second Ministry of Foreign Affairs."[9] Three days after the LDP Foreign Affairs Committee meeting, Inoue wrote a long letter to the president of the ICRC, Leopold Boissier, in which he reported "an indication that the Japanese Governmental party, the conservative party [i.e., the LDP] would start a movement to support the repatriation of the Koreans."[10]

These communications initiated an extremely energetic campaign by the JRC to persuade the ICRC to take up the repatriation of "North Koreans" as a humanitarian project. It should be noted, though, that the terminology was flexible. On March 19, 1956, Inoue wrote to the ICRC again, this time referring not to the problem of "North Koreans who wish to return to their homeland," but rather to the "mass repatriation of Koreans in Japan who cannot earn their living." The Governing Board of the JRC, Inoue reported, had given its unanimous support to a proposition that, in order to solve the problem of these indigents, it was "essential to repatriate at least 60,000 Koreans within this year."[11]

The Politics of Humanitarianism, 1956–1958

The JRC's lobbying activities resulted in the dispatch of a confidential mission by two ICRC officials, William Michel and Eugene de Weck, to Japan and the two Koreas in April and May 1956. During their stay in Japan, Michel and de Weck met Foreign Minister Shigemitsu Mamoru and officials of various Japanese ministries, who emphasized the Japanese government's enthusiasm for pursuing the repatriation, and echoed Inoue's figure of 60,000 as a possible number of returnees.[12] This figure, which repeatedly appears in the documents of the time, was alleged to have come from Chongryun and to represent the number of *zainichi* Koreans wishing to return to North Korea.

By the time Michel and de Weck arrived in Tokyo, a demonstration by Koreans demanding repatriation to North Korea was being held in front of the Red Cross headquarters in Tokyo. And indeed, there were Koreans in Japan who were eager to move to North Korea. They included some of the small proportion of *zainichi* Koreans who actually came from the north of the Korean peninsula and wanted to rejoin their families there; some students who wanted to continue their education at colleges in North Korea; and left-wingers who had been arrested for illegal immigration or other offenses, were awaiting deportation, and were terrified of the fate that awaited them if they were to be sent to South Korea, then ruled by the passionately anticommunist Rhee regime. However, the number does not seem to have been anywhere near the target of 60,000 cited by the Japanese government and the JRC. In fact, a Chongryun official, giving evidence to a Japanese parliamentary committee in February 1956, noted that the numbers demanding repatriation were rising sharply because of the government's increasingly stringent restrictions on benefits to the Korean community, but gave the grand total as 1,424.[13]

If the statistics employed by the JRC and Japanese government are enigmatic, however, there is no mystery about their motives for supporting the repatriation scheme. Foreign Minister Fujiyama Aiichirō explained to the U.S. ambassador to Japan in early 1959 that the mass repatriation of Koreans to North Korea was backed not only by communists and socialists but also by conservatives: the prospect of "ridding [the] country of [the] Korean minority is highly popular in view of their high crime rate, their political agitation and their pressure on [the] labor market."[14] He added that one of the principal factors for supporting repatriation had been internal security concerns (Koreans were seen as being left-wing). Another factor was economic: the "burden of destitute Koreans on Japanese government institutions at all levels totals 2.5 billion yen." Lastly, Fujiyama made it clear that the Japanese government regarded the repatriation scheme as a political tool that might be used to extract concessions from South Korea, particularly in negotiations about the contentious issue of fishery rights in the seas dividing Japan from Korea.[15]

Michel's notes of a conversation with Inoue in May 1956 cite the JRC official as highlighting "the desire of the Japanese government to rid itself of several tens of thousands of Koreans who are indigent and vaguely communist, thus at a stroke resolving security problems and budgetary problems (because of the sums of money currently being dispensed to impoverished Koreans)." Inoue went on to inform Michel that the Japanese government had "decided to undertake repatriation, if necessary by provoking individual demands to go to the North."[16]

Exactly how the government intended to "provoke individual demands" was not explained. However, it is important to consider an aspect of Japanese welfare policy unfolding precisely when this conversation took place. When Koreans in Japan were stripped of their Japanese nationality rights in 1952, they also lost the right to almost all forms of welfare. At the beginning of the 1950s, more than three-quarters of working-age *zainichi* Koreans were either unemployed or engaged in casual work with very unreliable earnings. To prevent complete social chaos in impoverished Korean communities, the Ministry of Health and Welfare, as a special act of "benevolence," agreed in 1952 that Koreans and Taiwanese in Japan, having been stripped of all other social entitlements, could continue to claim the most minimal form of assistance given to the very poor—Livelihood Protection Benefits, commonly known as *seikatsuhogo*.

But discretionary benevolence by the powerful is a two-edged sword. What is given may also, discretionarily, be taken away. In 1956, immediately after the LDP Foreign Affairs Committee addressed repatriation, the Ministry of Health and Welfare began an energetic and coordinated campaign to slash payments to *zainichi*. Between late 1955 and mid-1956, more than 70,000 *zainichi* Koreans had their welfare payments either reduced or canceled. This undoubtedly made the prospect of life in North Korea more attractive than it otherwise would have seemed, and appears to have been a major factor behind the growing demands for repatriation.[17]

Given the nature of the information received from Tokyo, in retrospect it seems remarkable that the ICRC was willing to involve itself in the repatriation at all. However, the Committee had very little background knowledge of the history of the Korean community in Japan. They evidently believed that they could control the process in such a way as to ensure a truly humanitarian return of those who were genuinely longing to leave Japan for North Korea. William Michel himself simply (and mistakenly) did not take Inoue's comments seriously.[18]

In the end, after considerable internal debate, the ICRC offered to verify the free will of returnees to North Korea provided that an agreement on the repatriation could be reached by the parties involved.[19] By then, however, rumors of a mass repatriation scheme had provoked ferocious opposition from the South Korean government, which claimed all *zainichi* Koreans as its own citizens. As a result, few shipping lines were willing to carry the returnees for fear of retaliation from the Rhee regime. Equally important, there was little sign in 1956 that the North Korean government was seriously interested in accepting a mass influx of Koreans from Japan.[20]

Kishi Nobusuke, who became Japanese prime minister early in 1957, was particularly keen to improve relations with South Korea. For this reason, he was extremely cautious to avoid creating any public impression of a connection between the Japanese government and schemes for repatriation to North Korea. But this did not mean that he opposed such schemes. On the contrary, moves to establish diplomatic relations with South Korea may have added to the urgency with which repatriation was viewed in government circles. There were fears that once relations with the South were normalized, repatriation to North Korea would become politically impossible. Certain key figures within the government were eager to "return" large numbers of *zainichi* Koreans to North Korea while preliminary negotiations with South Korea were still under way, and *before* moving on to the formal talks which would lead to the establishment of diplomatic relations with the ROK.[21]

In September 1957 Kishi reaffirmed the Japanese government's eagerness to obtain the ICRC's involvement in a mass repatriation program, and he strongly urged the JRC and the ICRC to counteract South Korean objections by "insisting on the humanitarian character of the problem."[22] In response to Kishi's comments, the JRC threw its enthusiastic support behind a resolution on the "reunion of displaced persons," which was put to the ICRC in New Delhi and passed unanimously on October 29, 1957, as the conference's Resolution 20. From then on, Resolution 20 was repeatedly invoked to generate international support in persuading South Korea and other countries to acknowledge the "humanitarian" nature of mass repatriation to North Korea. This seems a little curious, since more than 97 percent of *zainichi* Koreans originated in the southern half of the Korean peninsula, and very few had relatives with whom they could be "reunited" in North Korea. The JRC finessed the problem by claiming, as

Inoue Masutarō explained in a message sent to other national Red Cross Societies worldwide, that "the whole Korean Peninsula is the 'home' of the Koreans residing in Japan in the meaning of Resolution No. 20 of the New Delhi Conference."[23]

Korea Illustrated: The Democratic People's Republic, the Soviet Union, and the United Nations, 1958–1960

The situation was suddenly transformed in mid-1958. Until then, the North Korean government's interest in repatriation had focused on two quite small groups: *zainichi* students who had studied at Chongryun-affiliated schools and wanted to continue their education in the DPRK, and "illegal immigrants" and others held in Ōmura Migrant Detention Centre awaiting deportation to South Korea.[24] But in July 1958, quite abruptly, the DPRK altered its stance and threw its full weight behind a mass repatriation from Japan, and from August of that year on it began publicly to offer transport, jobs, free housing, and welfare to returnees.[25]

The reasons for this offer have been the subject of much speculation. One factor may have been a shortage of labor and skills in North Korea caused by a decline in Soviet technical assistance and the withdrawal of some 300,000 Chinese "volunteers" who had been sent to the DPRK during the Korean War and had stayed on to help with reconstruction. However, it seems clear that at least four other important Cold War strategic considerations were also at work.

The first was concern about the shifting balance of military power on the Korean peninsula following the withdrawal of the Chinese "volunteers." Since U.S. troops remained in South Korea, there were grave fears in the North that the DPRK would be strategically vulnerable when the Chinese withdrew. The United States, which had a dominant position in the United Nations at that time, was advocating free elections in both halves of the peninsula as a prelude to reunification—a suggestion bitterly contested by North Korea, who refused to discuss the possibility of elections while U.S. troops were still on Korean soil. To counter the U.S. proposal, North Korea (strongly supported by the People's Republic of China) attempted a major new initiative on Korean reunification, which, they hoped, would win support for the DPRK in the international community.

Second, relations between the USSR and North Korea had become strained following power struggles in the DPRK and a purge of pro-Soviet figures in the upper echelons of the North Korean ruling party [the Korean Workers' Party] (Lankov 2004: 121–174). The USSR appears to have used the repatriation movement as a means to reassert its influence over North

Korea, and to counterbalance the leverage that China was gaining through its collaboration on the reunification proposal. Material from the ICRC archives and from the archives of the former Soviet Union shows that the repatriation was enthusiastically encouraged by the Khrushchev government, whose officials acted as intermediaries in negotiations between North Korea and Japan. It was the Soviet Union that ultimately provided the ships used to take returnees from Niigata to Cheongjin in North Korea, as well as providing a discreet naval escort to guard them from a feared attack by the ROK.[26]

A third major consideration was that the Kim Il Sung regime was alarmed by Japanese moves to normalize relations with South Korea and hoped that the repatriation would hinder the improvement of Japan-ROK ties. In their covert contacts with Pyongyang, Japanese Red Cross officials, while asking the North Korean government to accept "returnees" from Japan, had stressed the need to carry out a repatriation in a discreet manner for fear of the reaction from South Korea. It is hard to avoid the conclusion that the North Korean government may have seen this as an opportunity to provoke South Korean antagonism toward Japan. Finally, the North Korean government (mistakenly) expected strong U.S. opposition to the repatriation and believed that this would help to drive a wedge between the United States and its major Asian ally, Japan.

On February 5, 1958, the Kim Il Sung regime put forward a proposal for a complete withdrawal of foreign troops from the Korean peninsula, to be followed by internationally supervised elections in both North and South. At the same time, the DPRK intensified its lobbying efforts to win international support, particularly within the General Assembly of the United Nations. They hoped that the mass "voluntary" return of Koreans, most of whom originated in the South, would be a huge propaganda coup for the DPRK.

In August 1958, a couple of months before the issue of Korean reunification was to be discussed in the UN General Assembly, Chongryun embarked on a mass campaign to promote repatriation. Rallies and marches were held across Japan, education campaigns on repatriation were held in Chongryun-affiliated schools, and the Association's newspaper *Chōsensōren* (Chongryun), which until then had focused mainly on news from North Korea and on the welfare problems of Koreans in Japan, began to run front-page stories in almost every issue highlighting the wonderful prospects awaiting returnees in the Fatherland.

Japanese media enthusiastically assisted Chongryun on this point. Here, as in the world of politics, the mass repatriation to North Korea won strong support across the ideological spectrum. Indeed, from the second half of 1958 to the early part of 1960, repatriation became the subject of a media boom not unlike the obsessive interest that more recently has greeted issues like the North Korean abduction of Japanese citizens. From *Akahata* (*Red Flag,* the Communist Party organ) to the mass-circulating *Asahi* to the *Sankei shinbun,* newspapers of every shade of opinion urged the Japanese government to resist South Korea's opposition and support repatriation to North Korea (Takasaki and Pak 2005).

Meanwhile, the DPRK was preparing the ground for a major propaganda assault on international public opinion. One vehicle for this was the illustrated monthly journal *Korea,* a lavish color magazine published and internationally distributed by the North Korean government in Korean, English, Japanese, Russian, and Chinese. The North Korean authorities pursued their propaganda campaign with care, waiting until they were sure that a sufficiently impressive number of *zainichi* Koreans had registered for repatriation before beginning to proclaim the story to the world. Once the first repatriation ship had arrived in Cheongjin in December 1959, however, issue after issue of *Korea* provided heartwarming illustrated stories of returnees overjoyed to be back in the bosom of the fatherland, and contrasted these stories with harrowing tales of the "living hell" that was South Korea.[27] Special material on the repatriation was also prepared for the 1960 meeting of the UN General Assembly.[28] Among the most widely circulated international propaganda on the subject was the book *Korean Returnees from Japan,* which, like the journal *Korea,* was richly illustrated, published in several languages, and filled with human-interest stories contrasting the joyful experience of return with the unhappy experiences of *zainichi* Koreans who had visited South Korea.[29]

A Meeting of Minds—The Calcutta Accord, 1959

As the mass movement for repatriation gathered momentum in the *zainichi* community and in North Korea, the Japanese government continued to follow its backdoor strategy, pursuing its aims through the intermediary of the ICRC. On February 13, 1959, the Kishi cabinet announced its "endorsement" of a mass repatriation. This endorsement (which, the government emphasized, was different from a formal cabinet "decision") was presented to the world as a humanitarian response to demands from the *zainichi* community that had taken the government entirely by surprise.[30] From that point on, the Japanese and North Korean Red Cross societies entered into intense negotiations. The discussions, held in secret in Geneva, were often acrimonious: although they agreed on the desirability of a large-scale repatriation, the two sides had fundamentally different motives, which dictated different approaches to practical details. By June 1959, however, they had produced a draft agreement and all that remained was to secure the blessing and supervision of the ICRC.

The main bone of contention in the negotiations was the role to be played by the ICRC. North Korea was reluctant to allow ICRC involvement, preferring the leadership of the national Red Cross societies and Chongryun. However, by the middle of 1959 the United States had begun to play a key background role in the process. South Korea was strongly lobbying the United States to intervene and prevent a repatriation accord between Japan and North Korea. At the same time, though, the United States was negotiating a crucial revision to its Mutual Security Treaty with Japan, for which it relied on the cooperation of the Kishi administration. Although some State Department officials clearly had misgivings about the repatriation accord, they were reluctant to pressure Kishi too hard on the matter, particularly since the repatriation of Koreans was good for Kishi's popularity with the Japanese electorate.

As the U.S. ambassador in Tokyo, Douglas MacArthur II, commented, the "American Embassy had checked Japanese opinion and found it was almost unanimously in favour of 'getting rid of the Koreans.'" MacArthur also added that he could "scarcely criticize the Japanese for this as the Koreans left in Japan are a poor lot including many Communists and many criminals."[31] As these comments suggest, key U.S. officials were concerned less about the fate of "returnees" in North Korea than about the repercussions for Japan's relations with South Korea. Ultimately, they decided that the best solution was not to oppose the repatriation outright, but to ensure active ICRC participation. This, it was anticipated, might partially allay South Korean concerns and would prevent South Korean opposition to the repatriation from gaining wide international sympathy.

While the ICRC debated whether to lend its name to the project, the intimate political connection between the Japanese Red Cross and the Japanese government became obvious. The ICRC was deeply divided on the repatriation question. Some members of the committee seem to have doubted that Koreans in Japan could really make a free choice about their futures, given the difficulties and uncertainties of their status in Japan. There were also concerns about the fate that awaited returnees in the DPRK. The task of allaying these concerns and winning the international body's consent was entrusted to Inoue Masutarō and the Japanese Ambassador to Bern, who together held intensive negotiations with ICRC officials. In the course of these discussions, the Japanese Red Cross passed on information from the government, assuring the ICRC (among other things) that Koreans received far more favorable treatment than other foreigners in Japan, and that Japanese law forbade employment discrimination on the grounds of nationality.[32] The government, via the Red Cross, also promised to issue a statement clarifying the residence status of *zainichi* Koreans who chose to remain in Japan.[33]

On the basis of such assurances, the ICRC agreed to supervise the repatriation process, and a formal agreement was signed in Calcutta on August 13, 1959. In response to pressures from North Korea, however, the Japanese government quickly watered down the commitments they had made to the ICRC. In particular, the encounter between ICRC representatives and "returnees" was reduced to a highly formalized ritual, carried out in the final days before departure from Japan (at a time when those departing had already left their homes and jobs and packed up their possessions). Rather than being seen individually, emigrants were interviewed in family groups in rooms whose doors had been removed, allowing others to hear what was being said.[34]

These compromises produced an angry reaction from the U.S. State Department, which called in the Japanese ambassador to demand an explanation: "[The] U.S. had been assured by the Japanese Government that it would not give way, nor would it in any way compromise [the] principle of voluntary repatriation. However, [the] Japanese now appeared to have done just these things . . . [The] State Department felt that [the] Japanese Government had not been completely frank and honest in the matter." Even now, however, the U.S. administration was reluctant to have a direct confrontation with Kishi, who sought to defuse their annoyance by professing himself to be "shocked when he heard about [the] way the U.S. had been treated."[35]

RETURN TO NOWHERE:
FREEDOM, RESPONSIBILITY, AND HOMECOMING

The Japanese Red Cross Society and the Japanese government, as well as the North Korean government and Chongryun, were generally successful in persuading the world of the voluntary and humanitarian nature of the return of Koreans to North Korea. An English-language history of the Japanese Red Cross, published in 1994, notes that the society faced criticism for its failure to protect allied prisoners of war during the 1940s, but that "the stand taken by the JRC in the post-war world in the matter of the repatriation of 100,000 North Koreans who had been forcibly removed to

Japan to work before and during the 1941–5 war did much to reestablish their position as an independent humanitarian organization" (Checkland 1994: 168).

In a sense, it was certainly true that most returnees to North Korea exercised a free choice to go, and that many went joyfully, full of hope for the future in the socialist homeland. It is also true that many Japanese people who assisted in the repatriation process—including rank-and-file Red Cross volunteers—did so genuinely believing that they were taking part in a humanitarian venture that might help to redress the wrongs inflicted by colonialism. However, the stories told here also suggest that the free choices of those who left were constrained and shaped by at least three forces.

Residence without Rights

The first, and perhaps the most important, force was the insecure position of *zainichi* Koreans in Japan during the 1950s and 1960s. In this case, the basic insecurity faced by ethnic minorities in many modern societies was compounded by the peculiarities of the postcolonial situation in Northeast Asia. The division of the Korean peninsula and the Japanese state's arbitrary abrogation of Japanese nationality for its former colonial subjects left Koreans in Japan in an unusually vulnerable position. Until 1965—when the normalization of relations between Japan and South Korea brought some improvements to the status of citizens of the ROK in Japan—they had no clearly defined residence rights under Japanese law. This also meant that they had no legal right to reentry if they left Japan; and those whose spouses, children, or other close relatives were still living in Korea had no right to bring family members to Japan.

Because of border controls introduced as early as 1946 by the Allied Occupation authorities in Japan, tens of thousands of *zainichi* Koreans who had made brief visits to Korea soon after the war to see relatives had, in so doing, violated migration regulations and turned themselves into "illegal immigrants" who, if discovered, were liable to deportation. The same threat hung over thousands more who had arrived as refugees from the massacres that followed the April 3, 1948, uprising on Jeju Island and from the Korean War. As I have already mentioned, the documents I have seen suggest that few if any ICRC members really understood this historical background, and the Japanese authorities, to put it gently, did little to enlighten them.

In the late 1950s, the first step toward providing a genuinely free choice for *zainichi* Koreans would have been to provide proper permanent residence rights in Japan. But instead the Japanese government actively intervened to *increase* the insecurity of Koreans in Japan by reducing their access to welfare. And no sooner had the ICRC's Resolution 20 on the "reunion of displaced people" been passed than the JRC's Inoue was writing to Geneva to seek reassurance that it would not be interpreted as giving relatives of *zainichi* Koreans the right to enter Japan, a reassurance that the ICRC's legal adviser, Henri Coursier, was happy to provide.[36] All of this, of course, had long-term consequences for *zainichi* Koreans who remained in Japan, as well as for those who left.

Information and Misinformation

A second force affecting the decision to stay or leave was the miasma of misinformation surrounding the repatriation process. While the information given by the Japanese government to the ICRC was (to borrow a phrase once used by a prominent British politician) highly economical with the truth, the information provided by North Korea and Chongryun to would-be returnees painted an utterly misleading picture of life in the socialist homeland. Returnees were, for example, repeatedly told that "all the necessities of life would be provided for," and visiting delegations were shown the modern "well-furnished houses . . . provided with a through-wire radio set" being built for *zainichi* Koreans in anticipation of their return.[37]

There is considerable anecdotal evidence that many Chongryun officials knew that the information they were distributing was misleading. Some returnees themselves may have had doubts, but left for North Korea all the same in the belief that socialism held the promise of a better future. It is important to remember that Japan in the late 1950s was a much poorer country than it is today, and that South Korea was a dictatorship where the standard of living was little higher, and may indeed have been lower, than it was in the DPRK. Nonetheless, it is also clear that returnees were often shocked by the sheer grinding poverty they encountered on their arrival in the North.

Many who went on the first repatriation ships indeed do appear to have been given houses and jobs in Pyongyang, where conditions were less harsh. But as the numbers grew, the conditions faced by returnees deteriorated. In a sense, the North Korean government became trapped by its own propaganda. By the middle of 1960, news reaching Chongryun, which was picked up by Japanese intelligence services and relayed to the JRC and in some cases also to the ICRC, showed that the DPRK was struggling to cope with the scale of the inflow. The North Korean authorities were apparently also taken aback to discover that many arriving *zainichi* Koreans spoke little Korean.[38] Letters sent back by returnees to friends and relatives in Japan, which were collected by the ICRC, contained thinly veiled criticisms of the conditions they were encountering:

> Every staple food is under government control and distributed. Rice, miso (bean paste) and shoyu (bean sauce) are specially cheap; the monthly expenses for these foodstuffs are about 8 yen in Korean money, but the cost of other and additional food is so expensive that I have to spend 30 yen per month. My income is 28 yen per month, so you can guess how it is. At present Korea is on the way to its reconstruction, so we cannot live as luxuriously as the Japanese do. However, we have hopes for a bright future.
>
> Four of us are suffering from something wrong with intestines, and our work is to go to the hospital every day. Medicine is also not so good. Moteru has stayed away from work since 2nd of this month. Mother lost her weight about 4 kilograms. I think it is the food.[39]

The Japanese government itself was clearly aware of such reports. Early in 1961, its Foreign Ministry, as part of an exchange of intelligence, provided the British Foreign Office with a report on the conditions of daily life in North Korea. It sought to refute Kim Il Sung's claims of rapid improvements in the standard of living by quoting from "letters addressed from those recently repatriated from Japan to North Korea to their relatives and friends." One of these letters comments that "urban life in Pyongyang is comparatively stable, but rural communities are suffering from the acute shortage of commodities including food." Others note that "only the inhabitants of large cities live on rice, while people in rural districts eat barley, wheat or soy beans for staple food," and that "in front of every shop there is a long queue . . . There is not even a scrubbing brush or a wooden spoon. Products of light industry are very scarce."[40]

Gender, Patriarchy, and Power in the Repatriation

The ritualized "confirmation of free will" which ultimately emerged from the negotiations surrounding repatriation also raises important problems concerning the power relationships within families, and within society more broadly. As we have seen, one of the more significant concessions to the North Korean side was that returnees confirm their wish to leave Japan not individually but in family groups. Indeed, the whole process was organized on the basis of family units. As Yi Yang-Su's experience (discussed above) shows, it was also organized in a way that reinforced the gendered assumptions of nationality law.

Among the former returnees I have interviewed is a Japanese woman, Ms. Yamada, who "returned" to North Korea in the early 1960s with her Korean husband and extended family. She recalls that as the time for departure approached, she felt increasing doubts. Together with her Japanese sister-in-law, she decided to take the opportunity of the "confirmation of free will" to tell the Red Cross representatives that they would rather stay in Japan. However, when the time came the entire extended family was asked a cursory question by officials, to which the (male) head of the family answered on behalf of everyone. In that setting, Ms. Yamada and her sister-in-law had neither the power nor the courage to make their voices heard. They both left on the repatriation ship and Ms. Yamada remained in North Korea for the next forty years. Her sister-in-law is still there today.

Of course, such stories raise complex problems. A truly individual "attestation of free will" might well have increased the already severe rifts within families caused by the repatriation. The structure of the Red Cross's confirmation, however, casts a harsh light on a problem that recurs in many "free migrations," past and present. Movement across borders is embedded in family power structures, which deeply affect the freedom of individuals to decide their futures. In the voluntary repatriation, many wives and younger members of families went reluctantly or halfheartedly. For women like Ms. Choi (introduced above) the "free choice" to leave for North Korea was a conscious act of self-sacrifice for the good of her children. Others, like Yi Yang-Su and his mother, were reluctantly forced to remain where they were.

Free choice involves assumptions about independent selfhood; these assumptions sometimes ignore the multilayered power relationships within both minority and mainstream communities. If one questions the "free choice" of Ms. Choi, it is also impossible to avoid uncomfortable doubts about the choice of Mr. Kim, who departed around the same time. Mr. Kim informed the ICRC representative that he had "escaped from a hospital for mental cases in Fukuoka Prefecture. Tokyo JRC officials checked the case and considered the man fit for repatriation. [He] showed no sign of mental disorder. He was most grateful for the possibility to get away from Japanese clinics." Before leaving for North Korea, Mr. Kim requested a special meeting with the ICRC representative, at which "he expressed again his gratitude and handed over to the ICRC representative a letter in which he pointed out that many more Koreans who were not crazy were held back in lunatic asylums."[41] Where do we place Mr. Kim's story in the narratives of "free" and "forced" migration? What multiple layers of force, and what complex meanings of "freedom," does this fragment of a life contain?

Homecoming is supposed to mark the end of diaspora. But those who "returned" to North Korea seem instead to have found themselves in the position of the exiles described by Mahmoud Darwish in his collection of poems *Victims of a Map:* "we travel like other people, but we return to nowhere" (Darwish 1984: 31). In North Korea, the returnees were readily identifiable as different and were colloquially labeled *kwipo,* an abbreviation of *kwiguktongpo*—"returned compatriots." Some returnees reciprocated by referring to the locals a "natives" or *genjūmin* (Ishimaru 2002: 148–150). From the perspective of local people, the returned compatriots became the object of mixed emotions: sympathy, support, suspicion, and envy (this last because of the consumer goods which many brought with them or received as gifts from relatives in Japan).

Returnees who have been able to speak about their experiences often acknowledge the kindness of North Korean neighbors who helped them settle in to their new lives and recall how special allowances were sometimes made for them by teachers, employers, and local officials. But as time went on, North Korean society came to be increasingly divided into an increasingly rigid hierarchy of groups defined by the revolutionary credentials of one's family. In this hierarchy, returnees from Japan found themselves placed near the bottom: excluded from access to elite education and prestigious careers. Those identified as "capitalists" or as particularly sympathetic to Japan were defined as "enemy elements," and in the early 1970s they and other returnees identified as politically suspect became the target of a purge, which, ironically, seems particularly to have focused on the ideologically committed. A large but uncertain number were sent to labor camps; some never returned.

The politics of the Cold War, in other words, magnified enormously the difficulties of an experience encountered by returnees from many diasporas. Like the ethnic Japanese from Brazil and Peru who have returned to live in Japan, like the ethnic Koreans from China [*Joseonjok*] who have gone home to South Korea, or the "overseas Indians" who have returned to Mother India, the returnees became a minority at home as they had been abroad. Unlike others, however, they would become a minority living on the last fault line of the still unfinished Cold War.

Today, former returnees from Japan are disproportionately represented among the refugees fleeing the economic chaos and repressive politics of the DPRK. Like the return itself, this new cross-border flow has become the subject of a disquieting mix of humanitarian ideals and political calculations, as governments and NGOs incorporate the refugee issue into the wider global rhetoric of "freedom" versus "the Axis of Evil." The story of repatriation told here can, I hope, contribute to a more nuanced understanding of the complex history behind that contemporary refugee flow.

I hope, too, that this story can encourage reflection on the problems of political responsibility so frequently obscured by the rhetoric of migration as free choice. The repatriation to North Korea was in one sense a "voluntary homecoming," but in another it was also the start of a new and yet unfinished journey. And the Japanese and North Korean states, together with the Red Cross societies of both nations, have yet to acknowledge their shared responsibility for creating the momentum that drew so many individual lives toward their first steps on that journey.

3. Visible and Vulnerable

The Predicament of Koreans in Japan

Sonia Ryang

Whereas the national security keyword in the United States since 2001 has been "9/11," in Japan it is "9/17." On September 17, 2002, the Japanese media reported that North Korea had abducted Japanese citizens during the 1970s and 1980s. With sensational and sentimental language, reporters relayed the shocking news that North Korean secret agents penetrated Japan's coastal prefectures and kidnapped a total of thirteen Japanese citizens, and then put them to various tasks including tutoring North Korean spies in Japanese. The victims of these bizarre crimes apparently were chosen at random, and many points, including the getaway route and other details, remain unknown or disputed to this day.[1] The news of North Korea's past crime was, needless to say, shocking for the world—perhaps not so much because North Korea did it, but because of the rather nonchalant manner in which Kim Jong Il admitted it. He literally threw the news in the face of Japanese Premier Koizumi Junichiro in what was the first ever meeting between the heads of the North Korean and Japanese states.

Within hours of the report, Korean schools, offices of the General Association of Korean Residents in Japan (Chongryun), and some Korean families and individuals began to receive death threats and other anonymous harassment.[2] In the following days reports began to emerge of Korean female students having their school uniforms slashed on crowded public transportation, being verbally abused, or even being spat at. Many Korean schools hastily organized security measures, while parents feared for their children's safety. For months and years to come, Koreans in Japan, especially those who were affiliated with Chongryun, would be vexed with worry and fear about their present and future in Japan.

To this day, the North Korean government has made no official statement or taken any action clarifying or disclaiming Chongryun's involvement in the kidnappings, which aggravates the situation for Koreans associated with Chongryun or regarded as supporters of the North. Only a handful of Koreans in Japan today support North Korea, while the majority claim no political association with either North or South. Many parents who send their children to Chongryun schools do so for the instruction in Korean language and heritage, and it would be safe to say that even Chongryun's full-time employees tend to stay with the organization because they cannot find viable alternative employment, not because they are ideologically committed to North Korea and its leadership. For those affiliated with Chongryun, therefore, the sudden eruption of hostility toward them came as a bewildering trauma and dilemma.

Even as strong anti–North Korean feelings abound, Japan has seen a boom in South Korean cultural products in recent years. Most notable is the popularity of the South Korean soap opera *Winter Sonata* [*Fuyu no sonata*] and the adoration of its lead actor, Bae Yong Joon, as well as the popularity (inspired by *Winter Sonata*) of products called *kanryū*. In November 2004, when Bae briefly visited Japan, about 3,500 fans, mostly women, rushed into the airport to have a glimpse of him—in the ensuing jostling some ten women were injured and sent to the hospital. News of Bae's visit was announced on TV via bulletins superimposed on the screen during afternoon variety shows, as if it was breaking news. The DVD version of *Winter Sonata* sold 360,000 copies in Japan, and one think tank estimated that in 2004 the series generated a massive 122.5 billion yen in Japan.[3]

Japan's postwar national reconstruction was energetic and successful, and in a way it directed the Japanese away from war and militaristic ambitions (the postwar constitution's renouncing war also played no small part in this outcome). And certainly the Japanese people made heroic efforts to achieve the goal of national rebuilding. But the postwar history of Japan was equally characterized by the emergence of a victim consciousness (due to the atomic bombings it suffered at the hands of the Allied forces) on the one hand, and an erasure of Koreans and other former colonial subjects on the other. This erasure was achieved primarily through a program of systematically imposed invisibility, most notably through the 1952 withdrawal of Japanese citizenship for all Koreans in Japan (see the introduction and chapter 6 in this volume). Koreans became an inexplicable population in the Japanese state's classification system. They disappeared—from the national census, from public service jobs, from national pension benefits. And they disappeared from the list of wounded veterans and atomic bomb victims. Because of their exclusion from postwar national membership, Koreans became invisible. Yet with the recent revelation of North Korea's past kidnappings, Koreans are becoming once again visible—almost hypervisible. In what follows, I explore this notion of visibility and invisibility—or more precisely, the paradox between the visible and the invisible—with reference to the Korean diaspora in Japan. I focus on so-called North Koreans in Japan, those affiliated with Chongryun, paying particular attention to female students—their visual image, their ethnicized agency especially as it is embodied in school uniforms, and their positionality in both the ethnic community and the host society.

Estimated at 100,000 out of a total of about 650,000 Koreans living in Japan, Chongryun-affiliated Koreans are an extreme minority in Japan today, and the female school-age population is, needless to say, even smaller.[4] As I have already implied, today's "Chongryun-affiliated Koreans" (I use the term "Chongryun Koreans" interchangeably) are in an ambivalent position with respect to Chongryun. They by and large are *not* Chongryun's political supporters or full-time employees. Rather, their affiliation with Chongryun came after the fact or as an afterthought, following the historical process of national partition, civil war, and Cold War. Most of today's Chongryun Koreans are accidental affiliates of Chongryun—their parents chose to have them educated in Chongryun schools, and they in turn tend to send their children to Chongryun schools at least part time. As such, their positionality vis-à-vis Chongryun has shifted drastically, even fundamentally, since the early 1990s when I launched my anthropological research into "North Koreans in Japan" (see, e.g., Ryang 1997b). Given the recent vulnerability faced by so-called Chongryun Koreans, one must be extremely careful in understanding and delineating the personal, historical, and social connections—however intermittent and unstable—that any Korean might have with Chongryun. Any such connection most likely does not embody any political commitment whatsoever.

Yet, with anti-Chongryun, anti–North Korean atmospheric pressure currently dominant in Japan's political climate, the media narrative of "Chongryun Koreans" who are loyal followers of the Kim regime and North Korea's state ideology has been noticeable; this in turn intensifies the vulnerability of those Koreans, sometimes endangering their very existence. Female students are singled out as the hypervisible targets, due to their ethnically (and hence politically) identifiable school uniforms. (Of course, every bully knows that girls are supposed to be the easiest to attack.)

In order to place these students and the situation they face in a more concrete context, I first present a brief history of Chongryun. Then, I look closely at the recent changes affecting the lives of Chongryun-affiliated Koreans. These changes are underpinned by the paradox of invisibility and hypervisibility I have already mentioned. I capture the moments where diversity and difference have led to clashes within Chongryun's community by briefly discussing a school meeting between mothers and administrators. In closing, I address the question of Japan as a host society, asking whether Japanese society qualifies as a "host" for Koreans—or for any diasporic people for that matter.[5] As I shall argue, the visibility (or the lack thereof) of a diasporic people reveals unexpected contours of shifting relations of power and deployment of agency in accommodating (or not) elements that are perceived as nonnational, i.e., different from or outside of the national.

BACKGROUND

Chongryun, or the General Association of Korean Residents in Japan, was founded in 1955 as a result of ten years of tumultuous expatriate politics and international conflict. It was founded by Korean nationalists in Japan whose aim was the eventual repatriation of all Koreans in Japan to a unified, communist Korea; as such, it defined all Koreans in Japan as North Korea's overseas nationals. This was a revision, historically speaking, of the previously understood position of Koreans in Japan. Immediately after World War II, the Korean left was actively involved with the Japan Communist Party in the joint cause of overthrowing the Japanese government. Leftist Koreans therefore defined themselves as Japan's ethnic minority; that is, though not Japanese, they assumed they had a life-and-death stake in the transformation of Japanese society. With the emergence of Chongryun, this self-understanding was radically altered. Chongryun declared itself to be a North Korean (i.e., foreign) organization in Japan and therefore made it clear that it would refrain from meddling in Japanese domestic politics and strenuously abide by the Japanese law. All forms of illegal activities were abandoned thereafter (Ryang 1997b: chs. 3–4).

In many respects, Chongryun can be seen as a successor to the original postwar Korean leftist expatriate organization, the League of Koreans. The League's activities did not start as pro–North Korean political activism, but as the tension on the Korean peninsula rose and the polarization of North and South became increasingly irreversible, the League became more inclined to side with North Korea. This was not welcomed by either the

U.S. Occupation or the Japanese authorities. Thus, in 1949 the League was suppressed under the Subversive Activities Prevention Law.[6] The merciless suppression of the League had been preceded by the forcible closure of Korean schools under the League's influence: during the 1948 closures by the U.S. military, numerous injuries and some deaths occurred.[7] After its emergence in 1955, Chongryun actively reconstructed the ethnic schools that the League used to operate. It placed top priority on turning students into North Korea's overseas nationals, not only by emphasizing Korean language education but also by emphasizing North Korea–focused nationalist ideology. Thus, schools emerged as the key apparatus for Chongryun's expatriate politics.

Chongryun's new policy of rendering every aspect of its activity lawful in the eyes of the Japanese state necessitated the state accreditation of Korean schools. Since Chongryun was not prepared to relinquish its pedagogical autonomy to the Ministry of Education of Japan, it pursued the astute strategy of accrediting its schools as miscellaneous [*kakushugakkō*], that is, not entitled to issue academic certificates and degrees. In this way, Chongryun schools all became fully legal, and yet the Japanese Ministry of Education to this day cannot interfere with its management, pedagogical philosophy, or curricular planning (Ryang 1997b: ch. 1).

Although the 1965 normalization of relations with South Korea allowed Koreans in Japan both South Korean nationality and permanent residence in Japan, Chongryun continued to enjoy the mass support of Koreans in Japan throughout the 1960s and 1970s, far more than its rival Mindan, the pro-South expatriate organization. In 1981, Chongryun-affiliated Koreans, who after 1965 typically would not have obtained permanent residence in Japan by applying for South Korean nationality, also became eligible for permanent residence in Japan. This was related to Japan's ratifying the UN Universal Declaration of Human Rights in 1979 and the International Refugee Convention and Protocol in 1982. These legal changes had clear impacts on Chongryun (see also Kashiwazaki 2000a). Chongryun-affiliated Koreans were now able to obtain a reentry permit to Japan, which enabled them to travel abroad. They also could visit North Korea, mostly under the pretext of reuniting with those family members who had been repatriated following the 1959 agreement between the Japanese and North Korean Red Cross (see chapter 2). But Chongryun systematically exploited this pathway by sending its activists for long-term reeducation and retraining courses, its teachers and education experts for consultation with North Korean experts in order to update Chongryun's textbooks, its artists for tutelage by North Korean artists, its students for "fatherland visitation" trips, and its affiliates for the "reward and recognition" of their devotion and cooperation. Thus, thousands of Chongryun Koreans eventually would visit North Korea (Ryang 2000).

What was intended as an emotional and moving visit to the "glorious socialist fatherland" (as Chongryun's rhetoric would have it), however, became an experience of sorrow and disillusionment, bitterness and dilemma. The North Korea that Chongryun affiliates saw with their own eyes was not the "paradise on earth" depicted in Chongryun propaganda, but a poor, struggling country, in which even the high-ranking personnel assigned to supervise visitors seemed completely out of touch with global reality. The stories they heard from their repatriated former classmates, neighbors, and, above all, family members were neither pleasing nor encouraging. They told of discrimination and distrust directed toward Chongryun returnees, including the realization that no returnee could possibly become a cadre in North Korea. The fantastic, dream-like stories that Chongryun Koreans were fed in the initial period of repatriation—of Kim Il Sung paying a surprise visit to the dormitory of Chongryun returnee children, for example, or of a repatriated family being given an enormous house and a comfortable living, complete with rewarding employment and social position for the parents and higher education and the bright future of becoming doctor or politician for the children—were either completely nonexistent or only partially and remotely true. Ironically, once Chongryun Koreans could actually go visit North Korea, their interest in and sympathy for the so-called fatherland waned; accordingly, Chongryun's authority and legitimacy began to fade away.

During the 1980s generational change within Japan's Korean communities became pronounced. The passionate homeland politics of the first generation was no longer mainstream in the Chongryun Korean population. Although younger Chongryun activists and officers were, in a way, better educated and indoctrinated into Chongryun's organizational doxa and North Korea–oriented values, they were also more realistic and practical with regard to the possibility (or the lack thereof) of the eventual repatriation of all Koreans in Japan to a reunified fatherland. Korea had been divided for close to four decades, and no positive sign of reunification emerged even as iron curtains were lifted in other parts of the world. In the meantime, younger Chongryun Koreans were growing up as perfectly acculturated, socioeconomically savvy, and linguistically masterful members of Japanese society. The standard of living for Koreans in Japan as a whole had improved thanks to the hard work of the first generation as well as Japan's long-lasting boom following the Korean War; in particular, education levels rose steadily.

At its peak, Chongryun had more than 150 schools at all levels, including K-12, college, and graduate school. Chongryun's Korea University (in Tokyo) provided higher education to future teachers for Chongryun schools. All Chongryun schools use a unified set of textbooks that are designed and written by Chongryun's teachers and education personnel, printed and produced in Chongryun's textbook company, and distributed free of charge to its students. Because Chongryun schools are not accredited as degree-granting institutions, the Japanese Ministry of Education cannot interfere with their textbook content or classroom teaching. Thus, the schools' focus on North Korea, their pedagogical orientation of enhancing students' loyalty to the North Korean leadership, and their North Korean–style organizational and political life (such as the Young Pioneers) all fall outside of the Japanese state apparatus.

Reflecting the changing political climate and generational shifts, among other factors, periodically Chongryun has updated and reformed its curricula systematically. By the time Kim Il Sung passed away in 1994, Chongryun was in the middle of its most radical curricular reform: it abolished all mention of Kim Il Sung's "revolutionary pedigree" in elementary and middle school. Thus, subjects such as the "Childhood of Father Marshal Kim Il Sung" and "Revolutionary History of the Great Leader Marshal Kim Il Sung," which used to be classified as ideological education [*sasang kyoyang kwamok*] and were taught ritually with a strict code of conduct, were abolished (Ryang 1997b: ch.2). In the early-twenty-first century, all portraits of Kim Il Sung and his son Kim Jong Il were pulled down from the classrooms of Chongryun's elementary and middle schools.

Today, the predominant majority of Koreans in Japan possess South Korean nationality. This does not mean they support South Korea, in my view, since the confrontational expatriate politics of the Cold War is long gone and many Koreans in Japan adopt South Korean nationality primarily out of convenience. Without South Korean nationality they would have no passport: the permanent residence that Koreans in Japan have become entitled to since the early 1980s, whether or not they possess South Korean nationality, provides them with only a makeshift laissez-passer called a "reentry permit" to Japan, and travel to all destinations except North Korea requires a preissued visa. This is an enormous inconvenience, and its cumbersome procedures got much worse after September 11, 2001. Overseas tourism or study abroad has become a relatively stable component of the lives of Koreans in Japan, as with any peoples in the industrialized world, and therefore, a passport has become imperative for many Koreans in Japan including those associated with Chongryun.

The majority of Koreans in Japan have no ability to speak or understand Korean, since only an extreme minority attends Chongryun schools—there are fewer than 12,000 total students attending approximately 120 schools of all levels[8]—and even those who study at Chongryun schools are not fully competent in Korean comprehension (see below). Chongryun's organizational publications are now predominantly issued bilingually in Korean and Japanese, and Chongryun offices are filled with activists who no longer can communicate in proper Korean. The old and new forces still clash, and the micropolitics of ethnic identity is still strained with division and disagreements, further frustrating younger activists and encouraging their attrition.[9]

Chongryun's local offices now face closure due to loss of membership, bank foreclosures, and the inability to pay rent and taxes. Financial scandals involving illegal transactions with North Korea and tax evasion in Japan produced wide-ranging investigations by Japanese authorities and resulted in some arrests. Chongryun-owned credit unions can no longer facilitate wire transfers to accounts in North Korea, formerly the only direct route for remittances between Japan and North Korea. Since 2006, all North Korean passenger ships have been banned from entering Japanese ports.[10] In the prolonged aftermath of the 2002 abduction scandal, the Abe administration in Japan has repeated the police searches, round-ups, and arrest of Chongryun offices and officers, evidently determined to take advantage of the situation to satisfy rightist ressentiment and thereby boost its popularity. The ever-closed nature of Japanese society as a receptacle for Koreans and other ethnic minorities is exacting a costly toll on many Koreans in Japan, who are genuinely at a loss regarding their children's future. Today, after half a century nurturing an expatriate movement in support of North Korea, Chongryun schools face the genuine and urgent need to transform themselves in order to cope with such acute issues as guaranteeing the basic security of students in addition to preserving its political identity. Predictably, the discrepancy between parents' concerns and expectations, on the one hand, and school authorities' management style, on the other, is widening, as the following shows.

VISIBLE AND VULNERABLE

In spring 2005, the T-1 Korean elementary and middle school mothers' association called for a meeting with the school's top administrators. The principal, deputy, and a few others were met by about thirty angry mothers whose daughters had to wear Western-style uniforms to get to school and then, once on the premises, had to change into Korean-style uniforms. Chongryun's Korean school system had implemented the dual-uniform measure to combat frequent incidents of slashing, cutting, and otherwise damaging girls' Korean uniforms by Japanese perpetrators. Each set of uniforms cost approximately 40,000 yen, for a total of 80,000 yen, a cost as well as a burden not born by boys, who wear one Western-style uniform both inside and outside of school. In the meeting, the administrators emphasized how important it was to preserve national heritage, even arguing that by wearing Korean uniforms, girls helped boys sustain their ethnic and national pride. The mothers were evidently agitated by this argument, since it clearly assumed that girls were subordinated and used as a proxy to educate boys, and yet the principal appeared clueless as to why the mothers were so critical.

In Chongryun schools, to this day a female principal is extremely rare, and good female teachers tend to hit a glass ceiling and end up leaving. According to a few mothers, while there are obviously exceptions, the female teachers who stay on tend to be the ones who are not very serious about education—as one mother cynically remarked, it's a better work environment than being a part-time cashier at a local supermarket. Male teachers, even when they are obviously less capable, are regularly given promotions. After three or four years, a young male Korea University graduate would be made the Young Pioneer supervisor, a political first step because membership in the Young Pioneers is mandatory for all students in Chongryun schools between grades four and nine. This position typically would be followed by his promotion to lower-grade-school administrator, which then would carry him smoothly on to a middle school administrative position. If he were to remain and cause no particular problems (even with no particular merit), he would eventually become deputy and then principal. Such a path is nearly completely closed for female teachers, who, upon appointment, are normally seen as lasting only three to four years before marriage and pregnancy.

Not surprisingly, then, on the day of the meeting all of the school representatives were male. What frustrated the mothers was not simply the way the principal handled their grievances but the lack of communication or common ground. For the mothers, choice of clothing was less important than learning Korean properly, for example. One mother quoted her daughter's yearbook, which was written by students in Korean, yet was full of erroneous spelling and incomprehensible expressions, and jumbled with Japanese-influenced foreign terms, all of which were placed in a nonsensical manner. This, for many mothers, was an urgent and serious problem that teachers should address, as opposed to forcing female students to continue wearing Korean uniforms. But teachers did not think so—for them, it was more important for girls to embody ethnic and national pride in their appearance. They labeled the mothers' demands "unpatriotic," "defeatist," and "rightist-opportunist," while mothers saw a crisis in the school's inability to identify what was most important pedagogically and make appropriate changes.

Frustrated, one mother stood up and almost shouted: "So, do you want us all to transfer our daughters to Japanese school? Their financial cost is double of male students' expenses. They are not even learning Korean properly. What, would anyone tell me, is the good reason for sending our daughters to Korean school?" The principal's answer was: "This is the tradition that has lasted for half a century. I will not be able to change it under my leadership." It was clear to the meeting participants that the school authorities were not open to listening to the mothers, and the meeting ended in discord.

For any observer familiar with Chongryun, it would have been very impressive that thirty-some mothers gathered signatures and came up with well-thought-out, concrete demands, as such action is not commonly taken in Chongryun schools. Perhaps for this very reason, school administrators saw it as a threat and intimidation—they were intimidated not simply by the mothers but also by the idea that they could be held responsible for any kind of unprecedented change. They ultimately were accountable not to mothers or students, but to Chongryun's higher authority. Mothers felt betrayed by the school's investment in a "tradition" that was only superficial (at the expense of the girls), while the genuine tradition (proper language education) was neglected and left to die out. In fact, I, a product of Chongryun education some decades ago, recently noticed that teachers at the Korean schools, although recent Korea University graduates, were unable to speak Korean fluently: their self-expression was impoverished and insufficient—sometimes embarrassingly so—while their Korean pronunciation was awkward, as if I was listening to the transliterated Korean words read out in Japanese enunciation. It was clear that they had a very limited vocabulary and were unable to communicate spontaneously in Korean. Perhaps the above mother's question is right: why send children to Korean schools that cannot teach Korean properly?

The primary concern that makes Korean mothers hesitate to transfer their children to Japanese schools is the possibility of isolation, discrimination, and ostracism by Japanese teachers and peers. In general, they worry about how rapidly violent Japanese society is turning.[11] Of course, this is a concern that any parent in Japan, regardless of ethnicity and nationality, has to deal with, since youth tend to be the most vulnerable members of society. But Korean parents must worry about another factor that can render their children vulnerable and on the defensive—their non-Japanese identity. Between stagnant pedagogical and administrative policies in Korean schools on the one hand and worsening conditions in Japanese schools on the other, Korean parents are truly in a predicament.

In any event, the majority of parents eventually transfer their children to Japanese schools for either the middle or high school. This, however, is becoming an increasingly costly operation. Since Korean parents are concerned with the deterioration of Japanese public education (especially in urban areas such as Tokyo), they try to place their children in private schools. The entrance exams for those schools require a higher GPA, however, so parents supplement the regular school day with evening cramming classes. One parent whose son takes these classes (from 7:00 to 9:00 P.M. five days a week) pays close to $400.00 per month. The following year, his younger brother will join him, doubling the expense. Not everyone has these funds at his or her disposal. In this light, the cost of a double set of uniforms for girls simply augments parents' burden.

And yet the debate over uniforms is not just one of cost, but of ethnic identity and its visibility. Since the colonial period, the visibility of Koreans in Japanese society was borne by women, who continued to wear ethnic clothing one way or the other. Indeed, the image of Korean womanhood as marked by clothing was captured in many renowned Japanese literary and photographic representations, including the lyrics of Nakano Shigeharu, *chōsen onna no fuku no himo* ("long ties of a Korean woman's dress"). Whereas men who had to work in factories or mines, for example, were unable to carry on wearing Korean costume and shifted to clothing more appropriate to their workplace, women kept the clothes they wore when they left Korea. The homebound existence of women in both Korea and Japan facilitated continuity in their dress. (Obviously, a different trajectory was created for Korean women who came to Japan as workers themselves, although they were a minority.) And practically speaking, most women simply could not afford to replace their Korean clothes with the clothes they saw in Japanese stores.

The association of the visual/visible marker of Korean ethnicity with women's clothing rendered it a gender-specific visibility. In this sense, it is unsurprising that school administrators internalized and reproduced this gender-specificity, insisting that the burden of ethnic marking is borne solely by female students. (Phenotypically, after all, a Korean is hardly distinguishable from a Japanese.) The logic behind it, according to the principal, is that it is a fifty-year tradition, Korean clothing embodies ethnic pride, and it helps nonbearers (such as male students) enhance their ethnic self-esteem.

As I have mentioned, before Chongryun schools adopted the double-uniform policy, female students' Korean-style uniforms subjected them to assault, harassment, and violence. For example, in 1994—when North Korea's nuclear weapons program was increasingly attracting Japanese media attention—a total of 154 incidents of abuse toward Korean school students was reported between April and July alone. The majority of the victims were girls whose uniforms were cut, torn, and soiled (Han 2004b: 118). After the September 17, 2002, revelation of North Korea's kidnappings, the harassment resurged and now included spitting and verbal intimidation (see, for example, Johnston 2002 and McNeill 2005).

On one level, Chongryun's burdening of young female bodies is analogous to the postwar silence around and ostracism suffered by former "comfort women"—women whose bodies were used by the Japanese imperial military, yet who were marginalized and dehumanized by a South Korean society that saw their violated bodies as the shame of the masculinized nation. In a larger sense, all of these bodies—of former "comfort women" and students alike—are treated as disposable, not only by violators (Japanese soldiers and anti-Korean citizens who harass students, respectively) but also by their own communities' dominant masculinist logics, which place female bodies on the front line as the first and most fragile sacrifice given to protect national orthodoxy or, in the case of Chongryun schools, to enhance the national pride of male students. In either case, young female bodies are reduced into a medium, an incomplete and derivative charade of national integrity, only to be used when they are convenient for the nation's manhood.[12]

This kind of exploitation of female corporeal visibility is widely seen in historically and geographically diverse instances of nationalism and anticolonial resistance. But at the same time, it is also true that female members of the colonized, resisting nation willingly participate in struggles for national independence, involving considerable sacrifice on their part. As such, female participation in nationalistic movements, and in particular the deployment of female bodies in such instances, allows for no simple or unidirectional understanding. Considered in the context of agency, subjectivity, docility, or disciplinarity, female bodies cannot be just disposable objects of male calculation. How should we, then, understand the complexity of the position in which Chongryun's female students are placed? And, how does that position relate to the larger Korean diaspora in Japan?

In order to place Chongryun's female students against the background of Japan's Korean diaspora, the research conducted by Han Tong-Hyun, a Korean scholar in Japan, gives us a helpful opening. In critiquing the assumption that traditional Korean dress is simply a symbol of patriarchy, she argues for the need to look closer at the agency of Korean female students, who, in the 1950s, voluntarily created Korean school uniforms by adapting them from traditional dress (Han 2004a, 2006). Han's interview data reveal that the adoption of Korean traditional clothing as school uniforms was itself an ethnic assertion in contradistinction from the Japanese mainstream. Around 1959, female students in Chongryun schools began to wear uniforms based on traditional Korean clothing, and by 1963 or 1964, the Chongryun school system standardized its uniforms for girls (in middle school and higher) with that style as a basis (Han 2004b: 111). Precisely speaking, it was a modernized or reformed version of Korean women's dress, which in fact Ewha Women's College had adopted for a short period of time under Japanese colonial rule, before the Japanese authorities in Korea banned all Korean-style school uniforms. The design adopted by Chongryun female students—apparently unaware of Ewha's precedent—was inspired by the ancient Korean female attire that included a pleated skirt, which conformed at least partly with the dominant design for female middle and high school uniforms in Japan—the sailor-colored top and pleated skirt (Han 2004a: 33–38, 42–43). The bodice of the Korean school uniforms was, however, unmistakable—it is a traditional Korean bodice with half-moon sleeves and long straps to be tied askance on the chest, much shorter than the bodice of the contemporary Japanese uniforms.

According to the recollections of Han's interviewees, Chongryun's female college students were the first to put on this style of clothing as uniforms. One of the women Han interviewed emphasizes that it was considered important to show the Japanese people that Koreans were different. Interestingly, another interviewee, a parent who otherwise is very proud of having disseminated the Korean-style uniforms among Chongryun's female students, is highly critical of how unprepared Chongryun has been to adapt to the shifting situations faced by Koreans in Japan, including the recent violent assaults (Han 2004a: 75).

What we can see here is a criss-crossing of the deployment of feminine ethnicity's visible signifiers with the changing contours of diaspora. In the early years of Chongryun's ethnic education, Korean female students projected visibility by making themselves look different from the rest of the Japanese society, even as Koreans became invisible in official Japanese national discourse. But even then, such an assertion was not directed solely at the Japanese nation: some women had to run away from their parents (or, more precisely, fathers) in order to attend Korea University in Tokyo, since their fathers would not accept the idea that girls should receive higher education (Han 2004a: 80–81). The adoption of traditional Korean clothing as daily attire, in this sense, was a visual demonstration not only of their non-Japanese existence to the larger Japanese society but also of their capability and willingness to participate in the patriotic cause of Chongryun, resisting and confronting the dominant values of their family and hometown. In this sense, traditional dress, which at a glance would seem to signify patriarchy and gender inequality, functioned as the signifier of the opposite, the embodiment of emancipation.

It is, then, an irony to see that this projection of female visibility, which was originally appropriated as a means to assert ethnic and gender identity, has made girls and young women objects of persecution in Japan's current tense, anti–North Korean atmosphere. It is no coincidence that these hate crimes target girls' clothing—by slicing the pleated skirt or bodice—as they aim to defile and deform the visible signifier of Koreanness, which, in the eyes of the perpetrators, should be invisible in Japanese society.

PREDICAMENT

The T-1 Korean School had enjoyed regular exchanges with the neighboring H Japanese Elementary School for twenty years or so. But a few years ago, H Elementary School officially requested that all exchanges between students and teachers cease. According to some mothers, since Ishihara Shintarō's election as the Tokyo metropolitan mayor, Tokyo public school teachers are regularly investigated and publicly criticized if they are seen as overly friendly with Korean school personnel. Rumor has it that the mayor calls out personally individual teachers who are seen as pro-Korean and publicly humiliates them and their schools. It is hard to substantiate the rumor, but it is generally true that being seen as pro-Korean is today tantamount to being seen as anti-patriotic, anti-nationalist, and anti-Japanese. This same mayor's government is being sued by twenty-five teachers in protest of its 2003 ruling that made it compulsory in public schools to stand with respect while singing *Kimigayo* (His Majesty's Reign), Japan's national anthem, which is closely associated with its imperialist past

(James 2005). In this climate, Korean parents perceive their school's future as extremely volatile.

As I have stated in the introduction and throughout this chapter, Chongryun Koreans have been made extremely vulnerable and insecure since the crisis of 9/17. Although this sense of crisis has been most keenly perceived by girls and young women and their immediate protectors, the general sense of bewilderment and crisis prevails throughout the organization at all levels and in all branches in the face of more intrusive state intervention and control. In a way, the hapless response displayed by T-1 School's administrators corresponds to the dilemma faced by the entirety of Chongryun. Just like some diasporic Muslim communities in the United States and Britain, for example, they are held responsible for the crimes committed by "other" (North) Koreans.

In the meantime, they do not even have North Korean nationality and citizenship: if they were to move to North Korea, there would be no guarantee of sanctuary. As Morris-Suzuki depicts in chapter 2, the life of returnees is harsh and trying. Kang Chol-Hwan's memoir is one among many stories about returnees from Japan being sent to concentration camps in North Korea for no particular reason (Kang 2002). Four brothers of Chon Wolson, a prominent Korean soprano in Japan, were repatriated in the 1960s and spent nine years in a concentration camp. One died there and recently two others died of unknown causes, while the remaining brother is missing (Chon 2006). Many Koreans in Japan whose families and friends have repatriated have heard and been faced with the news of exile and banishment in the North Korean camps (Ryang 2008).

Since 2002, Japanese state authorities—including taxation, police, education, immigration, and municipal authorities—as well as the mass media have been conspicuously targeting Koreans in Japan for dehumanization as retaliation for North Korea's kidnappings, as if to say that by persecuting those Koreans living in Japan, the kidnapping issue would be resolved. Numerous arrests, searches, and random inspections have taken place and are ongoing, on the basis of little more than a remote suspicion of past involvement with or donation to Chongryun.

On April 25, 2007, police searched the Tokyo home of a woman who was allegedly a former North Korean agent for her involvement in the 1973 abduction of two children on the northern island of Hokkaido. On the same day, in a manner reminiscent of the 1949 raid and suppression of the League of Koreans, police stormed premises housing a Chongryun-affiliated research office. Chongryun protesters resisted on site, resulting in numerous arrests for obstruction of justice ("Police Raid N. Korea-Related Facilities" 2007).

Such high-handed, forceful treatment of Chongryun would have been unthinkable even ten years ago, because of concern over possible protest by Japanese leftist, pacifist groups. But today, the Japanese government appears to be comfortable delivering such actions against Chongryun, since there is hardly any recognizable opposition in Japan's political and civic arenas. On the contrary, a tough line against Koreans (any Koreans) in Japan seems to earn mass support.

Witnessing Japan's social climate turning radically against North Korea, Chongryun Koreans are concerned but at a loss about where to turn; they trust neither Koizumi nor Kim. A few parents told me that they could visualize themselves as the first casualties of any hostility between Japan and North Korea: "If North Korea were to be crazy enough to launch a nuclear missile attack on Japan, the Japanese government would round us up and either send us to clean up the radioactive mess, or simply incarcerate us," one parent remarked. Among some Chongryun Koreans I have interacted with over the years, the scenario of a Japan–North Korea war sits as a heavy burden, a remote but nevertheless plausible menace. Anti–North Korean sentiment seems to suffuse Japanese society from the central government down to the level of the individual citizen, as manifested in the aftermath of a dispute over the bones of a Japanese woman who had been kidnapped and was said to have died in North Korea, a dispute that culminated in active discussion of sanctions, on the one hand, and isolated yet equally threatening reports of attacks on Korean female students, on the other (McCormack 2005, International Crisis Group 2005).

With this sense of crisis, concerned Chongryun Koreans worry about the animated debate over the amendment of Article Nine of the Japanese Constitution, the "no war" clause. With the proposed amendment aiming at enabling the deployment of the "Self-Defense Force" in a military *offensive*, Japan would once again be entitled to launch an attack. Having been aggressively indoctrinated into nationalism and now aware of its dangers, Chongryun Koreans are especially sensitive to such a move. As I have shown, the community has slowly come to the realization that North Korea is not the beloved homeland, but the decisive break came with the 9/17 revelations and the North Korean leadership's subsequent failure to display any concern whatsoever toward Koreans in Japan, who had supported the regime, financially and morally, for over half a century. Such a realization came as an anticlimax, since it followed a steady erosion of trust, yet it was an effective moment of awakening. With the possibility of any sanctuary in North Korea foreclosed, Chongryun Koreans became sensitized to the potential danger they face in Japan.

It is not just a handful of Chongryun Koreans who worry about today's Japanese society. According to Toru Hayano, the Asahi commentator I have already mentioned, voters and citizens who used to be attracted to Koizumi's reform-mindedness are today disillusioned by his inability to change society fundamentally, or are just bored with politics altogether and have shifted their passion to *Winter Sonata* and Bae Yong Joon. His worries about today's and tomorrow's Japan are encapsulated in a comment by Banno Junji, an emeritus professor from Tokyo University and prominent historian of prewar Japan, who compares today's Japan to the Japan of 1936–37 (Hayano 2004; Banno 2004, 2001).

The year 1937, of course, is the year of the Nanjing Massacre, more commonly known as the Rape of Nanjing, in which thousands of Japanese soldiers rushed into the ancient Chinese city of Nanjing, under orders to rape all females from toddler to elderly and kill all males, again, from toddler to elderly. This reverie of rape and massacre was carried out in the name of benevolent love for the emperor. One year earlier, in 1936, the Japanese media had been captivated by the obscenity of the Abe Sada murder and castration, which also was done in the name of love, albeit the love of one woman (Ryang 2006a: ch. 2). This violent mood swing from a single woman to the ruling and ruining of a nation is unmistakable. Do we see a parallel here, in that the energy and attention directed to Koizumi's political reform are now channeled to a South Korean soap opera, *Winter Sonata*, which brought to Japan the so-called *kanryū*, or South Korean popular culture boom? Could this same force swiftly produce the intensely anti–North Korean atmosphere in Japan?

The years 1936–37 saw the Sino-Japanese War become radically aggravated. Two years later, the Japanese government–initiated forced labor mobilization of Koreans officially began; four years later, the conscription of Korean males to the emperor's army became the law; in the meantime, hundreds of girls from the peninsula were hunted down and taken as military sex slaves. These were the times when an amorphous, otherwise dispersed population and its energy were quickly organized under a simplistic yet appealing slogan: the imperial destiny of Japan in East and Southeast Asia under the slogan of the East Asian Co-Prosperity Sphere.

It is against this background that worries arise when attention is lavished on the misfortunes of Japanese kidnappees in North Korea while hardly any public concern is shown (beyond a narrow circle of committed individuals) for the hundreds of Korean comfort women, themselves colonial hostages.[13] Commentators worry that today's parliamentarians have no idea what war means and that there is no real opposition to national mobilization, militarization, and defense, including the amendment of Article Nine (Littlefield 2005, McNeill 2006, Koike 2006, Yamaguchi 2006, and Nabeshima 2006). According to one survey, 62 percent of the population wants the Self-Defense Force to be granted the power to enter war ("Survey: 62% Want SDF Acknowledged" 2006).[14] At the same time, according to one poll, only thirteen percent believes that further apology to Asian nations is necessary (Horsley 2005). In a particularly egregious display, Prime Minister Abe rejected accusations that Japan coerced Asian (mostly Korean) women into military sexual slavery in a denial that has been described as "the clearest so far" compared to any of his predecessors (Onishi 2007).

In the meantime, Japan's closed nature toward non-Japanese members of society continues to be noticed. In 2005, Doudou Diene, a United Nations special rapporteur on racism and xenophobia, characterized Japan's racism as "deep and profound" (Hogg 2005). Is this a transient reaction in the face of the sudden influx of immigrants since the 1990s, or is it something that Japanese society cannot overcome? Conversely, is a society like Japan capable of having diasporic communities within itself?

Diaspora is talked about mainly in terms of diasporic people themselves, their identity, history, and above all suffering. Or it needs to be accompanied by the history and ongoing reality of persecution. Perhaps it would be useful to have a set of theoretical and empirical tools to assess the host society in terms of its capability of being a host to any diasporic community. A society such as Japan that firmly stands on the belief in its monoethnicity might be unfit to be a host society for modern diasporas. I state this with a certain urgency: it is public knowledge that since 9/17, North Korea has been roundly demonized and Chongryun-affiliated Koreans marginalized and isolated. The current situation creates constraints not just on the diasporic community but on Japanese society as well. How can this community survive as a diasporic community, if not as a North Korean community (which it never has been, as I have shown)? If the current association of Chongryun with North Korea is in part a product of the Japanese media, it needs to be noted that some Japanese and Western commentators also equate Chongryun and North Korea in a facile manner. Very little historical judgment is used in assessing the complexity of the historical raison d'être of the people known as "North Koreans" in Japan.[15]

POSTSCRIPT

Since the North Korean missile crisis of July 4, 2006—in which North Korea launched multiple long-range missiles into the Sea of Japan, refused to comply with a UN Security Council decision, and continuously threatened the world (more succinctly, the United States) that in case of any attack on its soil it would retaliate—parents of Korean schoolchildren have lived in a déjà vu of post-9/17 tension.[16] The T-1 Korean School practiced a group escort between school and home until summer break began. In August 2006, the Japanese Ministry of Justice announced a restrictive policy on non–South Korean nationality holders (many of them Chongryun Koreans), reducing the duration of their reentry permits from four years to a maximum of one year. And it made mandatory that they report the purpose and itinerary of their trips when applying for re-entry permits. Despite having identical permanent residence, South Korean nationality holders are not sanctioned in this way.[17]

As I write this, news of searches of Chongryun buildings and arrests of Chongryun personnel continue to reach me. A mother at T-1 school writes asking, "Why doesn't Abe just leave us alone? Surely, he knows that Chongryun will die away anyways and without him doing anything, Korean schools will go bankrupt on their own." Abe's "civil war" against Chongryun and Koreans in Japan is gaining ground, because Chongryun's destruction, in post-9/17 Japanese public discourse, has come to symbolize some kind of closure of the 2002 kidnappings. The long, strenuous search for safety and security for Koreans in Japan thus continues. When one's energy is diverted toward day-to-day vigilance, there is no mental room to introspect on one's ontological status, the meaning of life, or its beauty. When a diasporic community is denationalized, constantly on the defensive, there is no being at home.

4. Reinventing Korean Roots and *Zainichi* Routes

The Invisible Diaspora among Naturalized Japanese of Korean Descent

Youngmi Lim

INTRODUCTION: IS THE PERSONAL DIASPORIC?

Responding to my e-mail thanking her for an interview, Mika,[1] a fourth-generation self-identified "ex-*zainichi*" [*moto zainichi*], a naturalized Japanese of colonial Korean descent,[2] wrote:

> On my way home, on the train, I realized one thing that I could not instantly come up with an answer to; you asked me when or on what occasions I would feel I am a Japanese. Now I know what it is. When I run into ultra-thick *zainichi* [*monosugoku koi, baribari no zainichi*] such as the outspoken people on the mailing list,[3] I truly feel I am nothing more than Japanese.

Mika realizes her Japaneseness reflectively, in the presence of relatively "thick" *zainichi*. Perhaps one of the privileges of being "ordinary Japanese" in Japan, rather than Korean-Japanese or Chinese-Japanese (although such hyphenations are not widely used in Japanese), is that authentic Japaneseness is so taken for granted that there is no need to pause and reflect on it. Most of the time, Mika's identification with her Japanese nationality is something beyond her everyday concerns. Her Japaneseness can be defined absolutely by nationality but is only visible in relation to her exaggeratedly non-Japanese acquaintances.

Mika's otherwise forgotten *zainichi* background loomed large when she entered the marriage market. She and her family, although they had completely lost touch with *zainichi* organizations, reactivated those networks because of a tacit fear that Japanese suitors would exclude her based on her Korean lineage. Mika's parents assumed that being an ex-*zainichi* might affect Mika's marriage prospects among ordinary Japanese. But when they interacted with *zainichi*, Mika and her mother realized they were in limbo. On the one hand, "thick" *zainichi* were "too much"; they embraced their Koreanness too clearly, and hence (paradoxically) they were unconcerned about their Koreanness. On the other hand, Mika's family hesitated to identify fully with the so-called ordinary Japanese world, especially when it came to marriage, even though their Korean ethnic practices were minimal.

W. E. B. Du Bois remarked more than a century ago: "The problem of the twentieth century is the problem of the color-line, the relation of the darker to the lighter races of men in Asia and Africa, in America and the islands of the sea" (Du Bois 1961[1903]: 23). In the early twenty-first century in contemporary Japan, it is not color—i.e., visible shades of skin or phenotypes—but lineage that is the basis of exclusion. Lineage effectively makes abstract and invisible racial categories tangible and imaginable. Mika's case alludes to a persistent colorless color line between Japanese and *zainichi*; mutual repugnance results from phenotypically identical characteristics.

Mika's awakening to an otherwise dormant ex-*zainichi* identity is indicative of the ambivalent relationship between diaspora and assimilation. It is complicated in the Japanese context by questions of race, ethnicity, and nationality. In Japan, race, ethnicity, and nationality (each conflated with culture and lineage) are congruent with being a native of Japan and a native speaker of Japanese. The unthinking use of Japaneseness, be it racially, ethnically, or in the sense of nationality, relies on an implicit consensus about authentic Japaneseness; lineage trumps nationality, linguistic competence, or place of birth and upbringing (Fukuoka 2000: xxix, xxxvi; Morris-Suzuki 1998: 104–107; Weiner 1997: xiv; Yoshino 1992: 26–27). The supralegal definition of Japaneseness based on lineage continues to affect the identities of naturalized Japanese of colonial Korean descent. Throughout this chapter, I treat authentic Japaneseness, which is undefined in everyday language, as an implicit and invisible racial construct materialized through lineage. Regardless of cultural assimilation or the attainment of socioeconomic status, the invisible race question seems to be intertwined with the diasporic condition, in that colonial Korean lineage is perceived as a basis for exclusion, whether real or imagined.

After generations of residence in Japan, Mika's ethnic homeland is lost. She cannot claim a singular authenticity, which is, after all, a luxury that only people with a secure homeland can afford (and as the introduction to this volume makes clear). Japan is a conditional, step-homeland for Mika and her family, although they are no longer legally stateless. A claim to authenticity and secure homeland is precarious when invisible racial boundaries exist. Mika's case suggests a persistent boundary between authentic and inauthentic belonging to Japan's imagined national community, a community based on the idea that nationality = lineage = race.[4] But what is Mika's relationship to the Korean diaspora? Are culturally and legally-structurally assimilated *zainichi* detached from the collective diasporic consciousness of the more mainstream ethnic Koreans? Does the invisible racial boundary join them to the Korean diaspora, if only part-time?

The problematic intersection between the personal and the diasporic calls for a close look at everyday *zainichi* life, which is remote from the discourses of diasporic intellectuals and ethno-political organizations. To what extent can the personal be diasporic? This chapter explores how naturalized Japanese of colonial Korean descent reinvent and express their *zainichi* background—roots and routes—and in so doing how they constitute an invisible and apolitical diaspora in contemporary Japan.[5] In analyzing the cases of *zainichi* who, or whose parents, chose to become legally Japanese and official members of the Japanese nation-state and who neither express collective diasporic consciousness nor affiliate with *zainichi* institutions, I will examine the possibilities and limits of invisible diasporic identity formation. I argue that naturalized Japanese of colonial Korean descent can still be invisibly diasporic, despite their detachment from collective memories of displacement because of the understated, imagined persistence of symbolic racism.

In the following, I first give an overview of the relationships among assimilation, invisible race, and diaspora, as well as the visible and invisible aspects of assimilated/naturalized *zainichi*. Then I present and interpret six individual cases of naturalized Japanese of colonial Korean descent who consider themselves ex-*zainichi* and examine the ways in which they understand, express, and communicate their *zainichi* background. Applying recent critiques of the concept of diaspora, in the final section I return to the question: is the personal diasporic?

ASSIMILATION, INVISIBLE RACE, AND DIASPORA: IS THE RACIALIZED DIASPORIC?

As assimilation, cultural and structural, proceeds over generations through naturalization and intermarriage, the question arises: to what extent are *zainichi* diasporic? Can they retain diasporic identities without collective consciousness, especially after they have attained a seemingly post-stateless condition through naturalization?[6]

Being a stateless minority group that is structurally and symbolically excluded from an imagined national community facilitates the formation and reproduction of diasporic orientations (Clifford 1997; Safran 2004; Siu 2001; Tölölyan 1996). Conditions of statelessness, or of belonging to more than one nation-state, however, are by no means the early-twenty-first century's global standard (Friedman 2002). An individual (and his or her family) who belongs to and identifies with one nation is the modern norm; naturalization is the legal expression of that norm. A considerable number of *zainichi* legally possess sole membership in the Japanese nation. Approximately 10,000 Koreans naturalize each year (Japan Ministry of Justice 2007).[7] An instrumental approach to naturalization, or *kika*,[8] as an actively selected option is gaining in popularity (Asakawa 2003, Tei 2001). Naturalization—a structural form of assimilation through the acquisition of full legal membership—is pragmatic in that it guarantees comprehensive legal membership in a national community. Legal inclusion, however, does not automatically produce full social acceptance.

Behind the questions of authentic membership and unconditional belonging is the common use of nationality rather than citizenship in everyday Japanese language. Nationality is determined by parental lineage in the Japanese Nationality Law. Naturalization is a complex adoption procedure to become a formal member of the Japanese national community. For *zainichi*—whether second, third, or fourth generation—lacking a Japanese national parent, naturalization is the only way to acquire nationality. Nationality itself continues to be taken as a matter of fate, while citizenship connotes something optional and variable in everyday Japanese language (Lie 2001: 144). The sense of nationality as fate, transmitted through parental lineage, invokes race rather than ethnicity.[9] The acquired fact of Japanese nationality, therefore, tends to be regarded as strictly a private matter. When *zainichi* adopt Japanese names upon naturalization, as many do, they often lose the only public mark of their non-Japanese origin.

Jeffrey Alexander (2001) argues: "With assimilation ... the split between private and public remains in place; indeed, because the polluted qualities of stigmatized group membership are even more firmly restricted to the private sphere, this split becomes sharper and more unyielding" (Alexander 2001: 244). In segregated communities, it is possible to maintain a Korean lifestyle (invented or reinvented) in the public sphere or at private, family occasions, but for the Japan-born Korean with a Japanese alias, any public display will be undoubtedly seen as Japanese.

Because naturalized Japanese are no longer legally stateless, these "step-

Japanese," or "new" Japanese, do not belong to any politically committed, organized, or visibly diasporic community. They are caught in what John Lie calls "a paradox of oppression" in which the partially assimilated feel racism most acutely (2004: 258). The diasporically conscious bear the burden of symbolic racism precisely because the structural basis of racism seems to have diminished (Lie 2004: 256–257). Yet the possibilities and limits of diasporic identity matter theoretically and empirically to those who are situated outside of the conventional contours of a diasporic community. As was the case with Mika's concerns about the marriage market, they encounter symbolic exclusion that raises questions about their full incorporation in the Japanese nation-state. Subconscious fear of social exclusion in marriage and intimate relationships makes Japanese nationality among the naturalized a conditional, legal token of membership rather than an all-inclusive, unquestioned location, identity, and sense of national belonging.

Is this fear a necessary and sufficient condition for diasporic consciousness? In the introduction to this volume, Sonia Ryang identifies two models of diaspora: the classical model (which she associates with phylogeny) and the cultural studies (ontogeny) model. Individuals such as Mika, of Japan-born generations, have much closer ties to the home (i.e., Japan) than to the lost homeland (Korea), especially because they now hold Japanese nationality through naturalization. Their form of diaspora is ontogenetic, based on an appropriated sense of identity, as opposed to the classical/phylogenetic model of diaspora, which is based on collective memory and consciousness. Ryang is correct to question, however, the extent to which post-stateless *zainichi* can still be considered part of the Korean diaspora.

The uprooted are rendered diasporic not only through the search for the lost homeland but also by the process of making the hostland experience meaningful. James Clifford, a proponent of the cultural studies model of diaspora,[10] proposes a "decentered" model which emphasizes "a shared, on-going history of displacement, suffering, adaptation, or resistance" (Clifford 1997: 249–250), pointing out the limitations of a "centered" model which prioritizes the close and ongoing relationship with the homeland.

A "shared" history continues to be significant even in Clifford's decentered model. The decentered model's emphasis on the subjective realm of diasporic consciousness (as in collective memories) still indicates the juncture and disjuncture between diasporic individuals, the host society, and the diasporic community. It renders problematic the diasporic consciousness of individuals who do *not* share a history of displacement, suffering, adaptation, and resistance.

The *zainichi* case challenges both centered and decentered models of diaspora. Memories certainly connect personal experience to a collective past. However, this process cannot be taken for granted just because of shared lineage. Fukuoka Yasunori (1991: 220), in his life-course research on *zainichi* youths, found that grandchildren have heard little about their grandparents' migration or how preceding generations lived. Shared *zainichi* history is often of little importance to *zainichi* individuals, especially among those who do not maintain active *zainichi* networks. The formation of collective identity is difficult because *zainichi* are politically and ideologically diverse; the vast majority were born in Japan, educated only in Japanese schools, have few ties to other *zainichi*, and pass as Japanese using a Japanese alias (Fukuoka 2000; Kim 1978)—this last being a tactic that phenotypically invisible minority groups can adopt.

The extent to which structurally and culturally assimilated populations can remain diasporic depends not only on the social structures of the host society and the intraethnic community but also on their interpretations of exterior circumstances, present, past and future. Assimilated groups' precarious positions in the host society sustain diaspora as collective consciousness (Clifford 1997: 250–251). Is ignorance bliss? Does a lack of a collective sense of displacement and violent loss mean that Japanese of colonial Korean descent are no longer diasporic? What impact does structural prejudice have on the lives of *zainichi*, and how does it affect the meanings they attach to their existence in Japan?

VISIBLE AND INVISIBLE DIASPORAS

While researchers address the presence and diverse identities of *zainichi* as part of the twentieth-century Korean diaspora (Ryang 1997b; Sasaki 2003; Suzuki 2003),[11] it is important to note that some *zainichi* communities are more visible than others. *Zainichi* in general are phenotypically invisible (i.e., indistinguishable from the Japanese) yet racialized owing to their colonial legacy (Weiner 1997). Highly visible, organized *zainichi* communities, regardless of the content and the intensity of their political commitments, have provided rich and distinct subject matter for researchers of diverse disciplines and approaches. The studies have paid more attention to organized *zainichi* perspectives not only because of their accessibility but also because of the attractiveness of the communities themselves. Differences are more appealing than similarities because they illustrate diversity and challenge the assumptions of a monoethnic Japan and essentialism in general. The challenge is that difference perpetuates foreignness, imagined or real. The visible Korean minority can be used simultaneously to endorse the claims of both multiethnic and monoethnic Japan. The presence of a Korean minority, through its difference, highlights the idea that Japan is constituted by ethnic Japanese. Distinct and visible *zainichi*, along with other groups, on the other hand, legitimates the ideal of ethnic diversity in Japan.

An increasing number of scholars have become attentive to invisible sub-populations among *zainichi* often searching for alternative policies regarding naturalization.[12] Chikako Kashiwazaki (2000b), Kuraishi Ichirō (2000a), Mitsushi Sugihara (1993) and Eika Tai (2004) describe notable moves among Japanese of Korean descent who contest authentic and nation-bound Japaneseness, as well as Koreanness, by asserting Koreanness while maintaining Japanese nationality. These studies challenge the stereotypical portrait of Japanese of Korean descent who assimilate and reject their Korean ancestry in order to join the Japanese mainstream (e.g., Fukuoka 2000: 54–55).

Nevertheless, these studies infrequently incorporate the perspectives of organizationally inactive individuals. They focus on groups such as *Minzokumei o torimodosu kai* (Association for Reclaiming Ethnic Names) and *Paramu no kai* (Wind Society).[13] The activities of these groups are not well known among *zainichi*. Members of these groups selectively identify or reinvent Koreanness, which allows them to be fit neatly within a pluralist frame. Their voices thus find their way into mainstream academic discourse. Although some studies include the voices of unorganized Japanese of Korean descent (e.g., Fukuoka 2000; Sasaki 2003), those who express commitment one way or another to ethnic politics and organized ethnic movements are given more frequent representation.

By examining the invisible diaspora, this chapter questions an ideal-typical distinction between the ethnic and the diasporic, exploring the convergence between the racial and the diasporic. According to Tölölyan (1996: 14), diasporic peoples maintain intensive communal commitment to and connection with the homeland and other dispersed co-ethnic communities, rather than having merely sporadic, individual commitments. A diasporic population, however, is not always unified in terms of political commitment (as Tölölyan himself argues); individual and sporadic commitments may be more ethnic than diasporic. How individuals and groups understand themselves depends on the ways in which host societies receive them and the ways in which they interpret such conditions (Clifford 1997; Safran 2004). Naturalized Japanese of Korean descent do not always identify themselves as part of Korean diasporic politics. Nonetheless, is it possible that they engage in everyday resistance and challenge the hegemony of the Japanese legal system and social norms, which together define authentic membership in the Japanese nation-state? The following section introduces six cases of Japanese of colonial Korean descent.

NATURALIZED JAPANESE OF COLONIAL KOREAN DESCENT: SIX CASES

During my intermittent fieldtrips both to the Kantō and Kansai regions between 1998 and 2002, I interviewed 90 *zainichi* (45 Japanese and 45 non-Japanese). I also participated in events organized by different groups. I attempted to contact respondents through a snowball sample with diversified entry points. My snowball did not roll; although I asked interviewees to introduce me to someone, I rarely established another meeting, which was especially the case with Japanese nationals of Korean (or part-Korean) descent. I tried to reach organizationally inactive individuals as much as possible and did not use homeland, state-based organizational channels (e.g., Chongryun or Mindan). Each interview took approximately two-and-a-half to three hours. The interviews were conducted in Japanese, audiotaped, and transcribed. Some interviews had follow-up correspondence. I selected the following six cases based on gender (three male and three female) and different patterns of name use. I conducted the interviews with these six informants in 1999 and 2000. The translations into English are mine.

All six people have Japanese nationality. Four of them naturalized as minors because of their parents' naturalization. One followed her husband's decision. One chose independently to naturalize. The interviewees' ages ranged between 22 and 41 at the time of the interview, and they are all 2.5 or later generations. Their class backgrounds and educational attainment vary. None of them received full-time Korean schooling, but some had limited exposure to *zainichi* empowerment education within or outside school. None actively associate with *zainichi* or Korean diasporic politics. They are not actively engaged in local or state Japanese politics. None are active in conventional *zainichi* expatriate organizational politics, whether the pro-Pyongyang Chongryun or the pro-Seoul Mindan. While they all experience some moments in which their membership in Japanese society is marked as inconsistent and contingent, even precarious, the ways they cope with their *zainichi* background vary.

Following a brief description of the profiles of the six cases, I first discuss their responses across different (yet overlapping) themes, specifically focusing on their expressions of Korean roots in name usage. Name usage is the most intriguing point of reference, in that *zainichi*, regardless of nationality, can control the extent of their visibility by employing certain names in everyday use. Each case illustrates examples of minority "cultural logic" (cf. Ong 1999), indicating ways in which minority members accommodate and resist mainstream norms and racial stratification.

Second, I will introduce an illuminating case of the intergenerational transmission of *zainichi* routes, i.e., a family history of migration. In so doing, I point to a cleavage between a personalized immigrant family saga and the collective memory of diaspora; individual narratives of creating or reinventing *zainichi* routes can become isolated from any collective aspect of the group's past—be it suffering or resistance. Following a discussion of their fundamentally apolitical stances while indicating some critical awareness of the status quo, I shall return to the question of what makes invisible diasporas diasporic.

Chō Akio (b. 1963, third generation) was naturalized two months before our interview. In his family, he is the only one—so far—who has been naturalized. Akio works for a research institute while pursuing a professional degree. He naturalized primarily because "[i]t was so unnatural—I was born here, Japanese is my first language, and I don't know anything about Korea, and I am legally (South) Korean? Don't you think that's very strange?" He is not involved in *zainichi* politics or activism and had never heard of *Minzokumei o torimodosu kai*, whose members successfully sued in family court for the retrieval of their Korean (and Korean-pronounced) names, names that the Japanese legal system had replaced when Koreans became naturalized. His sole experience with *zainichi* empowerment education was compulsory participation in a series of seminars and lectures sponsored by a politically neutral Korean organization so he could receive college and graduate school stipends. When he naturalized, he chose his Korean last name, pronounced *Chō* in Japanese—*Chang* in Korean—and his Japanese-pronounced given name over the Korean-pronounced *Myeong-Nam*. It was simply the matter of continuity; Akio switched from his family's Japanese-style name, Nagata, to his Korean legal name, Chō, but using the Japanese pronunciation, when he entered university. Akio's undergraduate institution had a policy to use *zainichi* students' Korean names instead of Japanese-style names. Had his university not forced him to do so, he never would have activated his Korean last name, he admits. His name change was a result of institutional reinforcement rather than individual choice.

Pak Fumiko (b. 1963, 2.5 generation, father born in Korea) was naturalized with her parents and siblings when she was a high-school senior.

Fumiko and her family naturalized primarily to enable Fumiko's elder brother to find employment more easily after high school, although the naturalization procedure took longer than anticipated (they had to file twice in ten years; the first application was rejected). Although her father's siblings were active in the pro–North Korean Chongryun, Fumiko's family switched allegiance to South Korea following the 1965 Normalization Treaty (which guaranteed permanent residency among South Koreans, as detailed in the introduction to this volume). By the time the family naturalized, her parents were too old to enroll in the national pension plan. Fumiko supports her parents fully by working as a contract-based office clerk. About five years before I met her, she began using her Korean family name, Pak, in private, sending all her friends a postcard explaining the change. On choosing her name Pak (Korean; Boku in Japanese) Fumiko (Japanese; Moon-Ja in Korean), she explains: "I don't speak the language [Korean] so I liked my given name pronounced in Japanese." At her workplace, where her yearly contract-based employment is without guarantee of renewal, she uses her Japanese-style family name Kimura, now her legal name. She never used her Korean name when she was legally Korean. She switched her last name back to Korean in her private life to be explicit about her *zainichi* background. She wanted acquaintances, especially those who might become close or intimate, to know her background from the onset. Although she and her parents were never active in Korean organizations, Fumiko read widely on the topic during her twenties.

Saitō Dae-Won (b. 1974, fourth generation) naturalized when he was a high-school freshman with his parents and siblings. It was primarily to aid his elder brother's employment opportunities that his parents decided to naturalize. His brother, a graduate of a reputable four-year college, received an offer from a major Japanese firm before the family's naturalization application was approved: "So, in the end, our family's naturalization wasn't necessary after all. But for his future promotion or other opportunities, perhaps it was not a bad move. I myself do not care whether I have Japanese nationality or not. But I wish I had a choice—I did not have any reason to oppose it, and I did not have any knowledge to go for it either." The last name Saitō was chosen upon naturalization because it was more authentically Japanese than their former Japanese-style alias, which signaled the family's Korean origin. Some of his relative used to call him Dae-Won as a child, but his mother called him Hiro-Kun. Dae-Won went to a high school that had a constant enrollment of *zainichi* students, and a committed Japanese teacher encouraged *zainichi* students to switch to Korean names. After completing a vocational school where he used his

Korean name, Kang Dae-Won, rather than his legal (Japanese) name, and after working at several odd jobs, Dae-Won now works for a medium-sized Japanese company as a sales representative. His business card displays his legal Japanese name, Saitō Hiromoto, although he continues to use Dae-Won as a nickname.

Kuremoto Nami (b. 1958, 2.5 generation, father born in Korea) naturalized with her husband and children about five years before I interviewed her. Among those I describe here, she is the only person married and with children. She had been a full-time homemaker but had just started working part-time at the time of the interview. She worked to save for her children's education and perhaps to travel. Her husband, a third-generation *zainichi*, works for a large computer technology firm, having receiving a college degree from a prestigious institution, and makes a comfortable living. They live in a suburban detached house. Her father was strict and never allowed her or her sisters to attend coed schools. Trips and sleepovers were out of the question. He considered marrying his daughters to fellow Koreans as his supreme mission. So, Nami wants her children to travel outside of Japan. Her husband considered naturalization first, after his work began to involve overseas business trips. He was using his Japanese-style name at work and elsewhere, and he felt it inconvenient to carry a passport with his legal Korean name. They decided to keep her husband's Japanese-style name as their legal name after naturalization. Nami, who attended several Mindan-organized events, including a trip to South Korea, a rare event her father let her participate in, thought: "Kuremoto, to me, is apparently Korean! But my husband was not so aware of that."

Sokuhō Ikkyō (b. 1978, 2.5 generation, mother is not *zainichi* but a recent immigrant from South Korea where his father met her when he studied there) was born a Japanese national; his parents naturalized before he was born. His father, a Buddhist priest, created a new family name when the family naturalized. Ikkyō was a college junior when I interviewed him. He heard that both his grandfather and his parents naturalized for their children and grandchildren so that their life chances would not be affected by nationality differences. Ikkyō fully agrees with their idea. His first and last names are uncommon among Japanese, but his position as a son of a Buddhist priest, a follower of tradition, makes him appear more Japanese than the Japanese; his mother, whose Japanese is impressively accentless for a nonnative speaker, is a Korean from South Korea. Ikkyō's father leads two temples in separate locations: one is rural, passed on from his master, and serves the local Japanese, and the other is urban, serving *zainichi*. Although Ikkyō has used only one name from birth, he switches between a Japanese and *zainichi* persona, depending on the context. When Ikkyō participated in a Mindan-organized summer school for *zainichi* students visiting South Korea, a very rare occasion for him to get in touch with a *zainichi* organization, he asked the organizer to change his name badge to his family's Korean name, Ko, because he did not want to stand out from other *zainichi* members with Korean names.

Yamagami Mika (b. 1974, fourth generation), already introduced at the beginning of this chapter, said she was not sure whether her parents naturalized before or after she was born. She has never seen her family registry. Even if she had seen it, the details of naturalization might have been unclear without tracing the records. She never heard the details of why her parents naturalized and why her great-grandparents came to Japan. She graduated from a prestigious women's college and was working as a contract-based administrative assistant in a large Japanese company at the time of the interview. When the bubble economy burst, her age cohort, especially women, experienced difficulty finding employment. She describes herself as a *nanchatte* (fake) *zainichi*,[14] by which she means: "Well, I happen to be a *zainichi*, but not exactly—I do not know anything about it, sorry!" Mika's parents put her on the *zainichi* marriage market for a while, hoping to find someone of *zainichi* background with Japanese nationality. That was Mika's only contact with other *zainichi*, although one of her high-school classmates is a *zainichi* who used her Korean name. Mika learned that she is a fourth-generation *zainichi* when she was putting together materials to arrange her marriage. It was then that she first heard her parents' Korean last names and place of origin (she could not recall her father's Korean family name, but she remembered her mother's because it sounded "just funny"). Both Mika and her parents opted out of the *zainichi* marriage market when they realized that the families of *zainichi* men rarely exchanged photographs and the background information letter [*tsurigaki*] about family members, education, employment, hobbies, and the like. The lack of reciprocity made Mika and her parents feel prospects were bleak for meeting another *zainichi* who would treat her with fairness and respect.

ZAINICHI SIGNALING: REINVENTING KOREAN ROOTS IN NAME USAGE

For Japan-born Koreans educated in the Japanese school system, names are the only marker signaling their Korean origin. Leonard Plotnicov and Myrna Silverman define "ethnic signaling" as "the effort people make to find and express shared social and cultural attributes in order to enhance the basis for their relationship" (1978: 407). Korean signaling in Japan, however, is aimed at the Japanese majority, rather than at fellow *zainichi*. Whereas *zainichi* use of Japanese aliases allows them to blend in with the Japanese in everyday social encounters, *zainichi* use of Korean names in Japanese public spaces and conversations has the opposite effect, allowing them to stand out, with or without possible disruptions in social exchanges (see also the introduction to this volume). Some (not all) Japanese of Korean descent would rather express their ethnic Korean roots to selective audiences only, precisely because they are now officially Japanese, and, therefore, their national affiliation to the Japanese state is no longer questionable. Akio, Fumiko, and Dae-Won use this strategy, but Akio is the only person who has a legal last name signaling non-Japanese origin (Nami's last name, Kuremoto, may signal Koreanness as well, but not to everybody). Akio vividly recalled at the beginning of our interview:

> When I was granted Japanese nationality, I went to pick up the certificate; you have to go to the local bureau of the Ministry of Justice in person. There were about thirty people who were there to receive the naturalization certificate. Whenever a person's name was called, he or she would stand up and proceed to receive the paper with a bow and the bureaucrat handing the form would say "Congratulations." When my name was called—"*Chō-san, Chō Akio san!*"—every single person in the room turned around to see me! I was the only one whose family name didn't sound Japanese.

Seen from a more conventional majority point of view, having an unusual name is a nuisance in any society. Akio thinks had he been in business, he would have chosen a Japanese-sounding name. He is a researcher and consultant; expressions of individuality are more likely to be accepted. But he is reminded of his different status in everyday life. For example, each time he mentions his name on the phone, he has to repeat it, spelling it several times. He is often told how well he speaks Japanese. Regardless, Akio thinks: "It's easier to communicate my background at the beginning [of social encounters]. At least, my name gives people a chance to ask me if I am a Korean or some kind of foreigner, although some people don't ask about it at all."

Even for Akio, whose legal last name is Korean, it is difficult to be consistent in everyday life. For example, his landlord asked him not to put Chō on his apartment's mailbox: "I guess he did not want other tenants to be aware that he rents his apartment to a Korean." His landlord would not allow the mailbox to be blank, so he used his Japanese-style name Nagata, which he had not used since entering college. He did not insist, being overwhelmed by other routine matters in his life: "I could have argued with him, or looked for another apartment. But I was in a rush and it was too much trouble. The landlord lives right next to me, and I run into him so often. I don't want to have an issue with him."

He is not married and thinks it more likely that he will meet a Japanese woman. He is not sure what he will do if his future spouse rejects his family name when naming their child. The option of his future children using his Japanese mother's last name, against almost universal patrilineal naming conventions, would mean that he might be the last generation to use his once-lost-then-retrieved Korean name.

Among those whose legal names are Japanese-style, situational uses of Korean names are not solely based on personal preference. Both Fumiko and Dae-Won use their Korean names in their personal lives (Fumiko her Korean family name, and Dae-Won his Korean given name as a nickname). Both Fumiko and Dae-Won want their friends to know them well, and they prefer names that communicate their *zainichi* background. Fumiko feels strongly the need to clarify her Korean lineage. She experienced a stressful end to her relationship with a Japanese boyfriend, who, owing to her Japanese name, did not know her *zainichi* background:

> When I told him that I naturalized, he did not really understand what it meant. Even after he talked to his parents about me, he still did not get it. His parents were not happy about their son dating a *zainichi*. It was not surprising at all to me, but it was new to him. We never talked about marriage—we were both young. So I explained to him, "Many *zainichi* marry Japanese nowadays, but not every couple is celebrated by both families." But still he didn't understand what it really meant. He was not interested in understanding the situation. On the other hand, he did not assure me that it didn't matter to him. In the end, he just said, "Well, you'd better not speak up about it [having *zainichi* background]." I thought he was hopeless. Anyway, I thought it would be easier to let anyone I would be going out with know from the very beginning that I am *zainichi*.

Conversely, Dae-Won's experience is related to his connection with *zainichi* empowerment education and *zainichi* informal networks. He has been using his Korean name since he met a concerned Japanese high-school teacher who encouraged *zainichi* students to use Korean names at school. Dae-Won has many *zainichi* friends and acquaintances, and he is accustomed to be called by his Korean first name. He does not actively bring up his naturalization in front of his *zainichi* acquaintances.

Both Fumiko and Dae-Won chose not to use their Korean names at work. The paperwork involving taxes, pension plans, and health insurance conventionally uses legal names. In addition, the content of their work (Dae-Won's sales work requires a name easy to remember) or the form of employment (Fumiko works on temporary contract, afraid of introducing any factors that might affect her contract renewal)[15] influenced their name choice at work.

Akio, Fumiko, and Dae-Won are exceptional; the vast majority of *zainichi*, naturalized or not, use Japanese-style names. Even after the Ministry of Justice's naturalization guidelines ceased recommending Japanese-style names, choosing an ethnically signaling name has been uncommon among East Asians, as is illustrated by Akio's experience upon picking up his naturalization certificate.

When family names do not communicate Korean roots, mundane situations and random social encounters often raise the issue of when, how, and to whom to explain Korean roots. In Nami's case, she followed her husband's naming decision. Their Japanese name could possibly signal their *zainichi* origin to those who know *zainichi* names and typical aliases well. However, "in person, people never ask if we are Korean," and Nami dares not advertise her and her husband's Korean roots and naturalization to her neighbors or recent acquaintances. From early childhood, Nami revealed her Korean roots only to very close friends, even though many local Japanese knew the family's Korean origin because her father used to run a Korean barbecue restaurant. She never thought of marrying a Japanese man: "I thought, it's impossible because all the family and relatives would be against it." Because her parents insisted that she and her sisters not go out with Japanese men, she never dated any and so never faced the problem of revealing her background in an intimate relationship. Even with her rather unusual Japanese last name, Nami and her husband's Korean roots are in the closet. Many *zainichi*, like Nami, lack painful memories of being discriminated against, such as being bullied at school. Fear of discrimination, however, has framed their subconscious concealment of *zainichi* roots (Fukuoka 2000). Japanese neighbors and friends would never ask them if they are *zainichi*, either, because, according to Nami, "it is something you cannot bring up in person."

Ikkyō and Mika, though much younger, have a similar approach to revealing their Korean roots. They tell only those who are very close to them, and even in some fairly close long-term friendships they have yet to bare their Korean roots. If Mika and Ikkyō hear prejudiced utterances from friends who think they are Japanese, they neither embarrass them nor point out their prejudice. But such individuals will have failed Mika and Ikkyō's trustworthiness test, and they will never come out to them unless they have to.

Ikkyō is very outgoing and has maintained close friendships with his middle-school classmates. Some of them are his best friends. I asked if they all knew of his *zainichi* background. He told me that one of his best friends did not know, or, at least, Ikkyō had never mentioned his Korean roots to him. While he told me, at first, that he did not have an opportunity to say anything, Ikkyō later recalled his friend's utterance of a racial slur against Koreans. Ikkyō defended his friend, stating that he did not mean anything serious because he simply did not know anything about *zainichi*. Whenever Ikkyō starts dating someone, most often Japanese-Japanese, he explains:

> At least, I will wait for several months, figuring that if the relationship works out, then I will tell her that I am originally a [South] Korean. [Why?] Well, my family name is [Japanese-sounding] Sokuhō and I am a son of a Buddhist priest running a temple, and she would definitely think I am absolutely Japanese from a family of respectable, proper lineage [*yuisho tadashii ie*]; then I would feel as if I am lying. So I would tell [my Korean roots] at some point, but not right at the moment I meet someone.

While outspoken and proud of his Korean roots and his father's philosophy, being part of a *zainichi* family is a deviation from his image of a respectable Japanese family. His legal Japaneseness does not mean authentic Japaneseness, especially when it comes to a steady relationship.

Mika recently had a female-bonding dinner with three Japanese friends (two of whom knew Mika's *zainichi* background) to celebrate one of the women's having recently found a boyfriend; they called the dinner a victory celebration [*shukushōkai*], a deliberately ironic use of wartime terminology. When her friend mentioned her new boyfriend's name, the one who did not know Mika's *zainichi* family background said, "What an unusual name! What if he is a Korean?" and laughed, pretending that her comment was just a joke. Mika recalled: "You should have been there, Youngmi-san. Two of my friends who know I am *zainichi* totally froze! We, kind of, had eye contact, my friends not knowing what to do. The rest of dinner went on as if nothing had happened and nobody brought up anything not to embarrass the one who really didn't mean to say anything possibly offensive."

Ikkyō's and Mika's handling of their Korean roots illustrates well the reality that belies the official high proportion of cross-national marriage statistics. Lineage, not legal nationality, still matters in committed relationships and marriage, even among Japanese of colonial Korean descent who have assimilated culturally, socioeconomically and legally, and who have outgoing, fun-loving personalities. There are some moments when their otherwise comfortable lives become complicated [*yayakoshii*], in Mika's word.

The name usage of these six individuals indicates the presence of external pressures (both direct and indirect) either to pass or to differentiate. The expression of Korean roots is far from tension-free or constant because the messages conveyed by name choices pinpoint the moments of inclusion and exclusion (or the fear of exclusion). Even carefree young people like Ikkyō and Mika, who are often interested in settling down in a committed relationship, are very careful and strategic in communicating their roots, especially having encountered racist remarks.

THE JAPANESE HORATIO ALGER STORY: REINVENTING *ZAINICHI* ROUTES

As generations are born and age, details of families' *zainichi* routes, the trajectory and context of migration, tend to be lost. Moreover, more than *zainichi* routes, Korean roots have often been completely sealed. Some learn their (partial) Korean background as adults. Some parents were naturalized before their children were born, or one of the parents was naturalized before getting married to a Japanese. In those cases, the smooth transmission of Korean roots and *zainichi* routes is unlikely. Where the roots are known to children, they themselves may refrain from asking their parents the details, and if the parents are not getting along or the parent-child relation is full of tension, the overall lack of conversation inside the family may contribute to the obliteration of roots and routes.

Among the cases I have been discussing, Nami is the only one who has children and has been concerned with explaining her family's naturalization. For her, the emphasis was on how to put it in a positive light. Three years before I met Nami, she revealed to her children their Korean roots, remembering in vivid details how it went. The following is her account, which is worth quoting at length:

> My husband and I had talked about telling the children [about their Korean origin] at some point, but we had never discussed in detail when or how to do that. It was in the middle of summer vacation. The oldest was in the sixth grade. All the children were at home during the day with me. It just came to me that I should explain [that the

family naturalized] to the oldest one because he was to attend middle school in the following spring and he would start thinking about many complex things as he was reaching puberty. It just came to me out of the blue. So I called all the children. The middle one was in the third grade and the youngest was still at kindergarten, and I thought the younger ones might not fully understand it. I wasn't sure how to begin—I tried not to be overly serious; I tried to be casual and natural, just one of these things. They were all eating ice cream as they heard me talk. I first thought about explaining to each child when he was old enough to understand abstract things, but I also felt it strange to call up each child at a different time. The first one has a rather sensitive personality, and I also thought the explanation should be put in a way so that he was not shocked to hear of the family's roots. I first took out my passport and my husband's, showing them I said, "These are passports we used when we all went to Hawai'i, remember? You can also have passports but you were all very young so you are all listed in Mommy's passport, here you see your names. When we go abroad, we use the passports to prove that we are all Japanese. Here you see, it says, 'Japan.'" And next, I told them the story of one of the Doraemon movies.[16] Among different Doraemon movie episodes, there is the one called, *Nippontanjō* [The birth of Japan]. It explains that long time ago, the islands of Japan were geographically connected with China and Korea [*kankoku*; South Korea], and the story is situated in the prehistoric era. It says we all might share the same ancestry or something like that. A long time ago, everything [Japan, China and Korea] was connected and there was no border. . . . Then, I asked the children if they have noticed something different when we all visit the grandparents during summer vacation and New Year holidays. "Then we eat together and you play with your cousins, right? Have you noticed something a bit different, say, from your friends' house?" And the children all said, "Mmm, no idea." So I asked them, "What about the language Grandpa speaks? What about food?" And the middle one said, "I got it!" So I thought she would bring up *kimchi* or something like that. But she said, "Grandpa at Mommy's runs a pancake house, but Grandpa at Daddy's doesn't do anything!" I thought, "Ugh!" but I said, "That's true, well, but didn't you notice Grandpa sometimes speaks another language than Japanese?" Well, my father used to speak Korean a lot, but he now only uses some words sporadically. So it was not surprising that the children did not notice anything at all. . . . Then I brought back the story to the passport. "You see, these are Japanese passports so we are all Japanese," I pointed. I went on, "But Grandpa and Grandma are [South] Koreans. Mommy and Daddy were also [South] Koreans at first. But Grandma, Mommy and Daddy were all born in Japan, and Grandpa used to live in Korea when he was very young but he has been living in Japan, running restaurants, you see?" Then, I went back to the Doraemon story, "As you saw in the Doraemon movie, likewise, South Korea, Grandpa's country, and Japan used to be the same country. After the war was over, the two countries became separate again, but Grandpa used to be in South Korea and it's true that he is South Korean." I skipped the complicated part, but I told them like that.

Nami asked if they all understood the story and asked the oldest child if he was "shocked." The children said they more or less understood, and the oldest one said he was not shocked. Nami was worried that the children already had negative images about (South) Korea. She assured her children that they did not have to feel negative about (South) Korea no matter what was reported on the TV news. She reminded her children of their grandfather's achievements: "Grandpa came to Japan all by himself and built up that big restaurant. Not every Japanese could have done that, even with a college degree. He deserves respect. He came to Japan to study, but was cheated and ended up working in a coal mine in Hokkaido. He is a self-made man and truly extraordinary."

Nami's message to her children is that having Korean roots is something to be proud of, to feel good about. However, she added a cautionary note at the end of the long conversation with her children: "'But you don't have to tell your friends that you are Korean,' I told them. Because bullying was really a major problem at school, I was worried about it. So I told them not to tell their friends directly." Because the transmission of Korean roots and *zainichi* routes had to be a positive and easy-to-swallow story, the resulting narrative was consciously selective, especially about Japan's colonization of Korea. The problematic beginning of the individual migration history—Nami's father being deceived about being able to study in Japan, eventually being sent to a coal mine in Hokkaido—is obscured in the classic and universal immigrant legend of a man self-made through efforts and perseverance. Nami reinvented *zainichi* routes in a Japanese Horatio Alger story, a story of an immigrant's personal achievement against all odds.

The experiences of Japanese nationals of colonial Korean descent I have examined point to everyday challenges in expressing and communicating Korean roots and *zainichi* routes. Having Korean roots is still exceptional in Japanese society, where ever-increasing registered foreign residents still constituted only 1.69 percent of the population in 1007 (Japan Ministry of Justice 2008: 1) and the annual average between 1998 and 2007 was only 15,400 out of 127 million Japanese (computed from Japan Ministry of Justice 2007). The lure of blending in without challenging or subverting the Japanese national landscape might surpass the urge to exercise multiple belongings, except in very personal narratives. Assimilation while maintaining diasporic identity (Siu 2001) in this way becomes a challenge to ordinary Japanese of colonial Korean descent.

Nonetheless, one important factor in deciding whether to reveal one's Korean background or to use a Korean name is racism or the fear of racism, no matter how benign this Japanese brand of racism may seem. What made Fumiko decide to use her Korean name to reveal her Korean roots was related to the everyday concern of finding a potential spouse: lineage matters.

AN APOLITICAL TRUCE OF MIND:
PERSONALIZED INVISIBLE DIASPORIC CONSCIOUSNESS

Signaling Korean roots by name usage—which implies being socially a full-time Korean—itself does not automatically result in politically meaningful *zainichi* networking. For example, Akio, whose legal name is Korean (albeit with a Japanese pronunciation), has some *zainichi* acquaintances, but he has no interest in politics, whether local, national, or global, either Korean or Japanese. He is not particularly interested in getting to know other *zainichi*, either. His name is a matter of individual choice, and he does not attach any significant sociopolitical meaning to it—such as becoming a role model for other *zainichi*. Without imagining oneself to be part of the *zainichi* community, be it on the national, ethnic, or expatriate level, how can an individual like Akio be diasporic?

Ikkyō appreciates the opportunity he had during the Mindan student tour to South Korea to get to know people outside his neighborhood and school. He maintains friendships with his *zainichi* middle-school classmates and those whom he got to know on the tour. He, however, declines frequent invitations to recreational events organized by Mindan's youth organization, commenting: "I would say to myself, 'Don't you guys have anyone but [South] Korean friends!?'" Akio and Ikkyō are not the only ones uninterested in expanding their *zainichi* network. In this section, I discuss what I see as apolitical, unorganized diasporic consciousness.

Until very recently, Mika did not learn about her family's Korean name, which she could not even recall when I asked her; she has no way of and no interest in socially signaling her Korean roots with her name. She describes herself as totally apolitical; being *zainichi* is something complicated [*yayakoshii*], and she is not interested in dealing with it. Neither interested in Japanese national or local politics, she rarely votes in elections, unlike some naturalized Japanese who would never miss voting because voting rights are restricted to and the privilege of Japanese nationals. She told me after the interview that she had fun meeting with me, although she was reluctant at first to talk with me, a *zainichi* with a Korean-pronounced name, who approached her through an acquaintance's introduction. She said she had imagined someone who was stern and would preach to her about *zainichi* matters.

Even the self-proclaimed apolitical Mika has some empathy toward Korean issues. She sent me an e-mail several months later:

> Have you seen [on TV] a recent reunion of Korean families who were separated in South and North [Korea]? When I saw the news on TV, the families holding each other crying, I was so moved and almost about to cry. But then, my grandmother (second generation) who was at the dinner table with us, said to the TV screen, "overreacting! [*ōgesana!*]" and she burst into laughter "*gahahaha . . .*" at which I was so surprised that my tears dried up instantly! Well, I knew she had rather an unemotional nature to begin with, but I was shocked how detached she was.

Diasporic identification with Korean homeland matters can be blown up by the sanction of close family members who are emotionally less attached. A scene of a naturally moving moment of family reunification marks how unnatural any emotional association with the lost homeland can become. Mika's everyday life goes on without a fully activated diasporic identity, although here and there she faces some awkward moments associated with her ex-*zainichi* status, which would clearly make her identity different from her Japanese-Japanese friends.

Like Mika, Nami is at a distance from "difficult things" (her words). Her suburban motherhood requires her engagement in the Parent Teacher Association at her children's schools. While other mothers make up excuses not to attend the meetings, Nami attends meetings involving a larger unit of several school districts. At one event—a lecture and roundtable discussion for teachers and parents about the *dōwa* problem[17]—Nami broke out of her routine: "I usually do not say anything at the meetings. But at that time, only once, I spoke out that everybody was talking in the abstract. I said, 'Only those who experienced being discriminated against can understand the pain of being discriminated against.' I didn't say anything about my *zainichi* background at all. I could have, but I didn't. But I just could not stop expressing my opinion there."

Nami's comment there is connected with her personal experience as a *zainichi*. But her expression was not in the first person and was abstract enough that her speaking up did not bring attention to her own circumstance. Although Nami's breaking the silence here did not lead to any political awakening, as with Mika, Nami's overall lack of consciousness of any national or diasporic (Japanese, Korean, or Korean expatriate) political causes does not necessarily mean that her identity is identical with that of an average Japanese.

The people I have introduced in this chapter indicate a variety of ways in which naturalized Japanese of Korean descent reinvent and renegotiate their *zainichi* origins and their reasons for existence in Japan. It is intriguing to me that these nonorganized individuals take up with *zainichi* roots and routes typically when they are aware of or concerned with potential exclusion on the basis of family lineage. Such fear of exclusion is not framed as racism in their minds. This underdeveloped consciousness about racism among naturalized Japanese of Korean descent, or *zainichi* passing as Japanese, is imprinted through the accumulated small conversational and interactive episodes with Japanese-Japanese who do not necessarily have clearly malicious intentions.

Ien Ang, a Peranakan Chinese (of premodern migrant Chinese origin in Indonesia) who was born in Indonesia, grew up in the Netherlands, and resides in Australia, questions her imposed Chineseness, declaring: "[I]f I am inescapably Chinese by *descent,* I am only sometimes Chinese by *consent.* When and how is a matter of politics" (Ang 2001: 36, original emphasis). Imposed identities, however, often restrict the kind and nature of politics involved. Becoming Korean or *zainichi* by consent seems not really an option, if we consider how the reinvented roots and routes are the product of socially constraining milieus in the guise of sheer personal options and individual circumstances. The reinvention of Korean roots and *zainichi* routes is challenged by the mundane and individual. Nevertheless, as we have glimpsed, the mundanity of these individuals is overcast by a shadow of diasporic displacement, overtly or covertly.

The six individuals I have discussed do not imagine themselves part of the *zainichi* diaspora. Korean roots are something to be proud of, or even fun, as Dae-Won and Ikkyō mentioned several times during the interview. *Zainichi* routes are contained in accommodative, optimistic, and persuasive stories, as when Nami reinvented her multigenerational family experience. Her father's rise from humble beginnings, overcoming numerous hurdles including once blatant racism against Koreans, is an exemplary immigrant success story. These six stories illustrate ambivalent and awkward moments, which distinguish our protagonists from their friends whose Japanese lineage confers on them an unconditional, authentic Japanese identity, a secure patria that is literally a "home land." These interviewees, all Japanese by nationality, have not found a secure "home land" in their country of birth and residence over generations. Despite rarely identifying with their *zainichi* background, they are aware of subtle exclusion from the authentic national community. Their apolitical stance embraces ambiguities and burgeoning, unshaped, and isolated political discontent.

ASSIMILATION, RACE, AND DIASPORA REVISITED

Particular subgroups—minority intellectuals, especially—can more freely exercise their identity options than others (Tölölyan 1996: 16–17). The identity options for Akio, Fumiko, Nami, Dae-Won, Ikkyō, and Mika are optional in their minds, but their choices are influenced by their own mindsets, which subconsciously maintain a fear of exclusion on the basis of lineage in the contemporary Japanese context. The race question is frequently mentioned in diaspora literature in combination with various sources of oppression such as gender, sexuality, disability, and class. Race remains a significant source of discrimination in ordinary people's everyday life, whether in blatant, institutional forms or benign, symbolic ones (Winant 2001). Race, however, whether represented as phenotypical difference or encoded as lineage, seems to be losing its force as a source of alienation in the host society.[18]

Miri Song suggests that identity choices and claims have structural and cultural, obvious and subtle restraints: "Individuals can be creative about the ways they negotiate their identities, although this creativity is bounded by their resources and their location in specific social and historical times and places" (Song 2003: 55). Theorizing globalization and diaspora carries liberating tones, but it pays little attention to the factors that restrict people's experiences of identity and consciousness, factors that are more often than not bound to localities within the nation-state (Song 2003: 118).[19]

No matter what alternative identity claims are made, whether we prefer diaspora, hybridity, or transnationality over ethnic, national or racial identities, there always exists double-edgedness (i.e., contradictory elements of emancipation and oppression) and the threat of reification; the logic of inclusion and exclusion reproduces itself (Siu 2001, Ang 2003). Diasporic identity is no more unconditional in hierarchically structured ethnic groups than racialized identity in plural societies (Song 2003).

Diaspora, as a theoretical tool, challenges conventional teleological explanations of the trajectory of migrant groups, pointing out that tamed ethnicities thrive as do racialized hierarchical intergroup relations. Assimilation tends to be regarded as an inappropriate frame of reference, whereas identity politics has gained significance (Ang 2001: 9–11). No linear passage exists; racialized groups in the West can never be treated as authentic (Ang 2001: 9) and certain racialized groups, regardless of visibility, are considered unassimilable. In addition to such a response by the host society, immigrants themselves accommodate constraints. The intergenerational, gradual-incorporation model does not explain some racialized groups' strategic resistance to assimilation into dominant societal values in the United States (Alba and Nee 2003; Ong 1999; Waters 1999).

Assimilation, or adaptation of ethnicity behind the public display, is contingent on the negotiation of immigrant groups with host social structures and particular historical contexts (Alexander 2001) as well as those of the homeland (Ong 1999). Other groups, if they are racially invisible, practice part-time, symbolic ethnicity, although even in an officially plural society ethnicity is possible only in a contained way (Ang 2001, Song 2003, Steinberg 1989). Naturalized Japanese of colonial descent may or may not reactivate their ethnic culture and network. But the turning point is not leisure but necessity when handling their concern for being excluded just because of otherwise almost obliterated lineage.

On the one hand, assimilation is inevitable not only because it is imposed but also because many individuals find it an attractive option. Both identification with diaspora and assimilation into the host society have certain appeal (Ang 2001: 28). Naturalization is a form of legal structural assimilation, cumbersome but convenient enough for surviving the "either-or" pressure on identity. On the other hand, active, wholehearted associations with Japanese society are alien to many Japanese individuals of colonial Korean descent because of a desire to be free of societal expectations attached to their Korean background or legal membership in Japan. Akio, Fumiko and Dae-Won's personal resistance is symbolized in their Korean-signaling name use. Even Nami, Ikkyō, and Mika, who seem more accommodative, address moments of invisible diaspora in the context of their fear of exclusion.

I have explored in this chapter the everyday challenge of maintaining invisible and personalized diasporic consciousness faced by those unconnected to organized and self-conscious, collective politics. Individual cases point to the obscured boundaries between diaspora in itself and diaspora for itself. The personal and invisible diaspora cannot be denied outright as totally assimilated (and thus nondiasporic). The subgroup of apolitical *zainichi*, regardless of their legal inclusion in the Japanese nation-state, still face racism. They bear the social costs attached to *zainichi*ness, even if they identify themselves only as ex-*zainichi*.

Of course, in the context of, say, the United States, national citizens may be able to claim more easily their diasporic origin and reality in that citizenship is not granted on the basis of the singularity of ethnicity and lineage. In Japan, however, the treatment of naturalized Koreans, despite their membership in Japan's national citizenry, is impregnated with non-acceptance and singling-out, involving racialization of both positive and negative lineage cults. In this way, naturalized former *zainichi* are classified as outside of both the Japanese national community and the conventional Korean diasporic communities in Japan. Their ongoing reality, however, inevitably and incessantly demands of them the choice or strategic disposal of their non-Japanese origin, in an identical way in which the ontology of diaspora is accentuated with the added sense of the loss of home.

Zainichi might identify with Koreanness beyond the confinement of nation-state boundaries even after they have acquired Japanese nationality and even though they stay away from politics and organizational commitment. Such expressions of *zainichi* diasporic identity are hampered and fostered simultaneously by the contemporary geopolitics of Japan and the neighboring Koreas, as well as many other intra- and intergroup factors. When the interests of nation states are in competition, *zainichi* are not considered a neutral party and Koreanness is not an apolitical, cost-free ethnicity or identity-marker in Japan.

So is the personal diasporic? It depends. The personal is not visibly diasporic. The classic model emphasizes communal and constant commitment to homeland issues. It distinguishes the diasporic from the ethnic (Tölölyan 1996: 14). But if the expressions of Korean roots and *zainichi* routes are individualized and compartmentalized in private life, the distinction does not hold. Implicit fear of racism, for example, is fairly common among our six informants, although it remains remote from the political consciousness that a broader, structural arrangement affects personal troubles. The personal, however, can be invisibly diasporic. It is without clear collective and/or political consciousness. Moments of exclusion based on lineage, which make the naturalized aware of her or his inauthenticity, however, discourage active, wholehearted, and unconditional identification as Japanese.

Is, then, the diasporic racialized? Racialization in the contemporary Japanese context is the process of exclusion on the basis of imagined family lineage, which takes the form of subtle, invisible, and symbolic racism. The "paradox of oppression" (Lie 2004) indicates that symbolic racism generates intensifying protests. Racism against *zainichi* is now far more symbolic than during the colonial days, when *zainichi* themselves were more visible in language and other aspects despite their common phenotypes with ethnic Japanese. Naturalized Japanese of Korean descent have no structural barriers to block their holding public office or participation in electoral politics. They resist the arbitrarily drawn boundaries between the Japanese and the Korean. However, the segment of *zainichi* whose exposure to racism is the most symbolic because of their Japanese nationality remain silent. The unanswered question is, *for whom* is the personal diasporic? The cleavage between unorganized, atomized individuals and the proponents and critiques of diaspora is getting wider and deeper.

5. *Pacchigi!* and *Go*

Representing Zainichi *in Recent Cinema*
Ichiro Kuraishi

The highly regarded Japanese cinema magazine *Kinemajunpō* (Movie Times) named as its 2005 film of the year *Pacchigi!* (Head-butt), a film about love and friendship between ethnic Japanese and *zainichi* youth.[1] The magazine's decision came as a surprise: in 2001 the same prize had been awarded to the similarly themed *Go*, making it the second time in only four years that a *zainichi* movie had won.[2]

On the one hand, the recent attention given to *zainichi* youth films is a welcome turn in Japan's film industry in that it signals, finally, acceptance of the representation of *zainichi* by *zainichi* in popular culture. On the other hand, as with any representation of ethnicity or other identity politics, *zainichi* films are a double-edged sword. My intention in this chapter is to outline the plot of and characterizations in *Pacchigi!* and *Go*, and then comment on the essentializing as well as liberating effects of these productions on the representation of Korean identities in Japan. Recently, scholars have been engaging actively in discussion of the "consumption" of Asia in Japanese popular media (Iwabuchi 2001). I shall take up this discussion inwardly, so to say, by asking how a diasporic Asian community within Japan (here, the *zainichi*) is consumed by way of movies such as *Pacchigi!* and *Go*.

As Sonia Ryang details in chapter 3 of this volume, one of the most important recent events for *zainichi* was the North Korean government's official admission on September 17, 2002, that it had kidnapped Japanese citizens during the 1970s and 1980s. "Post-9/17" Japan has hence been rife with diverse forms of political activism and discourse among both ethnic Japanese and *zainichi* with regard to human rights, social justice, and national pride, from stances advocating for the rights of foreign students and ethnic minorities to those denouncing the Korean presence in Japan, demonizing North Korea, and emphasizing the threat of a North Korean attack on Japanese soil. The "9/17 shock" was the culmination of a series of crises in the 1990s between Japan and North Korea, such as the nuclear weapons crisis of 1994 and the missile issue of 1998 (and, more recently, 2006).[3]

The Japanese media's sensationalistic coverage of the kidnappings, the victims' families' grief and anger, the activities of support groups, and the government's reaction and overreaction, among others, make *zainichi* suddenly hypervisible, as Ryang's chapter makes clear. While broadcasts about North Korea shorten the distance between a *zainichi* and her putative homeland on the Korean peninsula, they also make Japanese aware of the existence of *zainichi*. Of course, Koreans have existed in Japan since the colonial period. But their existence has not been taught in compulsory public schooling, for example; what is seen as troublesome (whether Burakumin or *zainichi*) effectively has been censored in the Japanese media (Iwabuchi 2000).

The so-called ordinary Japanese audience normally would not have many opportunities to be exposed to *zainichi* existence and presence. Public education in Japan teaches virtually nothing about the history of Korean repatriation, and Japan's current younger generations would have few ways of learning about it other than watching a movie like *Pacchigi!* or *Go*. An encounter with cinematographic representations like these would remind the Japanese of the complex formation of *zainichi* as a diasporic community.[4]

In this chapter, by looking closely at *Pacchigi!* and *Go*, I'd like to inquire into the Korean diaspora in Japan and the way it is perceived in the two movies. By so doing, I shall explore the potential as well as limitations of each work as an exemplar of the diaspora-film genre in the context of the representation of Koreans in Japan.

PACCHIGI!:
THE JAPANESE VERSION OF THE KOREAN DIASPORA

In looking at *Pacchigi!*,[5] I wish to start with the following question: what makes this film not uncomfortable for the ordinary Japanese audience, despite its scenes featuring *zainichi* poverty, discriminatory and hostile Japanese attitudes, and the scars left by Japanese colonialism?

The story's outline is as follows: It is Kyoto, 1968. A trio of *zainichi* youngsters, An-Seong, Jaedeugi, and Bang-Ho, are students at a Chongryun Korean ethnic high school. They live in Kyoto's Higashi Kujō district, which spreads along the Takase River and is notorious for its poverty, delinquency, and adjacency to a Burakumin hamlet. The three peers are marked by deviant behavior, poor school attendance, and street fights with neighboring ethnically Japanese high-school students. On one such hopeless day, An-Seong out of the blue decides to repatriate to North Korea. Not just an undefeated street fighter but also an outstanding soccer player, An-Seong wants to contribute to his homeland, the North, with his athletic skill. Jaedeugi, a younger sidekick of An-Seong, feels deserted when he learns of An-Seong's decision.

Soon a "peace mission" from a nearby Japanese high school visits the Korean school and proposes a goodwill soccer game. One member of the mission, Kōsuke, falls in love at first sight with Kyeong-Ja, a female student at the Korean school who happens to be An-Seong's younger sister. Kyeong-Ja has been bewildered by her brother's decision to be repatriated and is reluctant to go with him. Although the "goodwill" soccer game results in a fiasco thanks to the violent intrusion of karate fighters from the Japanese high school, Kōsuke tries hard to earn Kyeong-Ja's attention. He learns some Korean, tries to master a Korean song on the guitar, and studies *zainichi* history. For his devotion, Kōsuke is invited to An-Seong's farewell party. He and Kyeong-Ja sing a duet, "Imjingang" (Imjin River), whose lyrics long for Korean reunification. Meanwhile, An-Seong is displeased with his sister's Japanese boyfriend. After the party, Jaedeugi confides in Kōsuke his worries about the loss that An-Seong's repatriation would bring; after a frank talk, the two promise to become good friends.

An-Seong himself has an ethnically Japanese girlfriend, Momoko, who discovers that she is pregnant as the day of An-Seong's departure fast approaches. In light of the baby's imminent arrival, An-Seong is in need of money. Jaedeugi comes up with an idea to sell An-Seong's school uniform—as the uniform of an undefeated fighter, Jaedeugi is convinced, it will sell for a lot of money. One night while Jaedeugi, clad in An-Seong's uniform, walks through downtown Kyoto, Japanese hoodlums attack him violently, mistaking him for An-Seong. He is badly beaten; on his way home, a truckload of iron rods accidentally breaks loose and hits him, killing him instantly.

A deeply saddened Kōsuke tries to attend Jaedeugi's funeral, but there he is harshly criticized by Jaedugi's Korean neighbors and friends for his ignorance of the colonial past and for Japan's discrimination against Koreans. Kōsuke falls into a serious depression, but after much effort to teach himself about *zainichi*, at last Kyeong-Ja returns his love. An-Seong and Bang-Ho take part in a revenge fight against the Japanese hoodlums, resulting in a draw. As the fight closes, Momoko gives a birth to a baby boy. As the credits roll, two couples are shown alternately: Kōsuke (now initiated as a Buddhist monk) and Kyeong-Ja drive in a car on a date; An-Seong, Momoko, and their baby boy journey on a train to an unknown destination—it could be Niigata, a port town where the repatriation boat to North Korea was harbored, but it is ultimately unclear.

Among the *zainichi* trio, Jaedeugi is the tragic character in terms not only of his premature death but also his lack of life prospects; the other *zainichi* youths more or less make their dreams come true: besides An-Seong and Kyeong-Ja, Bang-Ho enters Chongryun's Korea University in Tokyo, and his high-school classmate Gang-Ja, who drops out of school earlier in the movie, gets a certification and job as a nurse. All the *zainichi* characters, including An-Seong and his sister, leave Jaedeugi's memory behind and depart for other destinations, both personal and political.

I am particularly interested in the film's depiction of Jaedeugi and his premature death. Jaedeugi's death functions as a sacrifice that allows the other characters to survive and succeed. But Jaedeugi, with his loneliness and helplessness, ironically most reflects the real conditions of *zainichi* life in the 1960s, while the rest of the *zainichi* characters appear to be at odds with reality. Take, for instance, Gang-Ja. Without years of preparation, it would have been impossible for a *zainichi* girl who dropped out of a Korean high school to make it into nursing school and become qualified as nurse in Japan. The sequence of events in the film implies that she somehow became a nurse soon after dropping out of high school. Similarly unrealistic is the romance between An-Seong's sister and Kōsuke, which at best would have been met with scorn and ostracism. The romance between An-Seong and Momoko—resulting in childbirth—would have produced radically mixed reactions among neighborhood Koreans, while the Korean school authorities would have expelled An-Seong. Such interethnic romances did not exist in the 1960s as the cause for celebration depicted in the film.

The portrait of Jaedeugi as lonesome and downtrodden is truthful not only historically but also as an up-to-date description of *zainichi* youth, who face closure from all directions of Japanese society. Consider the scene in which Jaedeugi asks Kōsuke to be his friend just before his death:

> *On a street corner in central Kyoto.*
> JAEDEUGI: Honestly speaking, we, too, are afraid of fighting. . . .
> KŌSUKE: What?

JAEDEUGI: I've been tormented by many dreams that hundreds of [Japanese] hoodlums suddenly rush out on the street corner to beat me.

KŌSUKE: I never had...

JAEDEUGI: Well, Kōsuke, I have given up on my dream of becoming an action star for Tōei Movie Company [one of the major motion picture companies in Japan of the day]. Will you teach me how to play guitar?

KŌSUKE: I cannot...

JAEDEUGI: An-Seong will leave [for North Korea] and Bang-Ho will also leave me, so let us be friends from now on [*Oreto tsureni nareyo*].

KŌSUKE: OK...

Jaedeugi's phrase "let us be friends from now on" [*Oreto tsureni nareyo*] rings as if a message from Korean to Japanese society. Jaedeugi comes from a below-subsistence, single-mother household. His house is a tiny shanty whose front door is too narrow to let even his coffin pass through—Korean neighbors and friends have to break it open before his funeral. The scene symbolizes Jaedeugi's loss of belonging—in this life or the next. A Korean death, in which even one's coffin cannot make it to one's own home, resonates with the predicament of the Korean diaspora in Japan that Ryang depicts in her introduction to this volume. Nevertheless, in *Pacchigi!* Jaedeugi's death is not the culmination of a tragedy but a convenient solution to the complex pain to which *zainichi* are subjected. The elimination of Jaedeugi opens up possibilities for the rest of the *zainichi* characters. After emotional upheaval and wailing lament over Jaedeugi's death, each character goes his or her own way, each becoming successful or happy one way or another. Here I see an unfortunate resonance with the irresponsible attitude of Japanese society with regard to its own past. Once the most downtrodden is removed from the story, everything is fine; once we forget about the painful past (whether colonialism, wartime forced labor, or "comfort women"), everything becomes all right.

In this way, Jaedeugi's death is a salvation or solution for (Japanese) film audiences, and by extension for ordinary Japanese people: by eliminating this tragic figure and leaving only those who are capable of self-reliance and self-promotion (including An-Seong, Kyeong-Ja, Gang-Ja, and Bang-Ho), the film enables Japanese audiences to reconcile the *zainichi* tragedy as something that can be eliminated from memory. For it would be a mental burden to imagine Jaedeugi's future: anyone would predict hard days ahead for him, with no economic and familial means and very little personal strength. There is a clear contrast in this respect between Jaedeugi and the Japanese hero, Kōsuke. Kōsuke is the son of a Buddhist priest in Kyoto and is designated to succeed his father. The occupation carries little risk and provides the viewer with firm scaffolding to imagine his secure and stable future.

It is also important to note that Jaedeugi's death occurs not in the present but in 1968, a time now long past. The film's reliance on an irresponsible nostalgia is inescapable. Here it is possible to glimpse the Japanese version of *zainichi* experience: *zainichi* is a thing of the past and therefore something that can be removed from present reality. It is not painful for today's Japanese audience to talk about, to represent it, or to face it, as long as it stays in a box of memory.

How, then, should we understand the *zainichi* protagonist, An-Seong? Is he also a person of the past? One interpretation is that his (would-be) repatriation to North Korea follows the same line as Jaedeugi's premature death, that is, that of salvation and/or elimination. In other words, repatriation functions in the film as *symbolic death*. But An-Seong is not a tragic character; on the contrary, he is depicted as a gifted and strong person. In fact, he is a masculine leader, a dominant male ideal in the 1960s. Why remove him to North Korea?

Seen from the Japanese audience's point of view, envisioning An-Seong's future is a morally vexing task. An-Seong's social and family life with Momoko and their children would have been tough. There would be complications arising from their interethnic romance, illegitimate birth, poverty, lack of qualifications, possible unemployment, and so on—in a word, all the factors that today's post-affluent, peaceful Japan would rather not contemplate. Thus, though capable and sturdy, An-Seong and his anomalous family need to be eliminated so as not to confront Japanese audiences in any hostile way, but rather to give them hearty entertainment without incurring any sense of political or historical guilt or burden. In this context, North Korea is a convenient locale precisely because of its enigmatic unknowability. I must hasten to emphasize that the North Korea of the film is that of 1968, not the post-2002 North Korea that has been increasingly demonized in Japan. But perhaps precisely because of its current extreme demonization, the North Korea of 1968 seems even more alien and far away. The final scene's vague allusion to the family's repatriation is characterized by the happy smiles of young parents and a beautiful child, accentuating the sense of hopeful departure to an unknown land.

The convenience of North Korea as a locale to consign a potentially problematic protagonist requires its depoliticization: if North Korea is depicted as an ideologically confrontational place vis-à-vis Japan, an audience of Japanese citizens would be forced into a position of self-reflection, which is obviously not an appealing imposition from a commercial perspective. An-Seong's decision to be repatriated is thus depoliticized in the name of soccer:

> *In the restroom of the Korean high school.*
>
> BANG-HO: The World Cup Game! I was moved to tears... An-Seong, you aren't going to practice soccer today?
>
> AN-SEONG: I have decided. I'm gonna go back to my homeland.
>
> JAEDEUGI: What?
>
> BANG-HO: Why?
>
> AN-SEONG: Why? I would never become a member of the Japan national team no matter how hard I work, as long as I stay here. Instead, I'll go back to my country and play on the pitch at the World Cup Games.
>
> JAEDEUGI/BANG-HO: ...
>
> JAEDEUGI: ...OK, if so, can I get your bellyband as a memento?
>
> AN-SEONG: Ahh, I'll sure give it to you. I'll leave when the repatriation ferry comes in.
>
> BANG-HO: When is that?
>
> AN-SEONG: After the end of this summer, maybe. Bang-Ho, will you come with me [to North Korea]?
>
> BANG-HO: Mmm, well, I've got so many enemies I have to deal with here in Kyoto, so...

Like many conversations in the film, this one is gently comedic in its handling of the everyday. As the motivation for repatriation, becoming a member of the North Korean national soccer team and playing in the World Cup is presented as apolitical. (Of course, in North Korea sports are never free from politics.) Jaedeugi's and Bang-Ho's humorous responses never relate the repatriation to anything transcending their everyday life-world, as exemplified by Jaedeugi's question about the bellyband. The repatriation reference becomes even more tokenistic and, indeed, ironic when one realizes that in reality, all repatriation boats were suspended between 1967 and 1970 by the Japanese government (Takasaki 2005b: 49–50).

GO: THE INDIVIDUALIST VERSION OF THE KOREAN DIASPORA

Go[6] and *Pacchigi!* are similar in many senses. In *Go*, just as in *Pacchigi!*, a character's premature death is in order. The sacrifice in *Go* is the hero's best friend, a Korean high-school student felled, again, by an accident in a public space. Second, a central feature of *Go* is the winding road of interethnic romance, although the genders here are transposed, with a Korean male hero, Sugihara, and his Japanese girlfriend. Third, *Go* makes reference to North Korean repatriation, though to much lesser degree than *Pacchigi!:* in one scene, the hero's father is shocked by the news of the death of his younger brother who had been repatriated to North Korea in the 1950s. Here, repatriation is posited as the past segregated from today. Fourth, almost all of the *zainichi* characters in both films are committed to North Korea and Chongryun, though in the case of *Go* the commitment of the hero and his family is broken off as the story unfolds. Finally, both films are noted for their outstanding Japanese box office success beyond the *zainichi* film genre.

The outline of the story is as follows: Sugihara, the protagonist, is a third-generation Korean, a student in a Japanese high school who graduated from a Chongryun junior high school. His father runs a back-alley shop that specializes in exchanging pachinko-earned goods for cash—a "common" *zainichi* occupation. In the past, his father had long been committed to the cause of Chongryun and supported North Korea, but he obtained South Korean nationality in order to go sightseeing in Hawai'i (or at least so it is depicted initially—but see below), which required a South Korean passport.

Just like An-Seong, Sugihara's schooldays are filled with fights that always result in his overwhelming victory; he and his delinquent peers fill the rest of their time with all kinds of mischief. His best friend, Jeong-Il, with whom he shares an unbreakable bond, is a Korean high-school student who had been his classmate in junior high. When Sugihara decided to leave Korean schools for a Japanese high school, their classroom teacher harshly criticized him, calling him a traitor to their homeland; Jeong-Il supported Sugihara by saying: "We never have had what you call homeland."

One day, Sugihara attends the birthday party of one of his friends and falls in love with a mysterious Japanese girl whose family name is Sakurai (she is reluctant to use her first name). He takes her out on a couple of dates and they gradually become intimate. But sudden sad news dejects him: Jeong-Il is stabbed to death by a Japanese youth at a railway station. Jeong-Il mistakenly thought that the youth was about to attack a female Korean student at the station; the boy, who is carrying a knife, attacks Jeong-Il. Sakurai comforts Sugihara, and that night they attempt to make love. She freezes in bed, however, when Sugihara confesses that he is Korean. She declares that she is wary of a non-Japanese male entering her. Everything falls apart.

Sugihara's father, in the meantime, has been depressed by the news that his younger brother has died in North Korea. In sadness, Sugihara provocatively blames his father, stating that the second generation of *zainichi*, with its sentimentality and powerlessness, has caused *zainichi* much grief and difficulty. They fistfight, which is depicted with excessive violence, and the result is the son's complete defeat by his father. In the wake of the fight, Sugihara finds out that the true reason for his father's adopting South Korean nationality was that he wanted to make his son's life easier.

Six months later, on Christmas Eve, Sugihara is studying hard in preparation for college entrance examinations. He is trying to fulfill the wishes of the deceased Jeong-Il, who always wanted him to go to a (presumably Japanese) university. Sakurai calls him after a long period of silence and asks him to come to the place where they had their first date. As soon as he catches sight of her he shouts at her: "Who am I? *Zainichi*? Don't name us without our permission! I am I, or I am no man. Nothing!" She responds: "Sugihara is always Sugihara. You are the one and only. That's all for me. Your nationality or ethnicity doesn't matter." In this last scene, they recover mutual affection and leave for some unknown place together in a light snowfall.

As with Jaedeugi in *Pacchigi!,* throughout *Go* Jeong-Il is represented as a tragic character. But the tragedy lies not in his existence itself but in the fact that his hopeful future is foreclosed by his premature death. Unlike the dependent and helpless Jaedeugi, Jeong-Il is a wise, confident, and gifted person, who is introduced as "the most brilliant student in the history of Korean junior high schools [in Japan]." His dream is to be certified to teach in a Korean school. He is, at least on the surface, not presented as plagued with ontological insecurity and an ongoing identity crisis. On the contrary, he is self-assured in his declaration that he and other third-generation Koreans in Japan have never had a homeland. Unlike Jaedeugi's death in *Pacchigi!,* which was lamented by the entire Korean neighborhood, Jeong-Il's death in *Go* is an event that seems to be experienced only by the young people, both Japanese and Korean.

Pathos and sentimentality, embodied in *Pacchigi!* in the character of Jaedeugi, can be perceived in the father-son interactions in *Go*. It is in this connection that North Korea becomes important, but unlike the idealized and nonthreatening North Korea of *Pacchigi!*, in *Go* North Korea appears as a symbol of misery, inconvenience, and evil—a place where people die for no reason. Whereas in *Pacchigi!* An-Seong's (and possibly others') youthful hope is carried to North Korea, in *Go*, North Korea is passé, belonging to the old, backward-looking generation, which is immersed in unproductive and pathetic self-pity:

> *In the back seat of a taxi.*
> FATHER: Tong-Il [Father's brother] was good at painting.
> SUGIHARA: ...
> FATHER: When he was little, he painted a picture of the rising sun on the bow of a fishing boat. Three days later that boat was caught in a storm and went missing. Everyone gave up on it. But the next day the boat came back safely. Since then Tong-Il became a favorite painter. He earned living by painting on the boats. Ahh, [thanks to his earning] in those days we ate delicious crab for the first time in tearful pleasure. ... Ahh, I would have liked to ship the crab for him [to North Korea]. (in tears) Had he ever eaten crab in North Korea?
> SUGIHARA: ... Not cool [*Dasē*]!
> FATHER: What?
> SUGIHARA: Those stories of poverty are boring. (sarcastically) Why didn't you attempt to make revolution to get crab? What nonsense [*Kudaranē*]!
> FATHER: ...
> SUGIHARA: The days have passed when people are moved by such a sentimental episode. Just deal with your [generation's] problems on your own [*Temērano sedaide keri tsukeroyo*]. The laziness of you first- and second-generation *zainichi* is depressing!

Father's regret that he had not sent crab to his repatriated brother in North Korea presupposes and reinforces today's Japanese public image of North Korea—economic predicament, poverty, and starvation—and yet his words bear a certain nostalgic tone. Sugihara's comments, however—"not cool!" [*dasē*], "nonsense" [*kudaranē*], "just deal with your [generation's] problems on your own" [*temērano sedaide keri tsukeroyo*]—represent the impatience and annoyance felt by younger *zainichi* toward the older generations and the prolonged postponement of their realization that the national home is irrecoverable. Sugihara's claim, repeated in the movie, that he dares to erase the national borders—*kokkyōsen nanka orega keshite yaruyo*—in this sense embodies the *zainichi* generation gap, with the younger generation's eye on the possibility of going beyond the homeland orientation, as if to forget about the lost homeland, colonial history, and diasporic reality. But this desertion of the past obviously carries a conservative, almost reactionary message of antidiaspora and antiethnicity. Sugihara's "not cool!," in my view, symbolizes the attitude that devalues *zainichi* diasporic history, including repatriation; for Sugihara (and his generation), resentfully dwelling on past suffering is "not cool." In this way, *Go* becomes a movie about cooptation; in exchange for being cool, Japan's young people of Korean descent must drop their *zainichi* past as the "uncool" baggage belonging to poor, uneducated, and unsophisticated [*dasai*] old people.

This position is also visible in the climax, in which Sugihara and Sakurai reconcile:

> *On an elementary school playground.*
>
> SUGIHARA: What is my ethnic belonging [*orewa nanijinda*]?
>
> SAKURAI: . . .
>
> SUGIHARA: What is my ethnic belonging? No, what am I [*orewa nanimonoda*]?
>
> SAKURAI: . . .
>
> SUGIHARA: Answer me. What am I?
>
> SAKURAI: *Zainichi* Korean [*zainichi kankokujin*].
>
> SUGIHARA: How can you call me *zainichi* without asking me? What d'you mean when you call me *zainichi*? This means that I'm a temporary sojourner who goes out of this country some day. Do you really understand this?
>
> SAKURAI: . . .
>
> SUGIHARA: Sometimes an impulse to eradicate all of you Japanese people overwhelms me! You're scared of me, aren't you? You can't feel safe until you impose some name on me totally one-sidedly. Okay, I am a lion. The lion has no self-consciousness that he is a lion, [because] that's the name you give him one-sidedly. If you approach me, I'll jump on you to get you.

SAKURAI: ...

SUGIHARA: No matter what the name is. Scorpion or alien—all acceptable. I never recognize myself as an alien, though. I'm neither *zainichi* nor alien. I'm I. No, I don't even assert that I'm I. I am a question, an enigma, an unidentifiable object. Hey, are you afraid of me? So what? Say something! Damn it! So what? Shit!

SAKURAI: ... those eyes.

SUGIHARA: Eyes?

SAKURAI: Those eyes of yours fascinated me.

SUGIHARA: ...

SAKURAI: When I was first glared at by your eyes, I trembled all over. It no longer matters to me what Sugihara's ethnic belonging is. I have come to the truth at last. I should have known this the first time I saw Sugihara.

SUGIHARA: Mmm ... *(in tears)*

Sakurai's words, "It no longer matters to me what Sugihara's ethnic belonging is," superficially appear to endorse transnationalism, multiculturalism, and cosmopolitanism. Six months earlier, however, she had made racist utterances when Sugihara confessed his ethnicity in bed: "Daddy told me not to be associated with Chinese and Korean men because their blood is impure," "I'm scared of Sugihara's body invading my body," and so on. Her newly asserted logic of acceptance is therefore based not on the acceptance, endorsement, or understanding that Sugihara is Korean, but on the erasure or even denial of any ethnic identity. This acceptance, moreover, is asymmetrical. Sakurai's identity is never questioned: as a member of the Japanese majority, Sakurai has no need to try to be accepted. Only *zainichi* need to be accepted—by the Japanese, and apparently only through erasure.

This itself is a political theme, but in *Go* the dilemma for a *zainichi* of being accepted as a human in Japanese society is captured in distinctly individualistic terms: no perception of *zainichi* collectivity exists behind Sugihara's and Sakurai's reasoning. In other words, Sugihara's acceptance as a man by Sakurai as a woman is premised on the negation of his connection to or concern for his homeland, the erasure of his historical background, and the evasion of the recognition of the Korean diaspora as a reality. In this way, the reconciliation between the young lovers is placed—deceptively—in a zone devoid of historicity and relations of power. And in this way, this closing reconciliation scene functions as a salvation for Japanese audiences, because of its selective deployment of ethnicity—when creating the romantic conundrum, ethnicity is highlighted, when reconciling it, ethnicity is dropped. As such, in the final analysis *Go* allows young Japanese viewers a sigh of relief—by not pursuing the *zainichi* theme far enough.[7]

TWO DIASPORAS

Pacchigi! and *Go* represent an interesting transposition of the diachrony of diaspora. Although *Go* was produced a few years earlier than *Pacchigi!*, it depicts a time closer to the present. *Pacchigi!*, conversely, is saturated with consciously nostalgic reflection. If *Pacchigi!* reflects a longing for home, vaguely yet in reality shared by both old and young Koreans in Japan during the 1960s, *Go* shows the clear split between old and young *zainichi* with regard to their sense of loss of home and belonging (or non-belonging). If *Pacchigi!* shows the time when Korea's reunification was a living dream for *zainichi* Koreans, the young protagonists of *Go* have no concern over such an event. If *Pacchigi!* tries to speak to the nostalgic, collective recollections of *zainichi* (if only those affiliated with Chongryun), *Go* presents an indeterminable (if not wholly positive) future for *zainichi* youth.

As such, the films depict two different visions of diaspora. Whereas *Pacchigi!* relies on the existence of a diaspora that longs for a homeland and provides a subjective point of departure, the world of *Go* consists of atomized, individualized *zainichi*, young and old, who are no longer one and the same people in diasporic consciousness. The shift from the 1968 Japan of *Pacchigi!* to the more current setting of *Go* may be a reflection of the shifting reality of the Korean diaspora(s) in Japan.

Both *Pacchigi!* and *Go* end with scenes of leaving, or, more precisely, escape. This can be read in multiple ways, and in closing I wish to suggest two: the *zainichi* characters' escape can either symbolize a positive take-off to utopia or, contrarily, the elimination of a troublesome element and reality from Japanese society. In either event, the ways that both films use the image of the journey reflect the paradigm shift from "roots" of diaspora to "routes" of diaspora (see Clifford 1997). This shift suggests the possibility of resisting the master narratives of diaspora and ethnic identity politics, dispersing the centralized, monolithic subject of diaspora and leaving us instead with a decentralized, disrupted, and destabilized diasporic subject that is always on the run. It also should be evident that the concept of nostalgia plays an ambivalent role: for the majority host society, it is a warm, caring ethos that enables them to recover a memory that has been relegated to a long-forgotten historical past; for the diasporic community, it is an emotional atmosphere in which their current pain and struggles are repeated and reproduced. In a way, regrettably, the cool self-deception of *Go* or the commercial self-erasure seen in *Pacchigi!* might simply be two of the very limited modes of self-representation left for *zainichi* in Japan today.

6. The Foreigner Category for Koreans in Japan

Opportunities and Constraints

Chikako Kashiwazaki

The term *foreigner* in general signifies the status of an outsider, and is therefore likely to be employed by the dominant group in society to exclude such persons. In today's Japan, however, there are a number of instances in which the word *foreigner* [*gaikokujin*] is being used as a positive categorical term.

Gaikokujin mo jūmin desu (Foreigners are residents, too)

Gaikokujin tono kyōsei (Living together with foreigners)

Gaikokujin ga kurashiyasui shakai wa nihonjin nimo kurashiyasui (A society that is comfortable for foreigners to live is also comfortable for the Japanese.)[1]

Teijū gaikokujin no chihō sanseiken (Local electoral rights for resident foreigners)

These are a few examples of slogans aimed at advancing the position of foreigners in Japanese society. Advocates include *zainichi* Koreans, who have long struggled to gain their civil and social rights in their country of residence.[2] These phrases also represent a progressive cause for members of the majority Japanese in support of minority rights.

One may find something odd about the centrality of *gaikokujin* in these slogans, given that *foreigner* implies *outsider*. It may seem awkward, too, that *zainichi* Koreans should positively identify with the foreigner category. For one thing, the image of *zainichi* Koreans is far from the typical image of *gaikokujin* as it is used in everyday Japanese idiom. Second, having pride in being Korean is one thing, but having pride in being a foreigner is quite another. Unlike a specific ethnic group identity, the foreigner category appears less likely to provide a strong basis for group solidarity. Furthermore, in light of its general legal definition of being a foreign national, the term *gaikokujin* does not sufficiently capture the reality of today's *zainichi* Koreans. For example, Japanese nationality holders of Korean descent are on the increase (see chapter 4 of this volume). Nevertheless, politically active *zainichi* Koreans and their Japanese supporters have emphasized the foreigner category in their fight against social injustice and to maintain Korean cultural identity in Japanese society. Why should they?

One reason that immediately comes to mind is an ethnically exclusionary tendency among the Japanese. If it is difficult to become Japanese, either legally or in the form of social acceptance, then the non-Japanese or foreigner identity is likely strengthened. In other words, it may be an instance in which a minority group appropriates an imposed category. This is perhaps a good starting point but is not satisfactory, for it is not yet clear why *foreigner* should be a viable and attractive category. The goal of this chapter, then, is to better understand why foreignness became, and continues to be, a focal point in the construction of *zainichi* Korean identity for some. To that end I examine the changing relationship between the *zainichi* Korean community and *gaikokujin* as a social category in Japan.

In a consideration of diaspora, James Clifford (1997: 244) takes up the question of "what is at stake, politically and intellectually, in contemporary invocations of diaspora" and asks: "What experiences do they reject, replace, or marginalize?" I would modify these questions slightly and ask: What is at stake in invocations of *gaikokujin*—or active use of the foreigner category? What experiences do they reject, replace, or marginalize? These broad questions inform my analysis in this paper.

I would contend that the foreigner category for *zainichi* Koreans has represented (1) the *rejection,* or denial, of assimilation into the Japanese majority, and (2) the *replacement* of a vertical relationship based on colonialism with a horizontal one between sovereign nation-states and their respective citizens. I shall also suggest that at the same time, an emphasis placed on the term *foreigner* tends to *marginalize* alternative forms of Korean diasporic identity and helps reinforce the prevailing Japanese/foreigner dichotomy.

The chapter is divided into four parts. The first section begins with a discussion of the foreigner category and examines the change in the organization of legal status in Japan from "imperial-colonial" to "ethnonational." Under the latter mode of organization, the Japanese/foreigner dichotomy crystallized and came to be a dominant axis of social categorization in postwar Japan. The two sections that follow consider how mainstream *zainichi* Koreans and their Japanese supporters have appropriated the foreigner category as a resource to advance their causes. Analysis will mainly focus on two time periods: the years immediately following 1945, and the post-1990 period when Japan experienced a sharp growth in the number of resident foreigners. Despite all the disadvantages associated with it, the foreigner category was favored in both periods in the realm of politics because it allowed *zainichi* Koreans to maintain a respectable status, in sharp contrast with the earlier colonized status, and to protect themselves from the perceived danger of falling onto the "Japanese" side of the Japanese/foreigner binary. The final section discusses the recent institutionalization of the foreigner category in public policy and programs. This has occurred, ironically, when the need to part with the simple dichotomy of Japanese versus foreigners increasingly has been recognized.

THE DEVELOPMENT OF THE JAPANESE/FOREIGNER DICHOTOMY AND *ZAINICHI* KOREANS

The Category of Gaikokujin

In contemporary Japan the dichotomy between the Japanese [*nihonjin*] and foreigners [*gaikokujin*] often prevails over other categorizations related to race and ethnic origins. This can be compared, for instance, with the race-based dichotomy in American society, in which the demarcation between whites and nonwhites has been salient. Just as new immigrants of non-European origin are pulled toward the "nonwhite" category in the United States, so are people who do not share Japanese attributes quickly categorized as foreigners in Japan.[3]

Previous sociological studies have shown that the "Japanese" category consists of multiple dimensions. Whereas Yasunori Fukuoka (2000: xxix) discusses components of "Japaneseness" using lineage, culture, and nationality, Yoshio Sugimoto (1997: 171) gives seven aspects—nationality, ethnic lineage, language competence, place of birth, current residence, subjective identity, and level of cultural literacy—to show various types of Japanese. These exercises in deconstructing Japaneseness reveal that minority group members share, to varying degrees, some of the above components with the dominant population, and that they nevertheless tend to be placed into one side of the binary opposition or the other.

What, then, constitutes *gaikokujin*? Like Japaneseness, we can conceptualize foreignness using the several dimensions given in Table 1. The table also highlights the difference between "typical foreigners" and *zainichi* Koreans. The social construction of the foreigner category is a mirror image of the self-understanding among the majority ethnic Japanese. At its base is what a number of scholars have referred to as the "myth of ethnic homogeneity" (Ōnuma 1993: 339; Oguma 1995; Fukuoka 2000). This myth crystallized in the post–World War II period, and the majority population internalized it thanks in good part to the lack of teaching in school about ethnic diversity. This myth was further reinforced through the *Nihonjinron* literature that emphasized the uniqueness and homogeneity of the Japanese people (Yoshino 1992). Consequently, the majority Japanese have come to assume that ethnic origin (lineage or blood and appearance), cultural attributes (language and behavioral characteristics), and nationality status all go together.

"Typical foreigners," as they are commonly imagined, or "pure foreigners" in Fukuoka's typology (2000: xxxv), would therefore share none of these three aspects with the majority Japanese. They would stand out because of their appearance and behavior and would be recognized instantly as *gaikokujin* or *gaijin*.[4] Moreover, they would be assumed to hold foreign nationality. In contrast, *zainichi* Koreans today do not fit with the image of a typical *gaikokujin* held by the Japanese populace. Younger generation *zainichi* Koreans have been assimilated into the majority Japanese culture to a large degree, even though legally many of them remain foreign nationals. Korean ethnicity is often invisible, particularly because many *zainichi* use a "Japanese" name (alias, *tsūmei*) in their social life instead of their Korean ethnic name.

Consequently, ethnic Japanese people may be confused upon encountering a *zainichi* Korean. They cannot instantly comprehend the presence of a person who looks and behaves just like an ethnic Japanese but claims not to be.[5] They might wonder: "What does it mean that this person is *not* Japanese? Is s/he a *foreigner*, then?" However, foreignness is likely to be recognized once the person's Korean background is revealed. Both foreign national status and the use of a Korean-style name are major social markers of *zainichi* foreignness.[6] The term *Korean*, as both an adjective and a noun, invokes a sense of national differentiation.

Given the strong Japanese/foreigner demarcation in society, it may seem natural that people of Korean ancestry are categorized as foreigners. However, this was certainly not the case during the colonial era (1910–1945). It is important to recall that Koreans then were colonial subjects, and hence were legally treated as "Japanese." The contemporary association of Koreans with *gaikokujin*, therefore, cannot simply be assumed to arise from a preexisting Japanese/foreigner dichotomy. We therefore need to examine the interactive relationship between the development of dichotomous categories in Japan, on the one hand, and how Koreans came to be associated with the foreigner category, on the other.

TABLE 1. The Social Construction of the Foreigner in Japan

	Lineage or "race"	Culture	Legal status
Typical foreigners (*gaikokujin, gaijin*)	appearance, skin color	language, customs, behavior; ethnic name	foreign nationality, known or assumed
Zainichi Koreans	belief in difference in lineage	ethnic name	foreign nationality, known or assumed

NOTE: Items in the table indicate major social markers that differentiate a person from the ethnically dominant Japanese. The term *nationality* refers to formal citizenship.

The Development of Legal Nationality

A few conceptual clarifications are in order for this historical survey of the changing relationship among nationality, citizenship, and ethnic categories. To avoid terminological confusion, I shall use *nationality* to denote formal citizenship as recognized under international law.[7] It is a legal status indicating one's affiliation to a given national state vis-à-vis other states. *Citizenship*, on the other hand, is defined in this chapter as a bundle of rights and duties conferred upon individuals by a political community. Legally, the term *foreigner*, or *foreign national*, refers to persons who do not hold the country's nationality. It is common practice for contemporary democratic states to give full citizenship, including full political rights, to their own nationals, while allowing only partial citizenship to foreign nationals. Although foreign nationals can partially be citizens, the word *citizen* is normally used interchangeably with *national*. This overlap suggests the extent to which the concept of citizen has been strongly associated with nationality status.[8]

In historical perspective, the national/foreigner distinction is a by-product of modern nation building. In a given territory inhabitants were transformed into citizens, namely, members of a nation-state. In Japan, too, the legal distinction between nationals and foreigners developed as the country emerged as a modern nation-state in the late nineteenth century. The distinction was formally institutionalized by the Nationality Law of 1899.[9] This law, together with family registry [*koseki*], provided the administrative basis for defining a person's nationality status in accordance with international law.[10]

Internally, nationality represented common membership in a centralized state. Abolishing the hierarchy-based feudal order, the Meiji government declared the principle of equality between citizens. To be sure, democratization did not go very far; in imperial Japan, affiliation to the state primarily meant subjecthood—the status of being subject to the emperor—rather than equal membership in a political community. Yet nation-building projects fostered the idea of citizens [kokumin] bonded by horizontal, as opposed to vertical, ties in a national community. At the same time, the coupling of nationality status with family registry paved the way for the development of a concept of Japanese nationality that is more firmly rooted in ethnic Japanese lineage in postwar years.

*Institutional Frameworks:
From Imperial-Colonial to Ethno-National*

The legal distinction between Japanese nationals and foreign nationals did not from the outset correspond with the Japanese/non-Japanese differentiation based on ethnicity. By focusing on the changing relationship between legal nationality and ethnic group categories, we can understand how the shift from the "imperial-colonial" to "ethno-national" mode of nationality organization played a major role in the construction and reproduction of the Japanese/foreigner dichotomy, while prompting dynamic responses from *zainichi* Koreans.

Prewar Japan was marked by an imperial-colonial order that governed the legal status of the populations belonging to Japan. The presence of colonial subjects as a distinct category was at odds with a simple Japanese/foreigner dichotomy. The imperial-colonial mode of nationality organization had two distinctive features, which are displayed in Figure 1. First, being imperial, it was nonethnic, inclusive, and expansive in nature. Although it is often said that Japanese nationality is an exclusive status for the ethnic Japanese, or that a foreigner cannot become a Japanese national unless she or he is thoroughly assimilated, this certainly was not the case in imperial Japan. Japanese nationality was attributed to Okinawans and the Ainu even though they were ethnically differentiated. The Taiwanese after 1895 and then the Koreans after the annexation of Korea in 1910 were also incorporated as Japanese nationals.[11] In the context of international rivalry, imperial states, including Japan, competed with each other to gain new territories and claimed their rights to the population living in those territories. Manchuria is a case in point. In an attempt to prevent the growth of Chinese influence in the region, the Japanese government claimed its authority over Koreans, who were Japanese nationals, and

Legal framework	Japanese nationals (subjects)		Foreign nationals (sojourners)
	Persons from the mainland (*naichi*)	Persons from colonies (*gaichi*)	
Ethnic categories	Japanese (*nihonjin*)	Koreans (*chōsenjin*)	Foreigners (*gaikokujin*)

Figure 1. The imperial-colonial order.
Note: The distinction between *naichi* and *gaichi* was based on the location of one's family registration. This basically corresponded with the distinction between ethnic Japanese and ethnic non-Japanese (Koreans and the Taiwanese). Though defined as part of the *naichi* population, the Okinawans and the Ainu were also subject to differential treatment, such as a separate family registry (for Ainu) and the belated introduction of conscription (Sato 1988: 154–155).

prohibited them from switching to Chinese nationality (Mizuno 2001; Xu 2004).[12]

Second, the colonial component in the "imperial-colonial" order was reflected in status hierarchy among Japanese nationals, namely the distinction between colonizers and colonized. Put simply, Koreans were relegated to being second-class citizens/subjects. They were institutionally separated based on the location of their family registry, which was used to justify unequal treatment in legal rights and obligations.[13] To be sure, some policies and programs aimed at greater equality between the two people under the slogan of *naisenittai* (Japan and Korea as one). For instance, universal male suffrage was extended to Korean men residing in Japan proper (Matsuda 1995). However, any equalization was premised upon the idea of thorough cultural assimilation, as was most evident in *kōminka* policies (imperialization, or the project of turning colonial subjects completely into Japanese imperial subjects) in the last years of colonial rule (Kashiwazaki 2000a).

In sum, the legal framework during the colonial era was not a Japanese/foreigner dichotomy but had a tripartite structure: the Japanese, the colonized subjects, and foreign nationals.[14] Indeed, the term *gaikokujin* was not used to refer to Koreans; whether in official statistics or popular accounts, the term applied to them was *chōsenjin* or the derogatory *senjin*. Koreans were legally incorporated as Japanese nationals but were socially separated and placed in a lower rank as colonial subjects.

With the collapse of the Japanese colonial empire in 1945, this tripar-

Legal framework	Japanese nationals (full citizens)	Foreign nationals	
		Former colonial subjects	Other foreigners
Ethnic categories	Japanese (nihonjin) Okinawans Ainu	Koreans (zainichi kankoku chōsenjin)	Foreigners (gaikokujin)
		Resident foreigners (zainichi gaikokujin)	

Figure 2. The ethno-national order.
Note: "Former colonial subjects" were mostly Koreans but also included the Taiwanese.

tite structure was reorganized into a dichotomy. Koreans were no longer considered the Japanese emperor's subjects. Together with the Taiwanese, they uniformly lost their Japanese nationality and became foreign nationals in 1952, when Japan regained its independence from the Allied forces. As a result, the legal status of Japaneseness was redefined narrowly along ethnic lines. An ethno-national mode of nationality organization thus emerged to replace the imperial-colonial one. That is, ethnic categories came to overlap much more clearly with nationality status (see Figure 2).

The coupling of ethnic categories and legal nationality occurred in both public perceptions and institutional arrangements. In terms of perception, the ethno-national mode corresponded with an ethnocultural conception of Japanese nationhood.[15] Once colonies were cut off from Japan proper, it was deemed natural that only ethnic Japanese persons—in the sense of lineage and cultural attributes—should hold Japanese nationality.

New institutional arrangements were consistent with this ethnically exclusive concept of nationality. Under the patrilineal nationality law, access to the status of Japanese national was restricted. Naturalization was virtually the only way to acquire Japanese nationality for persons born to non-Japanese parents. Moreover, naturalization was to be permitted only on the condition that the applicant was sufficiently assimilated and would pose no threat to the putatively homogeneous society.[16] Family registry also acquired an ethnically exclusive character. Japanese nationality status was confirmed by the presence of one's record in a family registry, which in turn came to symbolize the idea of ethnic Japanese lineage.

Official maps and statistics provided another mechanism linking ethnicity and nationality in the mental picture of the general public. During the colonial era, the map of Japan included Korea and Taiwan, and the total population of Japan included that of its colonial subjects (Oguma 1995: 160–167).[17] In the postwar period, Japan's territory shrank; population statistics were compiled by nationality. Meanwhile, there was no ethnic subcategory under Japanese nationals based on ancestry.

Under the postwar ethno-national mode of organization, Japanese nationality holders were no longer imperial subjects but comprised a community of citizens, believed to be bounded by affiliation to the ethnonational group "Japanese." Japanese nationals came to enjoy full citizenship rights, including civil, social, and political rights. Consequently, democratization, or equalization among citizens, helped sharpen status differences between citizens and noncitizens. Its practical consequences would become increasingly pronounced with the inclusion of a nationality clause in a number of laws and regulations.[18]

DEFINING *ZAINICHI* KOREANS
AS *GAIKOKUJIN* IN THE POSTWAR YEARS
Seeking Respectable Status after Emancipation

Between 1945 and 1952, Japan was placed under U.S. occupation. It was during this period that nationality was reorganized as sketched above, and the dynamic interactions between the Japanese government and Korean residents reinforced the newly emerging binary framework. For *zainichi* Koreans, the legal nationality status was central to their identification with the *gaikokujin* category.

The Japanese government manipulated ambiguities in the legal status of former colonial subjects, usurped their rights, and antagonized them. On the assumption that Koreans still held Japanese nationality, the Japanese government continued to exercise criminal jurisdiction over them. At the same time, the government regarded Koreans as foreign nationals for the purpose of newly introduced immigration control devices, including the Alien Registration Order (1947) and the Immigration Control Order (1951).

School education is one domain where postwar legal flux fueled the tension between the authorities and *zainichi* Koreans, whose status shifted rapidly from colonial subjects to an ambiguous position and then to foreign nationals. As of April 1947, the Japanese central government held that citizens' obligations concerning compulsory education applied to Koreans, who were still Japanese nationals. In 1948, the SCAP (Supreme Commander of the Allied Powers) and the Japanese government ordered the closure of ethnic Korean schools (C. Kim 1997: 158–162). Once Koreans were officially stripped of their Japanese nationality in April 1952, rights and obligations concerning compulsory school education no longer applied to them. Public schools would accept Korean children as a favor but were not legally obliged to do so. Moreover, Korean parents were requested to sign a pledge stating that they would observe Japanese law and that their children would not cause any trouble (Nakayama 1995: 21–22; 53). For Korean residents, Japanese school was an institution for producing Japanese citizens, so they needed a place to educate their children as Korean nationals. The effort to establish Korean ethnic education was therefore closely related to their claim to the status of foreign nationals.

Resistance against the *daisangokujin* (the third-country national) category also illustrates well the sentiment of Koreans in Japan in the immediate postwar years. The Japanese government categorized Koreans and Taiwanese as *daisangokujin* to differentiate them from both the Japanese and other foreigners, mainly citizens of the Allied countries. *Daisangokujin* acquired a derogatory connotation, as it clearly indicated a lower status relative to other foreigners. This status distinction had concrete material consequences, such as receiving fewer food rations than Allied nationals (Miyazaki 1985). In short, the status of a full-fledged foreigner represented a privileged status.

To reject both Japanese nationality and the *daisangokujin* status, and to embrace *gaikokujin*, made sense given the nationalistic current in the Korean community.[19] For Koreans, redefining themselves as *gaikokujin* meant altering hitherto vertical relations vis-à-vis the Japanese based on colonial rule to a horizontal one—horizontal in the sense that all national states, be they small or large, poor or rich, theoretically have equal status in the international order, as enshrined in the one-country-one-vote system of the United Nations. Contemporary international order thus provided Koreans in Japan with a normative underpinning as they sought to establish a respectable status.

Political turmoil in the divided homeland also had the effect of strengthening foreigner identity among Koreans in Japan. In 1955 Chongryun was established as a pro-North organization, and it competed with the pro-South Mindan to gain support in the Korean community in Japan. Both organizations defined Koreans in Japan as overseas nationals of their respective states; they took it for granted that Koreans were living in Japan as foreign nationals.

To summarize, the status of colonial subject was gradually eliminated from the Japanese legal structure in the postwar years; what remained were the dichotomous categories of Japanese and foreigners. In the process, Japanese government policy demarcated nationality status, while Korean residents actively appropriated the foreigner category. On the one hand, foreign nationals were placed in a vulnerable position as a target of surveillance and control by the authorities and were restricted in their legal rights. On the other hand, the "foreigner" identity was a source of pride and had the connotation of privilege and respect, particularly when the reference point was past colonial subjugation.

Endorsing the Axiom

Zainichi Koreans' claim to full-fledged foreign national status found support among concerned Japanese. They endorsed the Korean leadership's international orientation, which emphasized one's national affiliation in interacting with others. A clear example is the position taken by Zainichi chōsenjin no jinken o mamoru kai (Association for the Protection of the Human Rights of *Zainichi* Koreans). This group was organized by Japanese lawyers in 1963 in response to frequent violence against ethnic Korean school students across Japan. Through research and advocacy the association addressed a wide range of injustices inflicted upon *zainichi* Koreans in those days, including problems in the immigration control system, lack of support for ethnic education, and infringement of human rights in every sphere of life. As the group's name indicates, the problems facing *zainichi* Koreans were framed as the human rights of foreign nationals. The basic premise was that *zainichi* Koreans were "foreign nationals with special historical circumstances" (Zainichi chōsenjin no jinken o mamoru kai 1977: 1). They declared:

> [T]he Japanese people are often not aware that *zainichi chōsenjin* are foreign nationals [*gaikokujin*]. However, Korea has become an independent state following Japan's defeat. It should therefore be understood that, in this postwar era, *zainichi chōsenjin* are no longer colonized people but are full-fledged foreign nationals with inalienable basic human rights. Just like American or British people, they have the rights conferred to general foreign nationals under international law. (Zainichi chōsenjin no jinken o mamoru kai 1977: 2; my translation)

This orientation echoes the sentiment expressed by resident Korean organizations in the early postwar years and was based on the understanding that the full-fledged foreigner represented a privileged status. Furthermore, we can see that although the concept of "foreigner" is multifaceted, its legal component was given extra weight.

An emphasis on the status of *zainichi* Koreans as foreign nationals was also salient among progressive educators. For instance, Nikkyōso (the Japan teachers' union) took up the issue of Korean ethnic education as one of the discussion themes in its annual meetings. The 1955 conference program included the following item: "Educational programs aiming at respect for human rights and deeper international mutual understanding [*kokusairikai*]" (Nakayama 1995: 69). Interestingly enough, the term *kokusairikai*, which would become popular in the 1990s with increases in resident foreigners, was already used in those days to emphasize respect for the people who belong to other sovereign states.

Japanese teachers maintained a similar attitude well into the 1970s and onward. Telling examples of an "international" orientation include statements issued by a major teachers' association in Osaka, the city with the highest concentration of *zainichi* Koreans in Japan. Osaka-shi gaikokujin shitei kyōiku mondai kenkyū kyōgikai (Osaka City Association for Research on the Education of Foreign Children) announced its basic plan for research in 1972, and stated in its "goals and issues to be tackled" as follows:

> The reason why we, as an Association, employ the term *gaikokujin* is because we wish true unification of the Korean people, with the expectation that Korean people will achieve the independence of the Korean nation by themselves. Moreover, it means that children of the Korean people truly are nationals of an independent state.[20]

Similar statements can be found in the School Education Plan issued annually by Osaka city's Board of Education. Beginning roughly in the 1980s, many local governments in the Kansai region compiled a "Basic plan for the education of resident foreign children" (Nakayama 1995: 217, 234). Consequently, the term *foreigner* entered into official vocabulary in local government programs, a trend that accelerated in the 1990s, as discussed below. Far from an exclusionary tone, such usage has symbolized a progressive policy.

The axiom that *zainichi* Koreans are foreigners also shaped the thought of legal theorists. Ōnuma Yasuaki (1983) conceptualized *zainichi* Koreans as *teijū gaikokujin* (settled foreign residents) and proposed a tripartite structure (Japanese/settled foreign residents/ordinary foreigners) to theorize their unique status. Shifting from a dichotomy to a tripartite structure appears reminiscent of the prewar period. However, this model is radically different from the prewar imperial-colonial model in that *zainichi* Koreans were now clearly on the "foreigner" side; the issue was a matter of a division *within* foreign nationals.[21]

By the later 1970s, some *zainichi* Koreans shifted away from their previous homeland orientation. The concept of *zainichi* (literally, resident in Japan) was actively explored. There was a wide, if belated, recognition that Koreans would continue living in Japan (Lie 2000). However, even after ties with, and the prospect of returning to, the homeland weakened, the importance of holding Korean nationality did not diminish. This is because nationality status had other meanings, such as a basis for anti-discrimination struggle, a source of ethnic identity, and resistance to the Japanese system of naturalization. Consequently, mainstream *zainichi* Koreans continued to identify themselves as both Korean *and* foreigner in Japan. Moreover, contested issues such as nationality-based restrictions on access to social security and civil service employment suggest that the legal element remained central among the multiple dimensions constituting the concept of foreigners.

REAFFIRMING FOREIGNNESS IN THE POST-1990 PERIOD

Since the late 1980s a new context has emerged, namely a sharp increase in "newcomer" resident foreigners. Foreign nationals living in Japan were no longer mainly *zainichi* Koreans but included such diverse groups as Asian migrant workers, South Americans of Japanese descent, Indo-Chinese refugees, and returnees from China. Whereas Korean nationals accounted for 85 percent of all registered foreigners in 1980, their proportion dropped to 49 percent in 1995 and then to 28 percent in 2007. Registered Korean nationals, at fewer than 600,000, were for the first time outnumbered by the Chinese in 2007 despite some increases in newcomer Koreans who partially offset the decrease in "old-timers."[22] Meanwhile, the total number of registered foreign nationals in Japan rose from 780,000 in 1980 to over 2.1 million in 2007 (Japan Ministry of Justice, and Japan Immigration Association, various years).

Crossroads

The *zainichi* Korean community was at a crossroads when an increasing number of foreigners arrived and settled in Japan. Japanese nationality holders of Korean lineage continued to grow as a result of increases in naturalization and international marriages.[23] The number of naturalizations by Koreans steadily increased and reached 10,000 persons a year in 1995 (Japan Ministry of Justice, various years). The label *gaikokujin*, in the sense of foreign nationals, was therefore becoming an even less accurate way to describe the population of Korean descent in Japan.

In fact, beginning in the 1980s, sections of the *zainichi* community began questioning the foreign nationality status that was hitherto taken for granted both within and outside the community. Yang Tae-Ho (1984: 36–37) called for overcoming the previous perception of nationality and proposed the acquisition of Japanese nationality as of right. There was also activity by a group of *zainichi* Koreans holding Japanese nationality to reclaim their ethnic names. They demonstrated a way of life as "Koreans with Japanese nationality [*nihonseki chosenjin*]" (Minzokumei o torimodosu kai 1990; Kashiwazaki 2000b). Among the majority *zainichi* Koreans who held Korean nationality, too, a "foreigner" identity seemed rather weak as of the early 1990s. For example, in a survey conducted in 1993 on Mindan-affiliated *zainichi* Korean youth (with South Korean nationality), 24.1 percent of the 800 respondents chose "not different from Japanese persons at all" as the best description of themselves, while another 10.1 percent identified with "Korean Japanese" [*kankoku/chōsenkei nihonjin*] (Fukuoka and Kim 1997: 70).[24] Just when there were incipient signs of conceptualizing "Korean-Japanese" identity, new waves of immigration led *zainichi* Koreans to pull back, invigorating their social and political activities on the basis of the foreigner category. As Seung-Mi Han succinctly puts it, "Globalization gave Japan-resident Koreans a new awareness of the emerging opportunity structures" (Han 2004: 55).

However, it seemed neither natural nor inevitable, if not totally unexpected, for *zainichi* Koreans to get together and work with newcomer immigrants. They were quite dissimilar. Consisting mainly of second- and third-generation residents, *zainichi* Koreans, as mentioned above, were further removed from the "typical foreigner" newcomer immigrants, who exhibited stark cultural and linguistic differences with the majority Japanese. Newcomers did not share the colonial past with *zainichi* Koreans, either, for new migration flows, including those from Korea, were not a direct consequence of Japanese colonialism. Indeed, in academic writings, it has been common to make a distinction between "old-comers" ("old-timers") and "newcomers" in light of differences in their historical trajectories.

Moreover, active self-identification with the foreigner category would not seem to be particularly profitable for the *zainichi* community because it can have negative connotations in Japanese society. In addition to the label "foreign workers" [*gaikokujin rōdōsha*], which usually denotes unskilled laborers, the term *gaikokujin* conjures other expressions such as "illegal workers," or "illegally staying foreigners" (mainly visa overstayers). Media coverage tends to associate the presence of foreigners with growth in crime and worsened public safety.

Consequently, rather than unity between *zainichi* Koreans and newcomer immigrants, a more likely scenario would be a further division in the existing categorization separating *zainichi* Koreans from other groups more readily classified as foreigners. Nevertheless, leaders and activists, albeit a small proportion of the *zainichi* Korean community, have reaffirmed their identification with the foreigner category, emphasizing commonalities and shared experiences with more recent immigrants. Instead of dissociating themselves from newcomers, they have sought to establish a common agenda for foreign residents in Japan.

*Response to the New Context:
Coalition Building for Foreigner Rights*

The term *gaikokujin* as an umbrella category turned out to have potential as a resource for mobilization and empowerment. We shall see some examples of the connections and cooperation among actors involved in foreigners' issues and consider factors that encouraged such development. They will reveal a repeated pattern, or continuity from the early postwar years, of appropriating the *gaikokujin* category. At the same time, the meaning of the term *gaikokujin* itself has undergone both a shift in focus and an expansion in scope: slightly less emphasis on legal status than before to incorporate Japanese nationality holders with their ethnic roots abroad, and greater emphasis on being a social minority.

Local communities are the sites where old-timers and newcomers have encountered each other to produce new types of social activities. It is probably for this reason that former leaders of Mintōren (Minzoku sabetsu to tatakau renraku kyōgikai; Network of Groups for Combating Ethnic Discrimination), a group that was instrumental in bringing about locally based reform in the 1970s, have come to play a major role in this new development.

In Osaka, some local ethnic spaces that *zainichi* Koreans had carved out for themselves expanded in scope to include newcomer immigrants. Tokkabi in Yao city and Mukuge in Takatsuki city—two well-known after-school clubs for *zainichi* Korean children that began in the early 1970s— now offer programs in which Chinese, Vietnamese, and Filipino newcomer children and parents can participate (Tai 2006).[25] Likewise, in Kawasaki city, a nursery that was initially opened to accommodate *zainichi* Korean children now offers multicultural nursery (day care) services for children of diverse cultural backgrounds. There are children from the Philippines, Brazil, Peru, and elsewhere in addition to *zainichi* Korean children, and some are of mixed cultural heritage.

Yet another example of an expansion of activities beyond *zainichi* Korean issues can be found in an Osaka-based nonprofit organization called Taminzoku kyōsei jinken kyōiku sentā (Multi-Ethnic Human Rights Education Center for Coexistence). This organization was launched in 2000 also by a former leader of Mintōren. The center organizes lectures, symposia, and other educational programs for local government officials, businesses, and the general public. Major topics include the protection of basic human rights, job discrimination in hiring and promotion, social welfare for elderly foreign residents, and ethnic identity issues. The previous agenda for *zainichi* Koreans has thus been reformulated as one addressing foreign resident issues and Japan's broader challenges in creating multicultural communities.

The established ethnic Korean organizations, Chongryun and Mindan, have generally confined themselves to serving the ethnic Korean community. However, the growth of the foreign resident population and the popular slogan of internationalization [*kokusaika*] gave them new opportunities to revitalize their organizational activities.

Chongryun opened Dōhō hōritsu seikatsu sentā (Consultation Center for Law and the Everyday Life of Compatriots) in Tokyo in 1997. Targeting both old-timers and newcomer Koreans, the center offers consulting services, in particular legal advice on issues such as visas, old-age pensions, taxes, and inheritance, which require expertise in law and the administrative practices of both Korea and Japan. Chongryun schools have also taken advantage of the local-level internationalization framework (discussed below) and engaged in exchange activities with neighboring Japanese public schools. Furthermore, Chongryun-affiliated ethnic Korean schools and Brazilian and other ethnic or international schools are beginning to work together for the common purpose of advancing ethnic education in Japan (Io 2006).

Mindan, with its strong ties to South Korea, has benefited from growing Japanese interest in Korea and Korean culture. Moreover, some local branches have actively broadened their clients. For example, Mindan's Kanagawa prefectural branch launched a nonprofit, the Mindan International Cooperation Center, in 1999 to offer programs and services for both foreign and Japanese residents. As Han (2004: 53–54) explains, the enactment of law governing nonprofit organizations in Japan in 1998 encourages generalized public service activities, giving Kanagawa Mindan an incentive to formulate its programs as international cooperation.

Meanwhile, the Mindan central headquarters since the mid-1990s has made local electoral rights its priority and has lobbied actively on both the local and national levels. Between 1993 and 1997, over 1,300 out of approximately 3,300 local assemblies have adopted a statement proposing voting rights for permanent resident foreigners. By April 2004 the number had increased to 1,519.[26] Although local electoral rights used to be regarded as an old-timers' issue, it is increasingly becoming relevant to newcomer foreigners as well.

The social movement demanding local electoral rights has a transnational aspect, as well. This can be seen in the activity of the citizens' group Teijūgaikokujin no chihōsanseiken o jitsugensaseru nichi, kan, zainichi nettowāku (Network of Japanese, Korean, and Foreign Residents in Japan to Realize the Suffrage of Long-Term Foreign Residents in Local Politics). Led by *zainichi* Korean and Japanese activists who have for many years engaged in antidiscrimination advocacy, the network proposes a new vision of Japanese society that is multinational [*takokuseki*] and not just multiethnic [*taminzoku*]. Here we see that the possession of foreign nationality is considered an integral part of a multicultural Japan. The network, moreover, calls for cooperation with groups in Korea who have demanded local electoral rights for foreign residents in that country.[27] In South Korea, in June 2005 the Diet passed a law granting permanent resident foreigners the right to vote in local elections, encouraging the movement in Japan. In the Japanese Diet, however, there has been little progress since bills to grant voting rights to foreign residents were first submitted in 1998.

With the development of policies toward foreign residents (discussed below), citizens' groups and nonprofits in support of the rights of foreign residents have become increasingly involved in policy making processes where the problems concerning old-timers and newcomers are joined. In 1998, Gaikikyō (Gaitōhō mondai to torikumu zenkoku kirisutokyō renraku kyōgikai; the National Christian Conference for the Discussion of Problems of the Alien Registration Law), an NGO, issued a draft proposal for the Basic Law for Foreign Residents, which would protect the human rights of foreign residents and recognize them as members of a local community.[28] Although the organization had worked for the cause of *zainichi* Koreans, the scope was no longer limited to them. From the newcomer side, Ijūren (Ijū rōdōsha to rentai suru zenkoku nettowaku), a major nationwide network of groups supporting foreign migrant workers and their families, announced a Proposal for a Comprehensive Policy Plan on Foreigners in 2002 and has been updating it regularly since then. Likewise, the Japan Federation of Bar Associations [Nichibenren] issued a declaration in 2004 requesting central and local governments "to pass a basic law and ordinances of human rights . . . for non-nationals and ethnic minorities" (Nichibenren 2004).

Here, the addition of the category "ethnic minorities" [*minzokuteki shōsūsha*] indicates the inclusion of Japanese nationality holders with immigrant background, even though the content of the proposal focuses primarily on foreign nationals. Indeed, while pushing for foreigners' rights, these nonprofits, NGOs, and other support organizations do not necessarily limit the scope of their activities on the basis of nationality status alone, recognizing a rapid increase in children holding Japanese nationality (including dual nationality). However, their presence tends to be subsumed under the foreigner category.

The Appeal of the Gaikokujin Category

How can we account for the move on the part of *zainichi* Korean groups and activists toward coalition building on the basis of *gaikokujin* identity? In what ways is the term useful as an umbrella category?

To begin with, there is a demographic factor. Given the steady decrease in the number of *zainichi* Koreans who are foreign nationals, and to the extent that *zainichi* Koreans are understood primarily as Korean nationality holders, there is a risk of diminishing their power as a group.[29] Building a coalition with newcomers gives them the chance to tackle the problems they face with a broader support base.

Second, such cooperation is not simply utilitarian but is based on a real sense of shared experiences and a common fate. To be sure, old-timers and newcomers have some obvious differences in their primary concerns. However, there are still many instances of discriminatory treatment based on nationality status, and foreign nationals are often subject to generalized suspicion. Housing discrimination is a case in point. In a survey of foreign residents in Kanagawa Prefecture, for instance, 255 out of 966 respondents—more than one in four resident foreigners—reported they had experienced housing discrimination because of their nationality status (Kanagawa jichitai no kokusaiseisaku kenkyūkai 2001: 87).[30]

Nonetheless, the term "foreign" can have positive connotations, too, and this is another important reason for actively using the category. Just as in the immediate postwar years, an international perspective is key. The discourse of internationalization [*kokusaika*] since the 1980s has encouraged the Japanese to overcome insularity and forge friendly relations with people from countries all over the world. Here we find a parallel with the past: the promotion of mutual understanding and respect between the Japanese and foreigners, or *kokusairikai*, is an agreeable idea for the majority population. As long as *zainichi* Koreans project themselves as foreigners—people from another country—they might qualify as counterparts in international exchange activities with the Japanese.

Finally, there is a paucity of terminological alternatives. When addressing problems concerning the non-Japanese population, the only viable category seems to be that of foreigner, a prevailing social construction to describe ethnic differentiation in Japanese society. Possible alternative terms such as "ethnic minorities" or "immigrants" have not yet been accepted as legitimate.

To summarize, the demographic factor, shared experience as "foreigner," positive connotation in the discourse of internationalization, and the lack of alternatives all combined to prompt some *zainichi* Koreans to forge ties with more recent settlers based on shared foreigner status. At the same time, we have seen a gradual recognition that the ethnic minority population in question is not necessarily confined to foreign nationals but should refer more broadly to anyone perceived to be non-Japanese. The continued centrality of the term *gaikokujin* in the post-1990 period is closely related with its use in the administrative domain, to which we now turn.

INSTITUTIONALIZATION THROUGH GOVERNMENT POLICY AND PROGRAMS

With rapid growth in the number of Japanese nationality holders with roots abroad, the scope of the term *gaikokujin* has become ambiguous. Meanwhile, it increasingly has been adopted in public policy. The development of foreign resident policy, though considered a positive trend, has also had the effect of reinforcing the Japanese/foreigner dichotomy. The centrality of the term *gaikokujin* in what could alternatively be called "immigrant" or "ethnic minority" policy has much to do with its course of development.

Three Currents of Foreign Resident Policy

Contemporary policy and programs for foreign residents in Japan have had three major sources of current: local government response to old-timers, internationalization policy, and programs for the growing newcomer immigrant population.

Local-level programs for foreign residents in response to demand by zainichi *Koreans.* In the 1970s, a number of municipalities issued an ordinance that made foreign residents eligible for the national health care plan, which had been available only to Japanese citizens (Yoshioka

1995: 53–57). They also removed nationality clauses for the provision of childcare allowances and access to public housing, ahead of national-level reforms that came only around 1980. The core idea behind these changes was that foreign nationals, too, were "residents" constituting local communities and thus were naturally entitled to receive public services. In particular, Mintōren, mentioned in the previous section, played a major role by addressing unfair treatment of *zainichi* Koreans in both public and private sectors of society. To date, municipalities have been a major site of struggle for *zainichi* Koreans to advance their rights as permanent resident foreigners. Contentious issues include the hiring and promotion of foreign nationals as local government officials and tenured public school teachers, and the issue of local electoral rights.

Internationalization policy driven from above. Internationalization [*kokusaika*] was made a slogan in the 1980s as central government ministries embraced it and integrated it into their policy programs. In particular, the then-Ministry of Home Affairs (Jichishō, which was later merged with Ministry of Internal Affairs and Communications, or Sōmushō) played a central role by initiating a comprehensive local-level internationalization plan. With the issuance of Guidelines for the Local International Exchange Promotion Plan in 1989, the Ministry instructed prefectures and major cities to prepare a policy package for the advancement of international exchange.

The policy framework of internationalization tended to perceive foreigners as guests and visitors rather than as residents and citizens of the local community. Specific recommendations listed in the Ministry of Home Affairs guidelines included the use of foreign languages for maps, signs, and public facilities; publication of foreign-language guidebooks for community life; and festivals and events where foreigners and Japanese residents could get together (Chiba 1989: 39–40). In the 1990s, however, a sharp rise in the foreign resident population generated demand for municipal services that were much broader in scope than the items described above.

Responses by municipal governments since ca 1990. In municipalities that experienced a sudden growth in the foreign resident population, problems arose in such areas as housing, social security, medical service, and education for children. Whereas citizens' organizations and volunteer groups played a major role in providing assistance to these newcomers, local governments also developed programs and services, including Japanese language classes, the publication of multilingual brochures, consultation services, and financial support for emergency medical care

(Ebashi 1993). These new challenges popularized a new slogan, *uchinaru kokusaika* (internal internationalization, or internationalization from within), which was contrasted with conventional, outward-looking internationalization.[31]

The core ideas in the concept of internationalization, whether externally or internally oriented, included respect for other cultures, other peoples, and other nations. These are in fact a mirror image of "our" culture, "our" people, and "our" nation, which is understood as an *ethno-national* community. As a result, the project of internationalization is likely to reinforce the cognitive framework of the Japanese/foreigner dichotomy.

The Emergence of Foreign Resident Policy

In the 1990s, the three currents converged. Foreign resident policy (variously called *zaijū gaikokujin shisaku, gaikoku-seki jūmin shisaku*, and so on) slowly emerged as a recognizable domain of local administration (Komai and Watado 1997). Its formulation was heavily influenced by the current of internationalization. For instance, prefectures and major cities issued comprehensive policy guidelines with titles such as "Basic Plan for Local Internationalization Policy" or "Basic Plan for International Exchange," following the instructions of the central government. At first, such documents typically devoted rather small sections to issues concerning settled resident foreigners, as opposed to international exchange with visitors from abroad. However, the focus shifted over time to the former. Some municipalities have issued a plan specifically about foreign residents in the community, with the aim of advancing their welfare and encouraging their participation in community affairs.[32]

While progressive in content, these basic plans issued by local governments reflect the Japanese/foreigner dichotomy. Typical phrases and expressions are suggestive: "living together with foreign residents" (as introduced at the outset of this chapter), "promoting mutual understanding between the Japanese and foreigners" and "creating a viable local community together with foreign residents." Though well-intended, and perhaps useful for the purpose of enlightening the public, these ideas are likely to help reify the binary framework.

Foreign resident policy has also been integrated into human rights policy. With the growing international pressure to adopt proactive policies for the protection of human rights, both central and local governments have worked to develop a human rights policy package. For example, after the United Nations declared its Decade for Human Rights Education (1995–2004), the Japanese government set up an organ in charge in the

Cabinet Office and issued a domestic Action Plan in 1997. In this plan, foreigners were included as one of the nine categories of social minorities whose human rights problems warrant special attention. The other categories were women, children, the elderly, people with disabilities, people from *buraku*, the Ainu, people with HIV/AIDS, and ex-prisoners (Japan Cabinet Office 1997). This is yet another way in which the normative use of the foreigner category would help raise awareness about problems faced by foreign nationals, while reinforcing the existing social categorization.

Despite the problem of reification, the administrative use of *gaikokujin* as an umbrella category has surely been fruitful in local-level reform. This is perhaps most notable in the social and political participation of resident foreigners. In 1996, Kawasaki city launched the Representative Assembly for Foreign Residents. Two years later, Kanagawa Prefecture followed suit, and several more local governments have set up a similar forum.[33] These assemblies provided a space for resident foreigners of varied backgrounds, both old-timers and newcomers, to get together. They gained the opportunity to express their concerns, to recognize common problems such as housing discrimination and education of children, and make policy proposals to the mayor or governor. *Zainichi* Korean representatives, having grown up in the society, are usually the ones who are the most versed in Japanese culture and society, including communication skills. They have therefore tended to assume a leadership role in these forums.[34] These assemblies to some extent have compensated for the lack of local electoral rights, which have not yet materialized.

Local referenda are another channel for facilitating political participation by foreign nationals. Although the chance of legal change on the national level remains slim, an increasing number of municipalities have allowed foreign residents to vote in local referenda, which could be decided upon and implemented with local initiatives. In 2002, Maihara city, Shiga Prefecture, became the first to legislate an ordinance giving voting rights in referenda to foreign nationals who were permanent residents. As of February 2005, 177 local governments had by ordinance extended voting rights for referenda to foreign residents.[35] This rapid increase was due to a large number of referenda planned and held across the country in the early 2000s concerning the consolidation of local municipalities.

Tabunka Kyōsei *and Its Limits*

Around 2000, foreign resident policy took another turn as a new slogan, *tabunka kyōsei* (living together in a multicultural society), gained currency. Roughly corresponding to "multiculturalism," this term has been increasingly adopted not only by citizens' groups but also by local governments in their basic plans or as titles of their policy programs. Municipalities with large Brazilian populations have been particularly active in this regard. In 2000, the mayors of thirteen cities and towns, mainly in central Japan, established Gaikokujin shūjūtoshi kaigi (Association of Cities with a Large Number of Foreign Residents) and issued a declaration concerning the need for legal and administrative reform to accommodate resident foreigners in local communities (Tegtmeyer Pak 2006: 68). The association has regularly held conferences since then and actively used *tabunka kyōsei* as a slogan.

The term is now incorporated into national-level policy, as well. In response to the accumulation of pressure demanding a proactive policy, ministries in the central government slowly began to develop policy programs on the assumption that newcomer foreign residents would be here to stay as members of local communities. In 2006, the Ministry of Internal Affairs and Communications (Sōmushō) published a report on the promotion of *tabunka kyōsei* in the local community and issued a model policy plan.[36] The ministry then requested that local authorities develop their own policy plans to assist foreign residents, particularly those who face linguistic barriers, in daily life and promote multicultural coexistence in local communities. In fact, Kawasaki city and Tachikawa city had already compiled Guidelines for the Promotion of *Tabunka Kyōsei* a year earlier, in 2005. *Tabunka kyōsei* has thus become part of the administrative vocabulary and has emerged as a distinctive policy area in local administration.

Tabunka kyōsei has been favored for several reasons. First, with its focus on residency the new concept appears more rooted in local communities than *internationalization*. Second, whereas the term *foreign resident policy* gives the impression that it targets minority groups only, *tabunka kyōsei* seems better suited to address challenges pertaining to the majority Japanese, such as raising awareness and removing prejudice against foreigners. Third, it also fits with the idea of recognizing resident foreigners as equal members of the community and encouraging their participation in community affairs. In other words, it could mean more than just providing assistance to vulnerable populations but also valuing cultural diversity. Furthermore, *tabunka kyōsei* is potentially useful in overcoming a narrow focus on the relationship between Japanese nationals and foreign nationals, for multiculturalism could surely include cultural diversity within the community of Japanese nationals.

In most cases, however, documents promoting *tabunka kyōsei* do not address ethnic diversity among Japanese nationals very much. If anything, it is mentioned only briefly, mainly with regard to the education and identity of children with mixed cultural heritage. Although it has become fairly common to use expressions such as *gaikoku ni tsunagaru kodomotachi* (children who have their roots abroad), there is still a lack of appropriate terms and a cognitive framework to incorporate Japanese nationals of diverse cultural backgrounds. In short, the discourse of *tabunka kyōsei* remains largely about *kyōsei,* or the relationship of coexistence, between Japanese and foreigners, where the latter has become increasingly ambiguous in its content.

This chapter has examined how the Japanese/foreigner dichotomy developed and was reinforced, and how *zainichi* Koreans have contributed to that process. The overall process can be summarized by dividing it into institutional arrangements, popular perceptions, and strategic responses by *zainichi* Koreans. In contrast with the dominance of racial categories as in the United States, the Japanese/foreigner binary is salient in Japan. The concept of foreigner is multifaceted and contains racial, cultural, and legal components. The term conjures up a variety of images—positive, negative, progressive, and exclusionary—generating complexity when applied or appropriated in intergroup relations.

A key institutional factor supporting the sharp binary was the strength of the legal definition of foreignness, namely that most people perceived as *gaikokujin* indeed have held foreign nationality. An important historical moment was the shift in the organization of nationality from an imperial-colonial model to an ethno-national one. The Japanese/foreigner binary crystallized once legal nationality status was linked with ethnic categories after the collapse of the Japanese empire. Decades later, calls for internationalization were conducive to the further institutionalization of the *gaikokujin* category with its growing use in administrative spheres.

On the level of popular perception, the dichotomy has been supported by the very idea of ethnic homogeneity, which has permeated postwar Japan. There has been a lack of cognitive channels to comprehend a case where ethnically non-Japanese persons may also be Japanese in the sense of belonging to the Japanese nation-state. Again, recent increases in newcomer foreign residents have provided the majority Japanese population with greater opportunity to apply their internalized binary framework rather than to deconstruct it.

Identification with the foreigner category has been a major strategic response by influential segments of the *zainichi* Korean population to Japan's changing mode of organizing nationality and its homogenizing forces. I have contended that there is a parallel development between the early postwar period and the post-1990 period. The foreigner category held promise for Koreans in the immediate postwar years as a means to break away from colonial subjugation. It allowed Koreans to raise their status from colonial subjects to members of another sovereign state, turning their vertical relationship with the Japanese into a horizontal one. Norms underpinning the international order—in which people of all nation-states stand on equal footing, at least in theory—encouraged the formation of identity based on foreignness.

The same pattern of finding promise in the foreigner category can be seen in a more recent period. With increases in foreign nationals in Japan in the 1990s, the term *gaikokujin* acquired renewed significance for *zainichi* Koreans as an umbrella category, which could be used to form coalitions with more recent immigrant groups to advance the cause of all foreigners. The tendency among the leaders of social movements to associate *zainichi* Koreans with the *gaikokujin* category has been both empowering and constraining for the *zainichi* Korean community. On the one hand, the strategy of demanding citizenship rights *as foreign nationals* has provided *zainichi* Koreans and their Japanese supporters with a progressive cause and a chance for effective collective action. In particular, given the declining proportion of *zainichi* Koreans among foreign nationals in Japan, cooperation with newcomers might be essential in creating a necessary critical mass. On the other hand, because *gaikokujin* literally denotes foreign nationals, identification with this category logically precludes the formation of alternative diasporic identities based on Japanese nationality, or full citizenship in one's country of permanent residence. It is legally constraining in that even if greater equality has been achieved, foreign nationals could not obtain full citizenship rights, including full political rights, which are available only to nationals of the country.

Precisely because advancing foreigners' rights is projected as a progressive and enlightening agenda, the proposal for a "Korean-Japanese" identity through the acquisition of Japanese nationality is often dismissed as reactionary and risky. In 2003, a small group of *zainichi* Koreans (former Mintōren members and their associates) launched "Zainichi korian no kokuseki shutokuken" kakuritsu kyōgikai (Association for Establishing the "Rights for *Zainichi* Koreans to Obtain Japanese Nationality") and began working to push for new legislation (Sasaki 2005). However, their movement has yet to secure wide support. Others pushing for the rights of foreign nationals tend to view such a move as weakening their cause. Moreover, the fact that in 2001 some conservative politicians participated in preparing a bill to grant special permanent residents (mostly *zainichi*

Koreans) the right to acquire Japanese nationality invited negative reactions among activists.

An emphasis on the Japanese/foreigner dichotomy is also socially constraining because it obscures ethnic diversity among Japanese nationals. There is growing awareness among groups working toward the formation of a multicultural community that *foreigner* is not the best word to capture the reality of the multiethnic minority population. Some NGOs have gradually come to adopt expressions such as *gaikokuni tsunagaru* (having roots abroad) or *tabunka no* (having multicultural background) to describe persons with non-Japanese ancestry. It is possible that the impetus for significant semantic change may come from newcomer communities as they generate an ever larger population of ethnic non-Japanese with Japanese nationality.

After all, identification with the foreigner category is based in part on the assumption that it would be impossible to gain a respectable status within the framework of the Japanese *national* community, as long as the category "national" overlaps with "Japanese" ethnicity. Appropriation of the foreigner category by *zainichi* Koreans represents one of many approaches toward achieving a greater equality with the dominant group while maintaining a distinct cultural identity. Though it is beyond the scope of this chapter, such orientation and strategies taken by influential actors, both *zainichi* Korean and Japanese, would have a significant impact on the rest of the members in the *zainichi* Korean community, be it empowering, constraining, or alienating.

7. The Politics of Contingent Citizenship

Korean Political Engagement in Japan and the United States

Erin Aeran Chung

Despite similarities in time period, country of origin, and labor composition, Korean migration to Japan and the United States from the late nineteenth century to the present has produced strikingly different communities. The current Korean resident population in Japan numbers a little under 600,000 and constitutes the oldest foreign resident community in Japan, with mass settlement beginning during Japan's colonization of Korea from 1910 to 1945. Spanning four generations, this community shows few signs of maintaining a strong Korean sociocultural identity through the traditional indicators of language, education, and marriage. For example, intermarriages between Koreans and Japanese now constitute over 80 percent of all marriages among Korean residents. Yet, because only about 30 percent of the population has naturalized in the past 50 years, foreign-born and native-born Korean residents continue to make up one of Japan's largest foreign communities.[1]

In the United States, the Korean population numbers a little over 1.2 million, and in 2000 it made up the fourth largest Asian-American group.[2] However, in contrast to Koreans in Japan, 57 percent were foreign born, over 70 percent spoke Korean at home, and over 85 percent classified themselves as Korean alone in their ethnic background, according to the 2000 census. Yet naturalization rates in the Korean community were slightly higher than the national average: according to the 2000 census, slightly more than half (50.8 percent) of foreign-born Koreans were naturalized U.S. citizens, compared to 43 percent of the total foreign-born population in the United States. The number of naturalizations among Koreans in the United States contrasts strikingly with those in Japan, especially given the fact that over 90 percent of Koreans in Japan are native-born, whereas over half of the Korean population in the United States is foreign born.

Thus, Korean migration to Japan and the United States has resulted in a highly assimilated, structurally foreign Korean community in Japan and a linguistically and culturally distinct, structurally incorporated Korean community in the United States.

The differences between these two communities may not be puzzling given the divergences between U.S. and Japanese processes of social and political incorporation. U.S. citizenship policies permit birthright citizenship and allow for relatively easy naturalization. The costs of naturalization are relatively low compared to the benefits, which include voting rights, protection from deportation, and the capacity to sponsor relatives for immigration. Indeed, when immigrants apply for permanent residency, U.S. Citizenship and Immigration Service officials provide them with information on proceeding to the next step of naturalization. Male applicants for permanent residency are required to register with the military Selective Service System. Although both countries share restrictive immigration policies, the United States nevertheless projects itself as a country of immigration, whereas Japan maintains closed-door policies toward immigrants and has the worst record in the industrialized world for accepting refugees.

Japanese citizenship policies are among the most restrictive of advanced industrial democracies.[3] Nationality is closely related with ethnic, racial, and national identity. Naturalization applicants not only must renounce their allegiance to their country of origin, but must demonstrate evidence of cultural assimilation. For instance, Japanese officials frequently pressure naturalization applicants to adopt Japanese names. While state statistics lump foreign-born and native-born permanent residents together, the media often depict both recent immigrants and long-term foreign residents as sojourners.

Racial politics in both countries contrasts starkly as well. Much of the scholarship on race and racism portrays the United States as the case study *par excellence* and overlooks Japan because of its putatively homogenous society. Until recently, Japanese minorities—including ethnic Koreans, Chinese, Ainu, Okinawans, and Burakumin—were invisible to outside observers because most are physically indistinguishable from the Japanese majority. Conversely, Asian Americans, like other racialized groups in the United States, have historically been hypervisible not only because of phenotypical differences but also because of apparently insurmountable cultural differences.

In sum, Japan is purportedly ethnically homogenous with highly restrictive citizenship and immigration laws, whereas the United States is racially diverse with relatively easy naturalization policies. Accordingly, we should not be surprised to find that Koreans in Japan exhibit low rates of political assimilation and high rates of cultural assimilation, whereas Korean Americans exhibit higher rates of political assimilation and lower rates of cultural assimilation. Based on these differences, we would expect to find a highly deprived Korean community in Japan with little or no political voice, and a cohesive Korean-American community whose interests are represented in U.S. politics. Instead, Korean activists in Japan have emerged as leaders of the burgeoning immigrant community and are often at the center of public debates on immigrant incorporation, Japanese citizenship, and Japanese national identity. Conversely, Korean Americans found themselves in the middle of interethnic minority conflicts in urban areas, especially in the early 1990s. The civil unrest in Los Angeles in 1992 following the Rodney King beating in particular exposed a Korean-American community that was largely powerless, voiceless, and marginalized as foreigners despite their legal status as actual or potential U.S. citizens.

Neither citizenship and immigration policies at the level of the state alone nor group characteristics of either community can explain this puzzle. This chapter examines the intervening variable: the mutually constitutive relationship between postwar American and Japanese citizenship policies formulated in the context of the Cold War and Korean community voluntary associations. The following section analyzes the intersection of citizenship, identity, and racial politics through an exploration of the contingencies of citizenship. The remainder of the chapter traces the trajectory of the political incorporation, exclusion, and participation of Korean immigrants and their descendants in Japan and the United States, focusing on the period immediately before and after the implementation of citizenship policies in both countries in 1952.

THE CONTINGENCY OF CITIZENSHIP

Rogers Brubaker's (1992) comparative historical study of citizenship policies in France and Germany is one of the most influential studies of national citizenship that has emerged in the last two decades. Brubaker illuminates how contrasting definitions of citizenship in the two countries—one expansive and assimilationist and the other restrictive and differentialist—have been shaped by distinct national traditions (political versus ethno-cultural) rooted in each nation-state's political and cultural development. While his work has been criticized for framing the concept of national traditions in static, foundationalist terms (Feldblum 1999: 6–7), his linkage between national citizenship and social closure points to a key tension within contemporary citizenship practices. That is, universalist notions of democratic citizenship, invoked by state and nonstate actors alike, are inconsistent with the nationalist tenets and practices of citizenship within the system of nation-states. As Brubaker writes in a later piece, the modern institution of citizenship is Janus-faced: "Its internal face, seen from within a single polity, is inclusive, universalist, egalitarian. Its external face, seen from the perspective of the global state system or of humanity as a whole, is exclusive, particularistic, inegalitarian" (Brubaker 1997: 414).

This chapter takes Brubaker's assertion a step further in arguing that the tensions between the exclusive and inclusive aspects of citizenship exist throughout the entire spectrum of citizenship, both externally and internally. Despite universalist aspirations, citizenship policies throughout the world have been devised according to specific social, economic, and political circumstances that often entail the exclusion of particular categories of people and social identities. As Brubaker (1992: 27–31) describes, they influence the articulation, regulation, and enforcement of formal social and territorial closure. Moreover, the particularistic categories that inform state membership necessarily bleed over into the practices of internal citizenship. While all citizens share the rights and duties of citizenship equally in principle, the implementation and distribution of these rights and duties may be highly unequal. As Judith Shklar (1991) and Rogers Smith (1997) characterize American citizenship, the tension between political equality, or civic ideals, and racial and sexual inequality may be an integral feature of the institution of citizenship itself.

Accordingly, we can argue that citizenship—as legal status, rights and responsibilities, identity, and practice—is contingent in at least three ways. First, citizenship policies define the categories of political membership within a nation-state and their attendant rights and duties. By distinguishing between who is and is not worthy of membership, as well as the terms of membership and nonmembership, the state makes citizenship contingent upon particularistic categories, such as race, ethnicity, class, religion, gender, and sexuality. Citizenship debates are invariably contentious because they involve struggles over what the nation represents, who is capable of exercising the rights and duties of full citizenship, and how relationships between citizens and noncitizens, as well as between the state and citizens/noncitizens, should work (Petit 2000).

Second, in the process of naturalization, citizenship is contingent upon the individual applicant's ability to demonstrate that she has met particular requirements, such as knowledge of the host society's history and language, history of "good behavior and conduct" (Japan) or "good moral character" (United States), and residency requirements.[4] In most countries, these requirements resonate with debates about assimilability and national identity. For example, Japan's naturalization procedures confer a great deal of discretionary power to individual officials who have been known to conduct meticulous verifications of cultural assimilation, involving home inspections and interviews of neighbors, and often pressure individual applicants to adopt Japanese names despite the abolishment of the official requirement to do so.[5] Recent additions to citizenship tests in the Baden-Württemberg region of Germany that implicitly target Muslim immigrants exhibit how definitions of cultural and civic assimilability vary according to historical circumstances.[6] While the current U.S. citizenship test focuses primarily on U.S. domestic history and state institutions, definitions of cultural, civic, and political assimilability have historically played prominent roles in determining who was eligible for naturalization. Asian immigrants remained ineligible for naturalization based on the "free white persons" clause of the 1790 Naturalization Law even after the law was amended in 1870 to extend the right to African Americans. While the McCarran-Walter Act of 1952 removed racial restrictions to naturalization, it also introduced legislation that not only barred the entry of suspected political subversives into the United States but allowed state officials to deport both immigrants and naturalized citizens who were engaged in "subversive" activities. Thus, at the height of McCarthyism in the United States, the Act made U.S. citizenship contingent upon the immigrant's political assimilability (which, in this case, proscribed any association with communism or any Communist Party) both at the time of naturalization and anytime thereafter.

This last example leads us to the third form of contingent citizenship. Citizenship rights and citizenship status itself are not inviolable; they are contingent upon historical circumstances. The ability of states to strip particular populations of their citizenship represents the outermost form of contingent citizenship. While this act may occur in the process of nation building, as was the case with Japan's unilateral decision to strip Koreans of their Japanese citizenship following World War II, it may also be one step in a larger project to marginalize or extinguish a specific population, such as the 1935 Nazi Nuremberg Laws on Citizenship and Race. The U.S. internment of Japanese Americans during the Second World War also demonstrates the ways that the state may temporarily revoke full citizenship status from a particular population based on historical exigencies. Moreover, the historical circumstances surrounding the implementation of citizenship laws may result in the creation of de facto partial or second-class citizenship categories in which full legal citizenship does not always correspond with full citizenship status, identity, or practice. For example, a 1955 article in *The Nation* noted that the McCarran-Walter Act made a significant distinction between native-born and naturalized citizens by "subjecting the naturalized citizen to denaturalization and deportation on tenuous grounds rather than grounds of provable fraud" (Bruce 1955: 458).

The conflicting principles of civic equality and racial exclusion not only deny racial groups access to citizenship, they also shape the practice of not acknowledging the *full* citizenship of racialized groups. For example, local officials may restrict, impair, or deny the right to vote to some citizens based on racial criteria, as was reportedly the case in numerous districts throughout the United States during the 2000 presidential elections. At the national level, racialized constructions of national membership may block, limit, or hamper not only political participation but also the protection of basic civil rights. For example, post–September 11 campaigns to detain potential foreign terrorists and their affiliates have involved the profiling of suspects based on race rather than on nationality and, consequently, have criminalized both citizens and noncitizens alike. Indeed, in the United States, racial profiling is more often directed at citizens, especially African Americans and, since September 11, 2001, South Asian and Arab Americans, than at noncitizens.

Conversely, legal citizenship status is not always a requirement for citizenship rights and practices. In advanced industrial democracies, the duties of citizens are almost completely shared by long-term foreign residents (with the exception of jury duty and military service in most countries). Furthermore, most, if not all, advanced industrial democracies have granted the basic goods of state membership to long-term foreign residents, with the exception of (national) voting rights.[7] Citizens and noncitizens alike are increasingly sharing the practice of citizenship in the form of civic participation. Noncitizens are often vital and active members of local community associations, labor unions, school boards, and political campaigns. While one may formally be a national of a particular nation-state, one may participate actively in the civil society of another as a resident.

The remainder of this chapter analyzes the contingencies of citizenship in Japan and the United States through the lens of Korean diasporic communities. In exploring the relationship between citizenship policies and

Korean community organizations, I will focus on the following questions: If citizenship is by its very nature contingent, then what is compromised in the process of becoming a citizen? How do we assess the benefits and costs of naturalization for particular communities? How do particular citizenship policies shape political engagement by noncitizens and naturalized citizens?

THE POLITICS OF CITIZENSHIP AND IDENTITY IN JAPAN'S KOREAN COMMUNITY

The Postwar "Korean Problem" in Japan

With Japan's surrender to the Allied powers in 1945, the Supreme Commander of the Allied Powers (SCAP) set about the task of transforming the authoritarian imperial state into a developing democracy, in what was to become "Japan's American Revolution" (Pyle 1978: 151–166). Koreans in Japan did not figure prominently in the Occupation's plans. Although Occupation authorities implemented a constitutional provision prohibiting "discrimination in political, economic, or social relations because of race, creed, sex, social status or family origin" (Article 14) in Japanese society, neither Occupation nor Japanese authorities applied such democratic idealism to the Korean population. On the contrary, Occupation policies regarding Koreans in Japan reflected the prevalent view that Koreans belonged outside of Japanese society and were obstacles to Japan's democratic revolution. Hence, SCAP's primary aim for the Korean population was repatriation. Shortly after the end of the war, almost two-thirds of the more than two million Koreans residing in Japan returned to the Korean peninsula. However, unstable conditions in Korea as well as the arbitrary division of the peninsula into American and Soviet occupation zones at the 38th parallel provided the approximately 600,000 Koreans who remained in Japan with little incentive to repatriate immediately (Lee and De Vos 1981: 59).

Despite their dubious positions as both liberated nationals and potential enemies, Koreans in Japan were above all a source of irritation for the Occupation authorities, as Edward Wagner observed in 1951:

> In the eyes of the Occupation authorities the Koreans have constituted an unwelcome additional administrative burden. The contrast between Korean defiance and apparent placid Japanese acceptance of American rule has been strikingly evident. Not only has this helped to heighten the esteem in which the Japanese have come to be held, but it also has fostered violent dislike as the typical attitude of Occupation personnel toward Koreans. (Wagner 1951: 2)

Japanese authorities were quick to point to the Korean community's involvement in illegal activities such as the black market and their subversive potential as hostile former colonial subjects and allies of the Japanese Communist Party (JCP). As the following statement by Shikuma Saburo, a Progressive Party member from Hokkaido, demonstrates, the liberation of former colonial subjects implied chaos for many Japanese:

> We refuse to stand by in silence watching Formosans and Koreans who have resided in Japan as Japanese up to the time of surrender, swaggering about as if they were nationals of victorious nations. We admit that we are a defeated nation but it is most deplorable that those who lived under our law and order until the last moment of the surrender should suddenly alter their attitude to act like conquerors, pasting on railway carriages 'Reserved' without any authorization, insulting and oppressing Japanese passengers and otherwise committing unspeakable violence elsewhere. The actions of these Koreans and Formosans make the blood in our veins, in our misery of defeat, boil. (quoted in Conde 1947: 42)

Assuming that all Koreans in Japan would eventually repatriate, SCAP made no clarification regarding their legal status. Without a uniform policy toward Koreans in Japan, SCAP's often contradictory responses to the "Korean problem" set the tone for the strained, ambiguous relationship between Korean community organizations and the Japanese state throughout the Occupation to the present day. On the one hand, Koreans were given special guarantees and privileges as liberated nationals. Several early directives from SCAP to the Japanese government prohibited discrimination against Koreans and other minorities in employment, social welfare distribution, and public assistance.[8] Other directives placed Koreans beyond Japanese criminal jurisdiction. On the other hand, SCAP did not include Koreans among Allied nationals because of their service—compulsory or not—in the Japanese military during the war against the Allies. Further, because Koreans in Japan remained Japanese nationals by law until 1952,[9] they were not eligible for the special supplementary rations that Occupation authorities gave to most foreign nationals in Japan.

The Japanese government exploited the Korean community's ambiguous position by heightening police intimidation and surveillance to control the population while denying them full citizenship rights. Defying SCAP's orders, local Japanese officials refused to release some Koreans convicted of political offenses unless they repatriated. In December 1945, the Diet passed an amendment to the Election Law that denied voting rights to those whose family registers [*koseki*] were not located in Japan. As was the case during the colonial period when the family registry system was first institutionalized, this legal loophole provided the government with a tool to demarcate colonial subjects among Japanese nationals. In September 1946, Osaka officials instituted a local registration system specifically for Koreans that resembled the prewar police surveillance system (Wagner 1951: 60). In 1947, the Diet passed the Alien Registration Law that identified Koreans as belonging to *chōsen* based on their family registers and required Koreans to carry alien registration cards at all times.[10] However, because the Republic of Korea (ROK) and the Democratic People's Republic of Korea (DPRK) did not come into existence until 1948, Koreans in Japan during this time were held to be stateless. Consequently, *chōsen* referred not to a nationality but to an ethnic group.

Based on the notion that Japan is a homogenous nation, the Diet passed the 1950 Nationality Act perpetuating without controversy the principle of *jus sanguinis* from the Meiji law of 1899 (Takenaka 1997: 291). Finally, when Japan concluded the San Francisco Peace Treaty with the Allied powers in 1952, Koreans in Japan were formally declared aliens. In effect, postwar immigration and citizenship policies provided the maximum solution to the "Korean problem" during the Occupation. While SCAP could not forcibly repatriate all Koreans in Japan because of its early commitment to voluntary repatriation, the arduous naturalization process virtually guaranteed the cultural, social, and political assimilation of Koreans who elected to become Japanese nationals and the constant threat of deportation ensured the docility of those who remained in Japan as Korean nationals.

Foreign Citizenship Status as Political Strategy

From the onset of the Occupation, Korean community members regarded themselves as part of the victorious Allied armies. Many Koreans demanded the rights and privileges of the Allied nationals. Some believed that they were no longer subject to Japanese law and openly engaged in the flourishing black market of the postwar economy. However, the greatest threat posed by the community was in the realm of politics.

The first postwar Korean organization of national significance, Joryeon (Chōren in Japanese, or the "League of Koreans in Japan"), was established in October 1945 with the primary purposes of repatriating Koreans and protecting their rights. In addition, Joryeon offered educational programs such as Korean language classes to prepare Korean children for their future lives in Korea. As repatriation slowed and the organization began to focus its attention on the issue of Korean liberation in Japan, Joryeon members frequently joined forces with the Japan Communist Party (JCP). They maintained that the welfare of Koreans in Japan could not be secured within the present Japanese political establishment that perpetuated the emperor system, which was a claim that paralleled the JCP's call for the overthrow of the emperor system and the creation of a "people's republic" (Lee and De Vos 1981: 62, 111). As Sonia Ryang (1997b: 80–81) notes, Joryeon's Japanese edition of its official publication, *Haebang sinmun*, closely resembled the JCP's official publication, *Akahata*, which highlighted the two organizations' overlapping interests and close ties. Joryeon and Korean members of the JCP exhorted Koreans to take the matter of Japan's democratic revolution into their own hands. This call to action involved not only working from the margins of society but also demanding political enfranchisement.

Hence, the leaders of Joryeon did not believe that their status as foreigners would preclude their participation in Japanese politics. After all, foreign nationals—specifically the Allied powers—were leading the project of rebuilding Japan. Indeed, most of Joryeon's protests were in response to their treatment as Japanese nationals rather than as foreigners or liberated nationals by Occupation authorities. Joryeon's fiercest protests—including the violent Kobe incident in 1948 that led SCAP to declare a state of emergency—concerned their rights as foreigners to operate Korean schools in Japan autonomously.

With the approach of the Cold War and the growing power of the Chinese communists in the region, American Occupation authorities engaged in a "reverse course" (1948–1952) that shifted the goals of American policy in Japan from rapid "democratization from above" to political and economic stability. The high idealism of the early Occupation days that made it possible for labor to become an explosive force in Japanese politics in 1947 quickly deteriorated into suspicion of all things red.[11] SCAP grew increasingly impatient with labor and social reformers and targeted the left, especially communists, in a revived purge that had originally been intended for prewar nationalists (Pyle 1978: 164).

With the change in the political climate, SCAP no longer deemed Koreans in Japan merely a source of irritation; on the contrary, the "Korean problem" became a security issue that required immediate attention. The mass protests organized by Joryeon, which sometimes led to violent clashes with the police, as well as Joryeon's ongoing alliance with the JCP threatened political stability and, thus, national security. Moreover, after the establishment of the two separate Korean regimes, Joryeon declared its solidarity with North Korea and referred to the Rhee government established in the South as an American puppet regime (Ryang 1997b: 80). In reaction to Joryeon's support of North Korea, SCAP issued a ban in 1948 against the public display of the North Korean flag, which Joryeon defiantly disregarded. At last, Joryeon's joint declaration with the JCP to "overthrow the Japanese government" and violent clashes with the Japanese police provided fodder for the enactment of the Organization Control Law in April 1949, which outlawed organizations construed to be subversive to the Japanese state and that promoted violence. With SCAP's consent, the Japanese government declared Joryeon a terrorist organization and dissolved it in September 1949, part of the red purge that began earlier that year.

While Joryeon involved itself heavily in Japanese politics, its successor organizations, the pro–South Korean Mindan, established in 1946, and pro–North Korean Chongryun (Chōsensōren in Japanese), established in 1955, made clear from their inceptions that they would submit themselves to Japanese laws but not involve themselves in Japanese domestic affairs. Rather than mobilize to gain rights for Koreans as residents of Japan, they centered their activities on homeland politics and repatriation for the Korean community and discouraged their members from acquiring Japanese nationality. Unlike prewar Korean groups and the short-lived Joryeon, Mindan and Chongryun focused their political activities on opposing each other, not on contesting Japanese state policies and social discrimination. Thus, under the leadership of two insular organizations that encouraged them to maintain their precarious status as foreigners with limited rights, Koreans in Japan remained a severely deprived minority for at least the first half of the Cold War era.

CONTINGENT CITIZENSHIP AND POLITICAL DIVERSITY IN THE U.S. KOREAN COMMUNITY

At about the same time that Koreans in Japan lost their political and social rights as Japanese nationals, Koreans—along with other Asian immigrants—in the United States were granted the right to American citizenship when Congress passed the McCarran-Walter Act in 1952. Because the act was aimed primarily at the control of "subversive activities," American citizenship for those who were the primary beneficiaries of the naturalization provision—Asian Americans—was contingent on extreme political patriotism or passivity, as one opponent of the act avowed:

> A naturalized American will never be able to rest secure that he will not be deprived of his nationality. He is restrained from political activities a native American might engage in. He is encouraged by the act

to become an hysterical patriot before he has learned to be a simple patriot. Or else he is encouraged to passivity. This is one more contribution to the political sterilization of the American population. (Alfred de Grazia, quoted in Tamayo 1996: 351)

Moreover, by conferring almost unlimited authority over foreign-born Americans citizens to the Justice Department, the act effectively set the basis for the legal surveillance of naturalized Asian Americans.

While the act removed the bar on Asian naturalization, it also institutionalized the particular racialization of Asian Americans as foreign and unassimilable—rather than simply as nonwhite. Although the prohibition on naturalization was eventually removed for Chinese, Asian Indian, and Filipino immigrants in the 1940s, the McCarran-Walter Act removed the *racial* limitation on naturalized citizenship (Ancheta 1998: 24). Because those of Asian ancestry constituted the only "race" ineligible for citizenship by 1952, the simultaneous removal of racial discrimination, based on their nonwhite status in the 1790 Naturalization Law, and the injection of a new type of racial discrimination, which formally linked the alien with political subversion in federal naturalization and denaturalization procedures, at the height of McCarthyism resulted in a highly contingent citizenship that severely limited the political freedoms and constitutional rights of Asian immigrants and naturalized Asian-American citizens alike.

Before World War II, Korean immigrants to the United States, like other Asian immigrants, were ineligible for citizenship as a result of their nonwhite status.[12] While they were constrained by a host of discriminatory laws against foreigners and nonwhites, a number were actively involved in homeland politics. For example, among the first Korean immigrants to arrive in the United States were Seo Jae-Pil (Philip Jaisohn), An Chang-Ho, Pak Yeong-Man, and Syngman Rhee (Yi Seung-Man), all principal nationalist leaders in the Korean independence movement. In fact, the majority of the almost 100 Korean immigrants who arrived to the United States prior to 1903 were students and political refugees.

As colonial subjects of Japan, Korean immigrants were subject to all local and federal legislation that discriminated against Japanese immigrants in the United States, including the San Francisco School Board's segregationist directive in 1906; California's 1913 Alien Land Law, which barred Japanese from owning property, and the precedent set by the 1922 case *Takao Ozawa v. United States*, which declared Japanese ineligible for naturalization. Furthermore, legislation affecting immigration from Japan directly affected Korean immigration patterns prior to World War II. In

1907, Congress passed an amendment to the Immigration Act declaring that any immigrant not holding a valid passport to the United States—for Koreans, this specifically referred to Japanese passports—would be excluded (Houchins and Houchins 1976: 136–137). This was the same year that the so-called Gentleman's Agreement was reached between Japan and the United States whereby the Japanese government refrained from issuing visas to laborers bound for the mainland. Finally, the Immigration Act of 1924, which excluded any "alien ineligible for citizenship," effectively proscribed Korean immigration until 1952 (Hing 1993: 33, 66).[13] Consequently, Korean immigration to the United States before World War II was relatively small compared to that of other Asian immigrant groups.[14]

Nevertheless, Korean immigrants established numerous mutual aid organizations, religious institutions, and self-governing bodies that aimed to promote the welfare of Korean communities in the United States as well as work to achieve Korean independence from Japan (Chan 1991: 74). Beginning with the establishment of Korean village councils, or *donghoe*, on every plantation in the Hawai'ian islands in 1903, Koreans in Hawai'i organized more than twenty different social, political, and cultural organizations between 1903 and 1907 alone (see Choy 1979: 99–100, 114). The first political organization, the Sinminhoe (New People's Association) was established in 1903 for the purpose of uniting the Korean community in Hawai'i to work for Korean independence (Choy 1979: 141). Christian churches in particular functioned as vital grassroots institutions, centers of social life, and the lens through which Koreans looked at the larger American society—in addition to serving religious needs (Yang and Park 1992: vii, 7–8). In fact, most of the early Korean community leaders were church members or ministers.

Despite the low wages that Korean immigrants received for their labor—the average daily wage of a Korean plantation worker was 65 cents in 1905—the Korean immigrant community raised substantial funds for overseas political activity in the United States as well as in other Korean diasporic communities in Mexico, China, Japan, and Siberia (Choy 1979: 123). For example, a special youth action guerrilla group trained by the Korean nationalist leader Kim Koo, which made several attacks on high-ranking Japanese officials (including an unsuccessful attempt on the life of the Japanese emperor in Tokyo), was funded almost entirely by Korean residents in Hawai'i. In addition, the Korean communities in Hawai'i and California were active in organizing defense efforts in the trial of Jang In-Hwan, a Korean immigrant and member of the group Daedong bogukhoe (Patriotism Association), who in 1908 assassinated Durham Stevens, an American hired by the Japanese government to defend Japanese policies in Korea. During the seven-month trial, Korean immigrants hired lawyers, provided interpreters, collected evidence, and raised over $7,000 in defense funds from overseas Koreans in the United States, Hawai'i, Mexico, China, and Japan (Houchins and Houchins 1976: 138).

In 1909, one year before Japan's formal annexation of Korea, the two leading Korean organizations in Hawai'i and the U.S. mainland united to form the Kukminhoe, or the Korean National Association (KNA). With 116 local branches, the KNA raised almost $60,000 in support of anti-Japanese quasi-military training programs organized in Hawai'i, California, Wyoming, Nebraska, and Kansas from 1910 to 1916 (Houchins and Houchins 1976: 140). Indeed, Frank Baldwin (1969: 45–46) argues that political activities organized by overseas Koreans following President Woodrow Wilson's "Fourteen Points" speech in 1918, including work by Korean-American activists to petition U.S. assistance in achieving Korean self-determination, mobilized key sectors of Korean society to organize mass demonstrations that eventually led to the March 1 Independence Movement in 1919. Thus, political organizations and churches in the Korean-American community not only provided rich resources for fostering Korean nationalism and ethnic solidarity but were pivotal to the Korean independence movement as a whole. With greater political and material resources, Koreans in Hawai'i and the mainland United States raised more funds for Korean independence than any other group inside or outside of Korea (Lyu 1977b: 97).

Although those who had participated in the Korean independence movement had the same goal, their proposed paths were highly divergent, often split across ideological lines. As mentioned earlier, a number of Korean immigrants to the United States were principal political leaders of the independence movement and the Korean-American community was a primary source of political funding; therefore, the conflicts that plagued the movement became the sources of political contention within the Korean-American community. In particular, the rivalry between Pak Yeong-Man, An Chang-Ho, and Syngman Rhee, as well as the division between conservatives and leftists, created factionalism within the Korean-American community. Pak Yong-Man advocated direct military action against Japan and organized military training for Korean immigrant youth in Hawai'i and the U.S. mainland. He founded a military academy in Hawai'i known as the Kundan in 1914 with about 80 students and established the Dongnipdan (League of Korean Independence) in 1919 with 350 members.[15] Conversely, An Chang-Ho, whose philosophy resembled that of Booker T. Washington, believed that education was the key to restoring Korean sovereignty. In 1913, he founded the Heungsadan (Corps for the Advancement of Individuals), which focused on training overseas Korean youth for future leadership positions in Korea's eventual reconstruction.[16] Finally, Syngman Rhee, a staunch anti-Communist, proposed lobbying and petitioning Western powers to put diplomatic pressure on Japan. As the first Korean to earn a Ph.D. from an American university, Rhee was among the most prominent overseas Korean activists and was designated president of the Korean Provisional Government (KPG) upon its founding in Shanghai in 1919.[17] He formally separated himself from the central Korean National Association and organized the Dongjihoe (Society for the Like-Minded) in 1921 (Choy 1979: 118).

The predicament of Korean immigrants' legal status as Japanese citizens became especially urgent following Japan's invasion of Pearl Harbor in 1941. Setting the stage for Occupation policies regarding Koreans in Japan in the postwar period, Koreans in the United States were classified as "enemy aliens" along with other Japanese citizens. For security purposes, the United Korean Committee advised Koreans to wear badges identifying themselves as Koreans (Takaki 1989: 364–367).[18] In 1942, the U.S. State and Treasury departments issued a special order stating that Koreans should enjoy the same treatment accorded to citizens of other Allied nations after representatives from the United Korean Committee intervened in talks about relocating Koreans to Japanese internment camps (Choy 1979: 173). While many second-generation Korean Americans were critical of the unjust internment of Japanese Americans, most first-generation Korean immigrants, who technically remained Japanese nationals until the end of the war, invested their energies in protesting their enemy alien status. As Lili Kim (2001) argues, Korean Americans at this time were more interested in protecting their own interests—gaining friendly alien status and achieving Korean independence from Japan—than in criticizing the U.S. government on behalf of Japanese Americans.

Most Korean nationalists welcomed the war and involved themselves in the U.S. war effort against Japan by purchasing war bonds, volunteering for the Red Cross, and working as Japanese interpreters in the intelligence service. In 1941, a Korean military unit—called the "Tiger Brigade"—was formed in Los Angeles in cooperation with the California National Guard. Choy (1979: 174) estimates that 109 Koreans from Los Angeles alone—over 20 percent of the total Korean population in Los Angeles—participated in military training with this unit. In a letter to Secretary of War Henry

Stimson dated May 17, 1943, Syngman Rhee wrote, "every Korean will grab the first chance, if it is ever given, to fight for the United States" because "by fighting for the United States he can fight for the freedom of his own nation" (quoted in L. M. Kim 2001: 149). Korean Americans' precarious positions as both voluntary supporters of the Allied powers and "enemy aliens" who looked Japanese during the war may have been the driving force for large numbers of the community to seek American citizenship a decade later.[19]

The change in political consciousness of the Korean-American community following World War II, and especially the Korean War, was consistent with the domestic and international political tenor of the times. The division of Korea into two separate states and the implementation of the McCarran-Walter Act decisively put an end to the diverse political activities of the prewar Korean-American community. First, even after Syngman Rhee's inauguration as the first president of the Republic of Korea in 1948, he continued to monitor the activities of the Korean-American community through the Korean consulate and Korean-American loyalists. While embarking upon anticommunist witch hunts to destroy the South Korean left as well as his political rivals in South Korea, Rhee and his diplomatic representatives in the United States employed McCarthy-type tactics against Korean Americans who were critical of his administration's policies. Even members of the Korean National Association (KNA) who had worked with Rhee when he was in exile were accused of being procommunist. As a result, a number of anti-Rhee intellectuals and Korean-American leftists became the targets of vigilant government surveillance by both U.S. and South Korean authorities. In the 1950s, the FBI deported some Korean Americans who were associated with the Korean National Revolutionary Party in Los Angeles, a group that criticized U.S. involvement in the Korean War (Choy 1979: 84–85, 182–183). One of the deportees, Diamond Kim (Kim Kang), fled to North Korea by way of European communist countries, while the remainder were deported to South Korea, where they were imprisoned and possibly executed (Cumings 1997: 441).

Second, in accordance with the McCarran-Walter Act (Sec. 212-a), Korean immigrants as well as applicants for U.S. citizenship were closely screened for any history of involvement or affiliation with any organization or individual that was known to "advocate or teach . . . write or publish . . . circulate, distribute, print, or display" anarchism, communism, or totalitarianism. For example, the case of *Kimm v. Rosenberg, District Director, Immigration and Naturalization Service* (1960) involved a Korean student who was ordered deported because of his suspected affiliation with the U.S. Communist Party. The Supreme Court's ruling against Kimm's petition for suspension of his deportation determined that the burden of proof of an alien's affiliation with the Communist Party was not on the government; on the contrary, the alien had the burden of proving that he was *not* affiliated in order to establish that he was a person of "good moral character." Consequently, in the post–World War II period, leftist political organizations that had existed in the Korean-American community prior to the war were almost completely destroyed, former Korean political organizations were transformed into nonpolitical groups, and the Korean-American community in general became less active in homeland politics for a time.

THE COLD WAR, CITIZENSHIP, AND RACIAL IDENTITIES

The conditions under which Koreans in the two countries were either granted or stripped of their citizenship were pivotal in shaping the forms of each community's political engagement in the host society. Specifically, the historical timing of postwar citizenship policies that were formulated on the eve of the Cold War made the costs of citizenship especially high for Korean immigrants in both the United States and Japan: naturalization was contingent upon a type of political assimilation that curtailed political engagement with the state. In effect, postwar citizenship policies in both countries sought to create docile subjects of immigrants eligible for citizenship, not active citizens.

The 1952 McCarran-Walter Act, which made Asian immigrants eligible for naturalization, created a category of partial citizenship that was contingent upon political passivity. As the act was aimed primarily at the control of "subversive activities," both successful and unsuccessful applicants for naturalization were carefully monitored, and those engaged in "anti-American" or "radical" activities were subject to deportation. Given that "subversive activities" in the United States have historically been linked with white communists, foreigners, and African Americans, we may also surmise that the act had a chilling effect not only on radical political activity but on socially transformative movements involving multiracial coalitions as well. Hence, a "model" racial minority of Americans emerged that, as Robert Lee (1999: 145) compellingly states, were "not black" in two notable ways: "They were both politically silent and ethnically assimilable." In this sense, postwar citizenship policies formulated during the Cold War were neither politically empowering nor socially transformative for their primary recipients, Asian immigrants. In the process of their naturalization, Asian immigrants became merely marginal Americans, naturalized but potentially subversive, legally American but racialized as foreign.

The McCarran-Walter Act, coupled with political developments in the homeland, had a chilling effect on political activities within the postwar Korean community in the United States. McCarthysim in the United States and Syngman Rhee's anticommunist witch hunts virtually annihilated any leftist activity within the Korean-American community. Former Korean political organizations were transformed into nonpolitical groups. Vocal Korean-American activists deemed subversive either fled to a third country (in at least one case, to the DPRK) or were deported to South Korea. Those who remained in the United States had two limited options: they could remain politically silent to maintain a friendly alien status, or they could naturalize and become politically silent Americans. According to census records, most chose the second option. Of foreign-born Asians who entered the United States before 1960, Korean Americans have the highest percentage of naturalized citizens (about 90 percent) according to the 1990 census.[20] The forced retreat to nonpolitical activities resulted in a type of "citizenship nullification" for the Korean-American community, the consequences of which would be most acutely felt during the Los Angeles civil unrest in 1992.[21]

In Japan's postwar Korean community, citizenship has been at the center of its collective identity and political activities. Indeed, the institution of postwar Japanese citizenship has been all-encompassing and its acquisition highly conditional. Under the heavy-handed discretion of the Ministry of Justice, naturalization entailed not only the renouncement of national allegiance to the homeland but also complete cultural assimilation, or "Japanization." Until the late 1980s, Justice officials frequently commented that the existence of ethnic minorities within Japanese society was highly undesirable and that efforts should be made to encourage Korean residents to assimilate to the point of "indistinguishability" (Takenaka 1997: 303, Y. D. Kim 1990).

Postwar Japanese citizenship policies stripped Koreans of their Japanese nationalities, yet Koreans were not merely victims of an oppressive Japanese government. On the contrary, Joryeon objected to their treatment as Japanese nationals by Occupation authorities. Foreign citizenship in the early postwar era was associated with the special rights, privileges, and status of the Occupation authorities and their allies. However, Joryeon's dissolution and the establishment of Mindan and Chongryun facilitated the creation of a politically docile community vis-à-vis the Japanese state.

Rather than challenge the exclusionary ideology of Japanese homogeneity, both groups have, until very recently, constructed their own ideologies of authentic identities for the Korean community based on blood ties and nationality. Their declarations of noninvolvement in Japanese domestic politics and their rigid anti-assimilationist stance—at the expense of gaining rights for Korean residents—relieved the Japanese state from the burden of administrative change in regard to citizenship policies. Consequently, for much of the Cold War, Koreans in Japan were also a model minority of sorts—they were law-abiding, culturally assimilated (despite Mindan's and Chongryun's anti-assimilationist rhetoric), and politically silent.

With the end of the Cold War, the legitimacy of traditional first-generation organizations weakened and the contradictions of Cold War–based citizenship policies began to unravel within Korean communities in both the United States and Japan. For Korean Americans, the 1992 Los Angeles civil unrest demonstrated the perils of contingent citizenship and the model minority myth. The community's focus on attaining economic prosperity at the expense of political empowerment, as well as its social and cultural insularity, left its members defenseless, voiceless, and, ultimately, powerless. In the rebuilding process, Korean Americans reevaluated their collective identities as well as their social and political standing in U.S. society. Accordingly, citizenship has become a central issue in the post-1992 Korean-American community. By emphasizing the "Americanness" of their Korean-American identity, by participating more actively in U.S. politics, and by engaging in multiethnic and multiracial coalitions, the Korean-American community, led by a new generation of activists, is at once operationalizing citizenship and challenging the formal and informal policies and practices that have denied its members full citizenship.

Meanwhile, Koreans in Japan have gained greater political visibility as foreign residents than Korean Americans have as citizens or potential citizens of the United States. During and immediately following the Los Angeles civil unrest, Korean Americans were unable to secure either police protection or political representation *despite* their legal status as actual or potential U.S. citizens. Koreans in Japan, in contrast, have become relatively influential as *foreign* citizens. Although they remain disenfranchised, their political presence rarely goes unnoticed by policy makers, as demonstrated by current debates in the Diet concerning local voting rights and reforms to naturalization procedures. Especially in the post–Cold War era, native-born generations of Korean activists have used their noncitizen status not as a means of participating in homeland politics but as part of a strategy to gain political visibility in Japanese civil society.[22] In other words, Korean residents are engaging in particular forms of political activities *because of,* and not despite, their legal status.

Postwar Japan's citizenship policies were contingent upon complete cultural assimilation. At the same time, Mindan and Chongryun focused their activities on repatriation and homeland politics and discouraged their members from acquiring Japanese nationality. American Occupation authorities, Japanese officials, and Korean organizations all expected that Koreans would either return to Korea or undergo the process of naturalization if they chose to stay in Japan. Yet as Japan emerged in the international spotlight as a major economic power in the mid-1970s and after, the contradictions inherent in having a highly assimilated population of permanent residents without citizenship rights—in effect, a community of second-class citizens—threatened Japan's claim as an advanced industrial democracy.

Following Japan's ratification of international conventions on refugees and alien residents, the Japanese state enacted a series of reforms from the late 1970s to the mid-1980s that made the residence status of permanent Korean residents more secure and conferred on them social welfare benefits. Meanwhile, Japan's demand for unskilled labor resulted in a rapid influx of foreign workers from developing countries in the 1980s and ultimately led to a phenomenal growth of immigrant communities.[23] These developments have presented Korean activists with the opportunity to shape public debate on the problems of immigration and citizenship in Japan. Accordingly, by mobilizing around their noncitizen status, younger generations of Korean activists have sought to highlight the incongruities of Japan's citizenship policies and thereby transform the meaning of Japanese citizenship itself, from a discourse based on cultural homogeneity to one based on a multicultural, multiethnic society.

Although postwar citizenship policies marginalized both communities in different ways, they also created political opportunities for specific forms of participation. Korean Americans have begun to reclaim their "Americanness" through efforts to mobilize their community politically and reinsert themselves in U.S. electoral and racial politics. Koreans in Japan have reconceptualized possibilities for the extra-electoral options through which they can engage in civic activities that aim to reinforce, revise, or transform shared values and public policies.

These cases challenge our conventional understanding of citizenship, which would lead us to assume that noncitizen political activities are aimed at the acquisition of citizenship alone, and that citizenship acquisition is always politically empowering. They point to the gray areas of citizenship where egalitarianism and particularism overlap, and where citizenship is both a source of inclusion and exclusion. Above all, Korean experiences in both Japan and the United States demonstrate the contingencies of citizenship, both upon the individuals who seek to become citizens as well as the historical context in which particular citizenship policies are embedded. Hence, it is the *terms* of a group's political incorporation (or exclusion)—rather than citizenship policies alone—that shape both their treatment by the host state and citizens, as well as the political opportunities for distinct forms of political engagement.

8. The End of the Road?
*The Post-*Zainichi *Generation*
John Lie

In the early years of the twenty-first century, South Korean stars illuminated television screens in many Japanese households. Fanatical fans flocked to the location of a popular South Korean soap opera, *Fuyu no sonata* (Winter Sonata). Less ambitiously, they snapped up expensive photo books of its lead actor. Enthusiasm for South Korean popular culture—variously known as Kanryu, Hanryu, or K-pop—was powerful enough to elicit a countervailing movement, Ken-Kanryu (anti-Korean wave). At the same time, North Korea remained a major external threat. In particular, the fate of Japanese women kidnapped in the early 1970s and the present danger of North Korean nuclear weapon tests repeatedly became headline news. The coverage of the enemy had a lighter side as well. Comic books pilloried Kim Jong Il's hairdo and elevator shoes, while television shows sensationally reported his luxury consumption amidst the poverty of his country.

As the existence of Ken-Kanryu and anti–North Korean sentiments attest, Japanese attitudes toward the Koreas and Koreans are at times virulently hostile. Yet the legacy of the colonial past and colonial racism was clearly waning sixty years after the end of Japanese rule. Although there were ethnic Korean superstars in Japan during the post–World War II period, they usually were carefully in the ethnic closet and sought to pass as ordinary Japanese (Lie 2001). In the 2000s, South Korean stars—and increasingly some *zainichi* Korean figures—were openly and proudly Korean. When Japanese tourism to South Korea took off in the 1960s, one of the primary attractions was sex tourism, bringing countless Japanese men to South Korean prostitutes (Lie 1995). Forty years later, Japanese tourists were much more likely to seek a taste of "authentic" Korean food or the luxury of conspicuous consumption. While Japanese elders still recall South Korea as a poor or "developing" country, Japanese youths are more likely to evoke the manifest wealth of Seoul and the dynamic nature of Samsung. In short, it would do considerable injustice to reality to insist on the relentless and recalcitrant nature of the Japanese dislike of Korea and Koreans.

Simultaneously, few contemporary Japanese people would characterize the population of ethnic Koreans in Japan in unremittingly negative terms. Indeed, the long-standing penchant for ethno-national generalizations is losing credibility. Whether the colonial-era Japanese prejudice that delineated a lazy, dirty, and treacherous people or the pro-Korean narrative that depicted an exploited, oppressed, and discriminated people, the very idea of the essential Korean or the essential *zainichi* seems quaint. (Henceforth, I will follow the common contemporary Japanese practice of designating the ethnic Korean population in Japan, especially those whose ancestors arrived during the colonial period, as *zainichi*.) In 1981 Changsoo Lee and George De Vos could conclude: "To be known as Korean in Japan today is still to court possible failure in many business or professional careers. It is dangerous economically to 'surface' even after gaining recognition" (Lee and De Vos 1981:363). In spite of persistent poverty and continuing discrimination, we can no longer produce facile generalizations about the oppressed and pathetic status of *zainichi* in contemporary Japanese society. Rapidly disappearing, too, is the widespread Korean-Japanese practice of passing as Japanese. Merely a decade after Lee and De Vos's book, Son Masayoshi emerged as the Bill Gates of Japan. He was at once successful economically and openly "Korean." As we will see, some of the leading intellectuals in contemporary Japan are ethnic Koreans who, in spite of considerable differences in outlook, are routinely identified as members of the ethnic minority group. In short, *zainichi* today inhabit a much more prosaic world.

In this concluding chapter, I explore the paradoxical dynamic of *zainichi* identity in the early twenty-first century. As I have argued, the Korean-Japanese population—however diverse and divided—was predominantly identified as "Korean" and belonged culturally and politically to one of the Koreas until the 1970s (Lie 2001, 2008). Hence, there were efforts—collective and individual—to repatriate to the homeland, and the unavoidable question of identity almost inevitably took the population to the peninsula, whether physically or spiritually. Few advocated assimilation, though to neutralize discrimination in employment and everyday life, the vast majority in fact practiced assimilation. That is, most *zainichi* in the postwar era were in the ethnic closet, passing themselves off as ordinary Japanese residents. By the 1980s, then, second- and third-generation Korean Japanese were linguistically and culturally Japanese, while the first-generation survivors were rapidly dwindling in number. That is, except for ethno-racial descent, the Korean-Japanese population had become largely assimilated into the larger Japanese society. Even as they have sought to come to terms with their distance from the Korean peninsula, many have begun to assert their specific ethnic identity as "Koreans in Japan," or *zainichi*. By 1992, however, the number of *zainichi* who opted to become naturalized Japanese citizens exceeded 10,000 annually and has been growing steadily. Paradoxically, then, the assertion of ethnic identity grew along with assimilation and naturalization.

TO BE *ZAINICHI* IN NORTHEAST ASIA

Let me begin by discussing Kang Sang-jung, who is a renowned intellectual in Japan and a professor at the prestigious University of Tokyo (supposedly the first Zainichi to attain this position). He occupies a role in Japanese intellectual and cultural life that is somewhat akin to that of Edward W. Said, one of Kang's intellectual heroes, in the United States in the 1980s and 1990s. That is, Kang speaks out openly and polemically on a variety of political and cultural issues, is identified as a man of the left, and retains a great deal of scholarly respect to boot. Rather than discussing his well-known work on nationalism or his frequent intervention in public life, I focus on his 2004 autobiography, *Zainichi*.

Kang was born in 1950 in a Korean ghetto in Kumamoto City in Kyūshū. Most Koreans eked out a precarious living by pig farming or illegal alcohol [*doburoku*] manufacturing. His parents maintained Korean customs and rituals. His mother remained illiterate in both Korean and Japanese and never attained fluency in Japanese. His father first worked in construction and later in scrap recycling. Kang went to Japanese schools using a Japanese pseudonym. In short, Kang's was not an atypical upbringing for a *zainichi* child in the 1950s.

Nonetheless, the diversity of the *zainichi* population is evident in Kang's description of his two "uncles." The "real" uncle was a university-educated military police officer who married a Japanese woman. He went so far as to decide to commit suicide at the end of the war (though he ultimately was dissuaded by Kang's father) because of his loyalty to the Japanese emperor and the Japanese nation. After the war, he returned to

South Korea, became a lawyer, and married a woman from an affluent family. By the time he returned for a brief visit to Japan in 1970, he had expunged his memory as a military police officer and of the Japanese family he had left behind. Unlike his father's younger brother, the other "uncle" was illiterate. Living as an "outlaw" and devoid of family relations, this "uncle" worked and lived with the Kang family after the war. By the time he passed away, he had in his possession only a few articles of clothing and cigarettes.

Between these contrasting life courses, Kang's childhood memory is at once melancholic and schizophrenic. Lacking a unified homeland, he found it problematic to call Kumamoto or North or South Korea his ancestral homeland [*sokoku*]. He couldn't make sense of the divided Korea or the whiff of criminality that was associated with the *zainichi* population. Thus, Japan and Korea became at once the most beloved and the most detested country. The very notion of *zainichi* cast a dark shadow even over Kang's affective life. Kang believes that his inability to smile for photographs and his youthful stuttering are both intimately intertwined with his problematic identification as *zainichi*.

Entering Waseda University, Kang feared the shadow of *zainichi* existence and sought to flee it. Unable to talk about his turmoil, he led a lonely life amidst four "worlds": the fading memory of the world of the first-generation Korean Japanese, the simultaneously attractive and repellent world of Tokyo, the newly discovered world of scholarship, and the world of fellow *zainichi* students. Against the background of student activism, Kang remained "non-poli," or politically indifferent, when he visited South Korea for the first time in 1972. His rigorous interrogation by the immigration authorities—Kang was carrying a Japanese magazine with photos of Kim Il Sung—quickly dissipated any warm and fuzzy feelings about the homeland. Nonetheless, the warm welcome by his relatives, the contrast between the wealth of his lawyer uncle's family and the prevailing poverty of Seoul, and the wonders of South Korea led him to seek out Waseda University's Center for Korean Culture. At the Center he began to explore the roots of Korean problems and the status of *zainichi*. He also found a new identity as *zainichi* by discarding his Japanese name and henceforth using his Korean name. Kang implies that this course was in stark contrast to another fellow *zainichi* student who had committed suicide in 1970. Having been naturalized, the student could not join the Center (which was open only to Korean nationals) and hence could not be accepted by either Japanese or Koreans. Kang believes that what prevented such an end for himself was the memory of his interaction with the first generation that provided the paper-thin margin that separates life from death. That is, *zainichi* meant life; its denial meant death.

Nonetheless, the path of *zainichi* intellectual life has been far from predictable or smooth. Unlike first-generation *zainichi* intellectuals who focused almost exclusively on Korea and *zainichi* topics, Kang's work has only intermittently dealt with Korea and Koreans. Kang's doctoral thesis, for example, was on the German social theorist Max Weber (though Kang claims that the pioneering theorist of modernity had suggestive answers for his questions about *zainichi* identity). His appearances on television talk shows have dealt with events beyond the Korean peninsula and the *zainichi* population. By participating in the national debate on Japan's role in the world, Kang claims that he is seeking to destroy the prevailing image of *zainichi*. After returning to Japan from his study abroad in Germany, Kang had trouble assimilating into the *zainichi* world. He is married to a Japanese woman, and he departed consciously from the traditional Korean practice in naming his son. In other words, it is not at all obvious how or why Kang is a representative *zainichi*.

Kang's advocacy of *zainichi* identity is far from singular. During the movement refusing the compulsory fingerprinting of resident aliens by the Japanese government, his refusal made him a minor celebrity. However, faced with the prospect of imprisonment, he decided to comply with the authorities. Against the palpable disappointment of his supporters, he was saved by the sympathetic words of an activist Japanese minister, who later helped him secure a job at a Christian university. Kang also argues that Japanese themselves are becoming more like *zainichi*. In effect, the corrosion of social safety nets has rendered the mainstream Japanese population in a similarly risk-filled state to that of the *zainichi* population. What Kang stresses above all, however, is the memory and history of the first-generation *zainichi* population. Thus, he steadfastly resists the path of assimilation and naturalization, keeping the memory of the first-generation *zainichi* alive.

Kang concludes his autobiography by answering why he was born *zainichi* and who *zainichi* are. For Kang, returning to the Koreas is not a viable solution given the brute fact of linguistic and cultural assimilation or accommodation in Japan. Rather than being trapped in Japan, *zainichi* should enhance networks with other Korean diasporic people and seek to expand ties across Northeast Asia. In short, *zainichi* should be neither Japanese nor Korean but be part of the larger Korean diaspora. "To live in Northeast Asia" is his proposed project and solution.

NOT TO BE *ZAINICHI* IN JAPAN

Few would dispute Kang's eminence as an intellectual in contemporary Japan. He is aligned closely with the progressive intellectuals and publishers who dominated the post–World War II era. Unlike earlier *zainichi* intellectuals, who were largely excluded from prestigious universities and media, Kang is not closely identified with either North or South Korea. Indeed, he embodies the very idea of *zainichi* as an autonomous ethnonational identity: neither Korean nor Japanese. It is an identity, as he himself articulated in *Zainichi*, that constantly refracts the brutal colonial relationship, the enforced migration of Koreans to the Japanese archipelago, and the overwhelming poverty and discrimination that greeted the Koreans once in Japan. The capsule history of oppression and resistance constitutes Kang's articulation of *zainichi* identity, and therefore his heavy reliance on honoring the memory of the first generation. If *zainichi* identity had to be forged against the centrifugal force that retained the two Koreas as the ultimate homeland of ethnic Koreans in Japan, it unleashes in turn a powerful centripetal force of assimilation.

Indeed, the most vocal exponents of *zainichi* assimilation in Japan are second- and third-generation *zainichi* intellectuals. They argue against Kang's position that links the present with the experience of the first generation and that stresses Korean victimization and Japanese racism. A representative *zainichi* intellectual Kang may be, he does not exemplify *zainichi* identity *tout court*.

Consider Tei Taikin (Chung Daekyun in Korean), who was born in 1948 in Iwate Prefecture in northeast Japan. Like Kang, he studied at a prestigious private university (Rikkyo) and abroad (UCLA) and is currently a professor at Shuto University Tokyo (if not quite as prestigious as the University of Tokyo, certainly a highly respected institution). Born two years apart as second-generation *zainichi*, both Kang and Tei are prominent intellectuals who speak out on *zainichi* issues. In other words, they are, sociologically speaking, virtually identical.

In spite of considerable similarities, they are poles apart in their perspectives on *zainichi* identity and identification. Whereas Kang asserts ethnonational identification, Tei advocates assimilation and naturalization. Kang delineates the early history of *zainichi* as largely that of enforced migration, exploitation, and discrimination; Tei paints a much more ambivalent picture. While Kang publishes prolifically in progressive magazines, Tei's writings appear in right-of-center outlets. Given their antipodal outlooks, there is a temptation to seek their source in their life course and background.

After arriving in Japan in 1922, Tei's father became the first ethnic Korean to author a Japanese-language novel and later became an ardent supporter of the emperor. Along with Kang's uncle, Tei's father represents a not insignificant population of ethnic Koreans who became Japanese nationalists during the colonial period. The end of World War II unleashed mental anguish, and Tei's father eventually returned to South Korea in 1960 (Tei and his siblings stayed behind with their mother in Japan). Tei would not see his father again for fifteen years. Unlike Kang, then, Tei is at best ambivalent toward his impoverished and paranoid father. Tei's Japanese mother, whose dominant identification was as a Christian, had reared him as linguistically and culturally Japanese. Far from being proud of his heritage, Tei was "ashamed of being Korean, and tried to hide it" (Tei 2006:71). He was embarrassed by the "poverty" and "ugliness" of other *zainichi*, and went so far as to avoid learning anything about Korea. His long sojourn in the United States (where he studied) and South Korea (where he taught) clarified his lack of identification in any simple way as Korean. As a native Japanese speaker (as most second- and third-generation *zainichi* are), he did not fit in with native Korean speakers. Indeed, being abroad solidified his sense of belonging in contemporary Japanese society.

Parental or social background is inadequate to make sense of the divergent political beliefs of Kang and Tei, however. Tei's older brother was long active in one of the *zainichi* political organizations. His younger sister gained a great deal of notoriety after she lost a 2005 suit alleging discrimination against the Tokyo metropolitan government for not accepting her application as *zainichi*. She was reported after the verdict as stating: "I want to tell the world: Don't come to Japan!" (Tei 2006:153). Clearly, having the same parents or growing up together did not generate the same set of responses to *zainichi* issues. Indeed, Tei relentlessly criticizes her sister's action ("verbal violence") and her account of their shared family background and of the status of *zainichi*.

Tei's perspectives on the past, present, and future of *zainichi* depart significantly from Kang's argument. His current position is encapsulated in the title of his 2001 book, *Zainichi kankokujin no shūen* (The end of *zainichi* South Koreans). The fundamental point of contention is the future status of *zainichi* Koreans. In contrast to the "progressive" position of continuing to live as foreign citizens, Tei advocates naturalization and assimilation. He blames progressive intellectuals of robbing *zainichi* Koreans of "life chances" by discouraging assimilation and Japanization. Unlike Kang, Tei seeks to sever the present from the past. Tei castigates the victim mentality that harps endless on the enforced migration of Koreans to Japan and the ensuing lives of discrimination and oppression. Rather than blaming Japan, Tei argues that *zainichi* should embrace their fate as culturally and linguistically Japanese residents by becoming naturalized Japanese citizens. He also seeks to sever the *zainichi* population from the Korean peninsula. Drawing on his experience abroad, he argues that it is stressful to be a "foreigner" in Japan or Korean when he is by most measures Japanese. Tei argues that *zainichi* in South Korea—including himself, as he spent some fourteen years there—rarely stay on or become assimilated. Indeed, he suggests that most South Koreans disrespect *zainichi*. In contrast, Japanese prejudice and discrimination are in decline, and the rate of intermarriage between *zainichi* and ethnic Japanese exceeds 80 percent. For Tei, being naturalized does not mean the end of one's ties to the ancestral land. He advocates being Japanese but "feeling nostalgia" for the ancestral land. The birth of "Korean Japanese" [*koria-kei nihonjin*] would not only improve the status of *zainichi* but also contribute to Japanese society. A similar proposal had been made as early as 1997 (Chi 1997).

Another source of contrast is North Korea in particular and the Cold War in general. Tei is highly critical of progressive intellectuals who highlighted South Korea's repressive policies but were silent, if not laudatory, about North Korea's authoritarianism. Tei argues that consequently these progressive intellectuals ended up supporting the authoritarian regime in North Korea. Because the Korean peninsula remains one of the last outposts of the Cold War, it is not a coincidence that Cold War lines are recreated among *zainichi* intellectuals. Just as Kang bears the mantle of progressive intellectual—his work appears under the imprint of the progressive publisher Iwanami Shoten and its longtime flagship journal *Sekai*—Tei publishes in politically antipodal publishers and journals, such as *Bungei Shunjū* and *Seiron*.

Tei is far from alone in disputing Kang's role as the representative *zainichi* intellectual. Asakawa Akihiro, born in 1974 in Kobe, is a third-generation Korean Japanese who became a naturalized Japanese citizen like Tei. Although a specialist on Australian politics, he has attracted considerable attention as a critic of *zainichi* and progressive intellectuals. Asakawa's critique of Kang, especially *zainichi*, is symptomatic of his general critique. He provides a searing attack on Kang's claim to speak for or represent the first-generation Korean Japanese, denying that many of them were coerced or involuntary migrants. Similarly, he chides Kang for being silent on the effort to repatriate *zainichi* to North Korea. Asakawa also defends the series of Japanese government efforts to ameliorate the status and condition of *zainichi*. Here he denounces what he characterizes as Kang's defense of *zainichi* as a victimized population. Finally, Asakawa is relentless in criticizing the solidarity between progressive *zainichi* and Japanese intellectuals. He points to the convenient way in which progressive networks generated a good job for Kang, leading ultimately to his University of Tokyo professorship. In short, Asakawa's position follows Tei's argument.

INTELLECTUAL RESOLUTION?

In reviewing two opposing perspectives, the intellectual temptation is to reconcile them: review the available historical and sociological evidence, assay the logical structure of argumentation, and conclude in a dispassionate, scientific manner. Yet the nature of peoplehood identification resists scientific objectivity and sociological reductionism. Quite simply, it is possible to assert a wide range of claims about one's descent, belonging, and identification (Lie 2004).

Personal, much less ethnic, identity is far from fixed for even an individual. Kang is not very clear about his youthful sense of ethnic identity, but we do learn that he did not begin to explore his Korean roots until college. He also used his Japanese name until then. Tei's father was an ardent Japanese nationalist during the colonial period, only to return to Korea and thereafter abdicate his Japanese identification. Tei himself spent considerable time doing research on *zainichi* identity, later to resist and ultimately reject it. There are no identity essences over an individual's life course. Neither is identity reducible to family or social background. Tei's siblings presumably would have agreed with Kang's description and prescription for contemporary *zainichi* identity. Although Tei grew up in the same family, his deviation is quite manifest.

Consider in this regard two well-known *zainichi* musicians. Chon Wolson is a second-generation *zainichi* who attended Chongryun schools in Japan and became an opera singer (Chon 2006). Ryu Yong-gi is a third-generation *zainichi* who studied at a seminary and became a hip-hop artist ("Turning Rapanese" 2007). Both experienced discrimination as *zainichi*, but it would be difficult to generate useful generalizations from their shared background or experience. To say that they are both musicians is rendered nearly meaningless by the chasm separating the two genres of opera and hip-hop.

I am not denying that there are historically specific generalizations one may make about a group. The societal and historical context of one's life inevitably shapes the horizon of individual possibilities. The very possibility of becoming a professor at the University of Tokyo would have been well-nigh absent in the 1960s. For a completely different reason, becoming a hip-hop artist then and there also would have been impossible. It may even be possible to argue that the socioeconomic constitution of the *zainichi* population would make it more likely that the *zainichi* population may do worse (or better) on standardized examinations or status attainment. What I am denying is the cogency of group essentialism or sociological reductionism that would presumably have precluded the concrete trajectories of a *zainichi* person becoming a University of Tokyo professor or a hip-hop star today.

Furthermore, history is easily and essentially contested. As much as we strive for objective historiography, it is a truism that history yields no simple agreements on facts or morals. As we have seen, Kang endorses the *zainichi* historiography of *zainichi* that delineates a past of exploitation and oppression, struggle and resistance. Tei remains profoundly skeptical about the extent of the generalization and resists the expunction of voluntary will. Kang's memoir endorses Tei's historical perspective insofar as he had an assimilated and privileged family member (his "Korean" uncle). Kang's uncle also reinforces the first point about the dynamic transformation one may undergo during one's lifetime—a patriotic Japanese military police officer becomes an affluent attorney in South Korea. Life of privilege, mainly, but not one that adduces a simple and consistent identity. Certainly, one should not expect political differences to disappear—along with their vicissitudes even during one's life course, as is evident in the difference between Kang and Tei.

Relatedly, the present situation—the stuff of economics, politics, and history—does not yield an objective and neutral description and evaluation. The successes of Kang and Tei weaken the sociological generalization of the Korean minority as an underclass. Certainly, it would be difficult to classify them as "victims" of Japanese racism or of Japanese society. Yet the eradication of legal barriers or the vitiation of societal prejudice do not necessarily improve the subjective sense of well-being. What may have been an ordinary event for a *zainichi* person in the immediate post–World War II years—say, an ethnic invective hurled at them—would be extraordinary and intolerable for Kang or Tei in the twenty-first century. Paradoxically, the improving lot of a minority group may in fact exacerbate its sense of discrimination and victimization (Lie 2004).

Ethnic identity is, after all, as much about the future as about the past or the present. Many discussions of ethnic identity draw on memory and the shared experience as the core constituents. Yet a putative community of fate is simultaneously a community of destiny. "Where should we be?" is the question; Kang answers that *zainichi* should live in Northeast Asia among diasporic Koreans. Tei and Asakawa argue that the future of *zainichi* is squarely in Japanese society. Each perspective may adduce various distinct evidence and arguments, but there is no objective or neutral way to adjudicate which is more cogent or compelling. Needless to say, each individual comes up with her or his conclusion, yet that conclusion is often influenced, at times profoundly, by reading or listening to intellectuals such as Kang and Tei. Legal and economic conditions may change beyond recognition. I doubt that Tei could have predicted that he would become a naturalized Japanese citizen in his youth; it is not impossible that Kang may advocate naturalization as the privileged and preferred course of *zainichi* in the future. In short, the banal point that the future is uncertain makes any number of claims about ethnic identity more or less plausible, but not any particular one definitive.

In short, intellectual resolution is impossible. Given the profoundly prescriptive character of identity assertion, it is impossible to reduce it to fact or logic, history or sociology. As constituted as it is with memory, politics, and the future, identity is fundamentally complex and labile.

DIASPORIC FUTURES

Consider the Jewish diaspora in Germany in the 1920s. The overwhelming fact was assimilation: the Jewish population spoke German and adopted German customs, the rate of intermarriage escalated rapidly, and more than a few intellectuals prophesied the end of Jewish identity in Germany. Needless to say, no one at the time predicted the near extinction of the Jewish diaspora in Germany. In turn, in the late 1940s, few, if any, would have predicted the revival of the Jewish community in Germany by the early twenty-first century.

The tumultuous history of Germany Jewry is unlikely to be repeated for the Korean diaspora in Japan in the next half-century. Yet at each point in history few, if any, correctly prognosticated even the near future. This is true both at the individual and the collective level. Would it have occurred to anyone in Kang's family, or Kang himself when he was collecting scraps with his "uncle," that Kang would end up as a professor at the University of Tokyo? Or that ordinary Japanese people would be spellbound by a South Korean soap opera in their lifetime? When did Tei envision the possibility that he would end up teaching in South Korea? Or return to Japan as a professor at a major university? Beyond the vagaries of individual lives, who would have thought that the Korean minority would persist as a community a half-century after the end of World War II? Few in the 1970s would have predicted the massive wave of naturalization that emerged in the 1990s.

Retrospectively we can begin to make sense of the dramatic transformations. Yet we should resist the intellectual temptation to hunt for deep and deterministic causes that may in turn be applicable to make sense of the future. What we should learn is the limitations of facile sociological generalizations, whether to assume a singular identity in a population or to reduce identity to history and sociology.

Notes

INTRODUCTION

1. There are a number of reasons why Koreans in Japan are studied more as an ethnic minority (and therefore as a bastardized branch of Japanese studies) than as a diasporic population. The most important and relevant to this study seems to be the way Japanese studies have been carried out in the west, especially the United States. In postwar area studies, Japan generally has been regarded as homogeneous, and its minority invisible, with only a few scholarly exceptions (e.g., De Vos and Wagatsuma 1966; Lee and De Vos 1981). My *North Koreans in Japan* (Ryang 1997b), despite its discussion of diaspora, appears to have been read mainly as a "character study" of a minority group in Japan. Although an enormous amount of scholarly energy both in Japan and beyond has been devoted to exploring Japanese cultural uniqueness, Japan's ethnic and cultural diversity is still underexplored (see, e.g., Ryang 2004, chaps. 5, 6). This trend is changing, however; see, for example, Weiner (1997, introduction), Lie (2001), and Tsuda (2003).

2. Safran (2004) is a good example of this school of thought. For a summary of recent studies of diaspora, see Kokot, Tölölyan, and Alfonso (2004). See also Ong (1999, introduction) for a useful recounting.

3. Since the Japanese Ministry of Justice's statistics group Koreans with diverse residential categories into one category according to their alien registration, statistical analysis requires some digging. See chapter 6 by Kashiwazaki in this volume for more details.

4. I expand on this point in Ryang (2007).

5. Of course, the reform met resistance in Japan proper, on the logic that making Korean household registry identical with its Japanese counterpart would give too much privilege to Koreans, ultimately making them indistinguishable from Japanese. See Miyata, Kim, and Yang (1992), for example.

6. For a recent comment on Japan's wartime sexual slavery in connection with the Emperor's position as the restored ancient sovereign, see Ryang (2006a, chap. 2).

7. Statistics and other basic data on Koreans in Japan immediately after the war can be found in Wagner (1951) and Morita (1996), among others.

8. The *lex domicilii* of Koreans in Japan, however, was not clearly agreed upon in Japanese legal circles. While the government saw as late as the 1960s that the *lex domicilii* proper for Koreans in Japan in the area of private law would be South Korea because of the United Nations' acknowledgment of the latter, legal precedent did not conform to this view. Some cases show that North Korea was regarded as a homeland for Koreans in Japan, especially in rare cases in which the litigants claimed northern Korean ancestry, while others regarded Japanese private law to be proper for them. See Ryang (1997b: 120–125).

9. This is the situation described by Hannah Arendt in her "Perplexities on the Rights of Man," notably, that in the post–World War II era, a person with no nationality does not possess basic human rights. Conversely, only when one has obtained a nationality can basic human rights be extended (Arendt 1958). Only when a Korean in Japan obtains South Korean nationality does she secure a basic right of residential security in Japan and freedom to travel outside of Japan. I discuss this in depth in my work on autobiographical writings by Korean women in Japan and the United States. See Ryang (2008).

10. The only exception is Han Deok-Su, the deceased chairman of Chongryun, who was "elected" member of the Supreme People's Committee of North Korea. But this instance tells us more about the North Korean electoral system than the legal status of Koreans in Japan. Also, when Chongryun Koreans happen to be in North Korea during the "election" of the Supreme People's Committee, they get to join in the token voting. These, however, pertain to the genre of farce, rather than to any truly democratic election process.

11. As of 1959, only 1.7 percent of all Korea-born Koreans in Japan had come from the north, while 1.1 percent came from Kangweon province, which was divided into north and south in 1945 (Morita 1996: 40).

12. For work in this area, see Koh Sun Hui's energetic studies (e.g., 1995). See also Ryang (2002).

13. On exchanges between Kang Sang-Jung and Yang Tae-Ho on this subject, see Kang (1991a, 1991b) and Yang (1991a, 1991b).

14. Individuals with Japanese nationality but Korean heritage (such as those persons who were naturalized Japanese) assert their identity as *daburu*, i.e., double, as opposed to half. See Kashiwazaki (2000b) and Lim in this volume. Similarly, an option of "Korean Japanese" or *kankokukei nihonjin* was suggested by a veteran immigration officer. A veteran bureaucrat, Sakanaka Hidenori, proposed that Koreans be identified as "Korean Japanese" after naturalization. For more on this issue, see Tai (2004), although I am not sympathetic with Tai's argument in that "Korean Japanese" identity has very little (if not totally negative) viability in today's Japan—as such it is, in short, not an available choice for the majority of Koreans living in Japan.

15. I owe this information to Youngmi Lim.

16. As of October 2006. a high-ranking officer in Chongryun informed me

that an internal survey showed that about 5,000 Koreans in Japan did not have South Korean nationality.

17. The name- or naming-oriented approach to the issue of Koreans in Japan continues to be popular among research carried out in Japan. See for example Kim (1999), Kuraishi (1996, 2000a, 2000b), Miyauchi (1999), Pak (1999), Takeda (1996), Kawagoe (2000), Takenoshita (2000), Taira, Kawamoto, Chin, and Nakamura (1995), Fukuoka (1993), and Harajiri (1998).

18. On NSA eavesdropping, see Eggen and Pincus (2006) and Abramson (2006), to cite only a few.

19. For further investigation and interpretation on this subject, see Morris-Suzuki (2007).

CHAPTER 1

1. The Korean national flag first appeared in 1882. The Japanese prohibited the Koreans from displaying the flag and punished those who did. The most famous incidences of Korean defiance were during the March First (1919) movement and in 1936, when Korean newspapers superimposed the Korean flag over the Japanese flag atop the shirt of Son Gijeong, the Berlin Olympics marathon winner, who was Korean but participated on the Japanese team.

2. Scholars use different sources for this information. The most frequently quoted source is Wagner, who estimated that about 2.4 million Koreans were found in Japan in 1945 (Wagner 1951).

3. Sonia Ryang (2005b), in our view correctly, argues that the Korean diaspora in Japan is a postwar, rather than colonial, phenomenon.

4. This was the primary reason that the British gave for limiting the Korean participation at the 1952 San Francisco Peace Conference to that of observers (Cheong 1991: chap. 6).

5. Only POW informants were identified by name. The records of other interviewees were "sanitized," that is, they had all private information erased before being made public.

6. Close to 90,000 Koreans participated in the Japanese military. Many (along with Taiwanese soldiers) were given the tasks of guarding and punishing prisoners of war and were convicted of war crimes at a higher rate than their Japanese counterparts. Utsumi Aiko reports that twenty-three Koreans and twenty-one Taiwanese were executed for these crimes (2001: 211).

7. We see one of the more tangible results of this confusion over Korea's wartime status in the postwar discussion over reparations. Because the United States did not consider Korea among the Allied forces, Koreans were ineligible to accept property on the peninsula formerly occupied by Japanese as war compensation. This left the future possession of these assets in question until late 1948, when the Republic of Korea was founded (Cheong 1991: chap. 4).

8. Mindan's official name was changed on October 4, 1948, to Jaeilbon daehanminguk keoryu mindan, replacing "joseon" ("Korea," but can also denote North Korea) with "daehanminguk" ("Republic of Korea").

9. This report was issued on December 26, 1945. An earlier report issued just after the U.S. Occupation forces arrived (dated September 23, 1945) listed the following prices in Seoul: sugar, 35 yen per *kin* (1.32 lbs); rice, 25 yen per *shō* (3.18 pints); pumpkin, 13 yen per *kan* (8.27 lbs.); and cigarettes, 10 yen for three packs (Murai 1945: 75). The Occupation administration revised this provision on at least two occasions. In January 1946 it allowed Koreans to bring financial documents such as postal savings and bank passbooks to allow them to have their financial estate transferred at a later date. This adjustment period was insufficient, as financial transactions between Japan and Korea remained suspended from the end of the war (Lee 1981: 59). In 1948, after most Koreans seeking repatriation had returned, SCAP increased the limit to 100,000 yen.

10. One letter advised Koreans to hide this extra money in women's undergarments and water vessels (November 1, 1945; in United States Armed Forces in Korea 1988).

11. Wajima Eiji, Director of the Control Bureau of the Japanese Foreign Office, revealed this in a discussion with Richard B. Finn, who served in SCAP's Diplomatic Section (Finn 1949).

12. A 1947 letter signed by eleven U.S. soldiers stationed in Korea complained that the "living conditions are some of the worst they have yet experienced," a telling statement considering that these soldiers had arrived in Korea from Okinawa (see Brown 1995: 178).

CHAPTER 2

1. Accounts of the repatriation are given in Chung (1997), Kang (2003: 70–81), Kim and Takayanagi (1995), Okonogi (2004), Ryang (1997: 113–116), Takasaki (2004), and Takasaki and Pak (2005), and Morris-Suzuki (2007), for example. Chang Myeong-Su (2003) gives a somewhat sensationalized version of events, but is correct in highlighting the significant role played by the Japan Red Cross Society in the repatriation plan.

2. "Le CICR et la question des Coréens au Japon" (press release, August 11, 1959), ICRC Archives, B AG 232 105-011.05, Communiqué de Presse "Le CICR et la question des Coréens au Japon," 11.08.1959–11.08.1959.

3. All personal names that I cite as my interviewees and informants (except for Yi Yang-Su, who is publicly known) are pseudonyms for reasons of privacy.

4. "Report Concerning Operation 12, of the 34th Ship," ICRC Archives, B AG 232 105-018.01, *Rapports sur les convois*, 11.01.1960–20.12.1960.

5. Interview with Yi Yang-Su, June 2, 2005. Yi has also published several accounts of his experiences, including a series of articles distributed by the Kyōdō Tsūshin News Agency and published in numerous Japanese newspapers between August 13 and August 15, 2003; see also Yi Yang-Su (1987–1988).

6. Letter from Shimazu to Boissier, December 13, 1955, ICRC Archives, Geneva, file no. B AG 232 105-002, Problème du rapatriement des Coréens du Japon, dossier I: Généralités, 17.2.1953–11.10.1957.

7. On Okazaki's involvement in the 1950 deportation proposal, see "Korean Mission Releases Statement on Deportation of Koreans," translation of a report by Jiji Press, January 13, 1951, and "Communist Koreans to be Ordered Deported," translation of report by Jiji Press, December 24, 1950; in United States Department of State GHQ-SCAP Records, Box 2189, "Immigration—February 1950–March 1952," held in National Diet Library, Tokyo, microfiche no. GS(B) 01613.

8. "Nisseki gaijibuchō ni natta Inoue Masutarō," *Asahi shinbun*, July 2, 1955; "Memorandum of Conversation between Ambassador Inoue, Minister Shimoda, Howard P. Jones and Howard L. Parsons, Department of State, Washington, 12 February 1958," National Archives and Records Administration (NARA), Washington, D.C., section RG95, CFDF 1955–1959, box 2722, document no. 694.95B.

9. "Nisseki gaijibuchō ni natta Inoue Masutarō."

10. Letter from Inoue Masutaro to Leopold Boissier, president, ICRC, January 19, 1956, in ICRC Archives, B AG 232 105-002, Problème du rapatriement des Coréens du Japon, dossier I: Généralités, 17.2.1953–11.10.1957.

11. Inoue to Boissier, March 31, 1956, ICRC Archives, B AG 232 105-002 (emphasis added).

12. "Déroulement de la Visite des Délégués du CICR au Japon," p. 2, ICRC Archives, B AG 232 105-002.

13. Evidence by Li Ki-Ju to the Foreign Affairs Committee of the Lower House, Kokkai gijiroku, shūgiin gaimu iinkai, February 14, 1956. Available at http://kokkai.ndl.go.jp.

14. Telegram from MacArthur, U.S. Embassy, Tokyo, to Secretary of State, Washington, February 7, 1959, in National Archives and Records Administration (NARA), Washington, section RG95, CFDF 1955–1959, box 2722, document no. 694.95B/759.

15. Ibid.

16. Michel to ICRC, May 23, 1956, ICRC Archives, B AG 232 105-002.

17. See for example *Nihon Keizai shinbun* May 24, 1956; *Tokyo shinbun* May 24, 1956, translations of articles in ICRC Archives, B AG 323 105-004, Problème du rapatriement des Coréens du Japon, dossier III: Rapatriement de 48 Coréens en Corée-du-Nord, 18.5.1956–03.12.1957.

18. Michel referred to Inoue's statement as "puerile." Michel to ICRC, May 23, 1956, op. cit.

19. The formal proposal from the ICRC was sent to the Japanese, North Korean, and South Korean Red Cross societies on February 26, 1957. See Annex 1 to Aide-mémoire by J.-P. Maunoir for the ICRC Plenary Session of July 6, 1959, "Rapatriement des Coréens du Japon en Corée du Nord," p. 6, ICRC Archives, B AG 232 105-007, Problème du rapatriement des Coréens du Japon, dossier VI: Accord entre la Société de la Croix-Rouge du Japon et la Société de la Croix-Rouge de la République démocratique populaire de Corée du 24 juin 1959 et pétitions, 29.01.1959–13.08.1959.

20. During the visit by Michel and de Weck to Pyongyang, the North

Korean Red Cross expressed concern about the deportation of convicts and illegal immigrants to South Korea and asked that they be given the choice of being sent to the North instead. The North Korean government also offered to support Korean students in Japan who hoped to study at North Korean colleges. However, there was no sign of any plan to accept tens of thousands of returnees from Japan at this stage.

21. See, for example, letter from Inoue to Boissier, May 31, 1957, ICRC Archives, B AG 232 105-005.01.

22. See French translation of letter from Kishi to Shimazu, September 20, 1957, forwarded by Shimazu to Boissier, October 1, 1957, ICRC Archives, B AG 232 105-005. 01, Problème du rapatriement des Coréens du Japon, dossier II (Copies pour information transmises par la Croix-Rouge japonaise), 16.01.1956–18.12.1957.

23. Inoue Masutarō, "Why Is the Question of Repatriation an Urgent Humanitarian Issue?" document for circulation to national Red Cross societies, January 29, 1959, p. 4, in Archives of the International Federation of Red Cross and Red Crescent Societies, Geneva, file no. 22/3/4, Coréens au Japon.

24. Annex 4 to "Déroulement de la visite des délégués du CICR à la République democratique populaire de Corée," April 5–12, 1956, p. 4, in ICRC Archives, B AG 232 105-002.

25. "Record of Conversation with Comrade Kim Il-Sung, 14 and 15 July 1958," in Diary of V.I. Pelishenko, July 23, 1958, Foreign Policy Archives of the Russian Federation, archive 0102, collection 14, file 8, folder 95. I am very grateful to Dr. A. Lankov for drawing my attention to this document.

26. According to the Soviet ambassador in Pyongyang, the North Korean leader, Kim Il Sung, thanked the USSR soon after the arrival of the first repatriation ship, stating that the "Soviet sailors worked magnificently. As far as he [Kim] was aware, the [repatriation] vessels had been protected by Japanese naval forces while in Japanese waters and by Soviet naval forces in neutral waters. The government of the DPRK heartily thanks the government of the Soviet Union for the immense support and help, provided both during negotiations with the Japanese and in carrying out the repatriation." Dnevnik posla SSSR v KNDR A.M. Puzanova za period s 8 po 18 dekabrya 1959 g., entry for 16 December.

27. See, for example, "Welcome to First Group of Repatriates from Japan!"(1960), "In Quest of a New Life" (1960), Pak Chul Soon (1960), Li Dong Kang (1960), "We Are So Happy" (1960), Kim Yung Gil (1960), "Interview with Returnees from Japan" (1960), "I Grow Young" (1960), "In the Bosom of the Fatherland" (1960).

28. Dnevnik posla SSSR v KNDR A.M. Puzanova za period s 24 avgusta po 9 sentabrya 1960 g., entry for September 2, file 60-1-2.

29. *Korean Returnees from Japan* (1960).

30. See, for example, telegram from Angst to ICRC, February 13, 1959, in ICRC Archives, file no. B AG 232 105-009.01, Problème du rapatriement des Coréens du Japon, dossier VIII: Première partie, 12.01.1959–10.03.1959.

31. These comments were made by MacArthur to the Australian ambassador in Tokyo, A. Watt. See confidential telegram from Watt, Australian Embassy, Tokyo, to External Affairs, Canberra, July 15, 1959, in Australian Archives, series no. A1838, control symbol 3103/11/91 Part 1, Japan, Relations with North Korea.

32. Inoue to Gallopin, August 3, 1959, ICRC Archives, B AG 232 105-011.06, Problème du rapatriement des Coréens du Japon, dossier X: Décision du CICR de prêter son concours à la Croix-Rouge japonaise dans la question du rapatriement des Coréens (Notes et procès-verbaux d'entretien avec Masutaro Inoue, directeur du Département des Affaires étrangères de la Croix-Rouge japonaise, lors de son séjour à Genève), 01.07.1959–13.08.1959; Inoue to Gallopin, July 30, 1959, ICRC Archives, B AG 232 105-011.06.

33. Confidential letter from Gallopin to Inoue, "Concerne: Coréens résident au Japon," July 24, 1959, and confidential letter from Inoue to Boissier, July 28, 1959, in ICRC Archives, file no B AG 232 105-011.03, Aide-mémoire du 24 juillet 1959 transmis la Croix-Rouge japonaise et projets de communications, réponses, 03.07.1959–12.08.1959.

34. See "Supplementary Explanations on Certain Aspects of Actual Operations of Repatriation Work," and confidential minutes of meeting between M. Miaki, Gaimucho [sic], Asian Department, Messrs. Kasai and Inoue JRCS and, for the ICRC, Messrs. Lehner, Hoffmann, Gouy, and Borsinger, October 31, 1959, in ICRC Archives, file no B AG 232 105-013, Problème du rapatriement des Coréens du Japon, dossier I: Généralités pour la période Septembre–Décembre 1959 deuxième partie, 11.10.1959–29.12.1959. Interestingly, Chongryun's case during the negotiations was argued by an "M. Hoashi," presumably the Japanese Socialist Party politician Hoashi Kei.

35. This information was given to Australian diplomats in Washington by a senior official responsible for Korean affairs in the U.S. State Department; see telegram from Australian Embassy, Washington, to External Affairs, Canberra, November 3, 1959; telegram from Australian Embassy, Washington, to External Affairs, Canberra, November 13, 1959, in Australian National Archives, series A3092, control symbol 221/12/5/5/2, part 1, Japan–South Korea Relations.

36. See letter from Inoue to Gallopin, February 19, 1958, and letter from Inoue to Gallopin, April 18, 1958, both in ICRC Archives B AG 232 105-006.04, La résolution no. 20 de la Conférence internationale de la Croix-Rouge à New-Delhi, le regroupement des familles dispersées, le problème de la liberation et du rapatriement des détenus Coréens au Japon, 13.11.1957–03.07.1958; also "Re: Reunion of dispersed families," memo attached to letter from Gallopin to Inoue, March 31, 1958, in B AG 232 105–006. Coursier reassures the authorities in Tokyo that "the New Delhi Resolution only indicates a wish. The Resolution urges governments to intensify their efforts for humanitarian reasons. It could no more be mandatory than the Universal Declaration of Human Rights itself which, as Mr. Inoue rightly remarks, should be interpreted in the light of the two final articles concerning the duties of individuals. In the last analysis,

individuals, in exercising their rights must not thereby prejudice the rights of other individuals or communities."

37. *Chōsensōren*, September 21, 1958; *Korea* 40, 1959, p. 26.

38. Memo re: call on Messrs Satoshi Kurisaka and Nobuo Miyamoto, Section 2–Koreans, of the Public Peace Investigation Bureau, Hyogo District, August 24, 1960, by Max Zeller, ICRC Archives, B AG 232 105-017, Problème du rapatriement des Coréens du Japon, dossier IX: Géneralités concernant l'année 1960, deuxième partie, 12.04.1960–21.12.1960.

39. ICRC Archives, B AG 232 105-017, Problème du rapatriement des Coréens du Japon, dossier XIV: Géneralités concernant l'année 1960, deuxième partie, 12.04.1960–21.12.1960.

40. "Information for Judgment of North Korean Situation," English translation of report by the Japanese Ministry of Foreign Affairs, sent to the British Foreign Office by British Embassy, Tokyo, August 2, 1961, in British National Archives, file no. FO 371-158554.

41. "Note no. 66 to ICRC Geneva," ICRC Archives, B AG 232 105-018.01.

CHAPTER 3

Acknowledgments: I thank mothers from the T-1 Korean School, who allowed me to share in part of their lives and offered me invaluable information and insights. I am indebted to Dr. Hesung Chun Koh, who organized the panel on the Korean diaspora for the Association for Asian Studies meeting in March 2005, at which this paper was originally presented. I also wish to thank Dr. Do Hyun Han, who chaired the panel and offered valuable comments. A slightly different version of this paper was later presented in the "Gender in East Asia" seminar at Swarthmore College, and I am indebted to Dr. Aya Ezawa for her hospitality and helpful comments and suggestions. I wish to acknowledge Marc Epstein of *l'Express*, who interviewed me for an article—the conversation with him made me realize many aspects of the current situation faced by Koreans in Japan that I had not previously considered. I am indebted to Youngmi Lim, who drew my attention to the work of Han Tonghyun, and to Han Tonghyun, for conversation that gave me new angles for thinking about Koreans in Japan.

1. For critical updates with regard to the negotiation between North Korea and Japan, see for example McCormack (2005) and International Crisis Group report (2005).

2. As I discuss later in this chapter, since its foundation in 1955 Chongryun has consistently and tirelessly supported North Korea, functioning almost as the latter's representative or liaison office in Japan.

3. "Japanese Marriages Falling Victim to 'Yongfluenza,'" *Crisscross News Japan*, July 17, 2004; "Women Swarm Narita for Arrival of 'Yon-sama,'" *Japan Times*, November 26, 2004; "10 Women Hurt While Jostling for Glimpse of 'Yon-sama,'" *Japan Times*, November 27, 2004; and Kaku (2005). See also Ryang (2006a: ch. 4).

4. Marc Epstein of *L'Express* estimates that Chongryun has about 100,000 affiliates as opposed to a total of about 400,000 affiliates of Mindan, the South Korea-supporting organization (Epstein 2005). One needs to remember that the number of affiliates does not denote the number of "North Koreans" (i.e., those Koreans who do not have South Korean nationality) in Japan (for more on this topic, see the introduction to this volume).

5. In the past decade or so, scholars of Koreans in Japan (myself included) have tended to focus heavily on internal matters—power relations, gender relations, ethnic identity, and so on—inside the Korean community itself, thereby blurring our vision of Japanese society itself as a receptacle for the Korean community. In this chapter I wish to propose a corrective, or at least an addendum. The attention to intracommunity affairs was a reaction to an earlier dominant trend (see Lee and De Vos 1981 for a classic study) that represented Koreans in Japan as collectively oppressed, dehumanized, and therefore hopeless. This view reduced them to a faceless mass while obscuring internal stratification, unequal gender relations, and uneven power relations within the community.

6. The suppression of the League of Koreans was the first application of the Subversive Activities Prevention Law in postwar Japan, the next being against Aum Supreme Truth in the 1990s.

7. The fiercest clash was recorded in April 1948 in Kobe, where three Koreans were killed and martial law declared. See Kim (1997), Koshiro (1999), and Inokuchi (2000).

8. Epstein (2005). This is a considerable decline. As of the late 1980s, a total of about 20,000 out of 150,000 Korean students in Japan attended some 150 Chongryun schools (Fukuoka 1993: 55).

9. For example, in 2004, through the Internet, the memo entitled "A Proposal for Reform and Resurrection of Chongryun in the Twenty-first Century" was circulated. Although the content of the circular was nothing radical, the fact that it was carried on the mass-accessible media (Internet) offended the Chongryun leadership immensely. Also, the fact that the author was then an active Chongryun officer did not please the leadership, either.

10. Reports abound in recent Japanese media about Chongryun's illegal activities and courtroom defeats. See, for example, "Court Axes Tax Cuts for Chongryun Hall" (2006), "Police Search Chongryun Affiliate over '80 Abduction"(2006), "Pro-Pyongyang Group Searched" (2006), and "Sin Guan-Su's North Korean Spy Ring under Investigation" (2006). The real extent of what Chongryun did or did not do with regard to the North Korean abductions or illegal transactions is hard to determine, not least because of media sensationalism..

11. Japan's crime rate has been reported to have dramatically increased over the past decade. See the reports by Curtin (2004), "Japan's Crime Rate on Rise" (2002), and "Japan's Crime Rate Soars" (2001), for example.

12. On "comfort women," see, for example, Choi (1997), Suzuki (1993, 1996), Kim and Yang (1995), Kurahashi (1994), Yamada (1991), Nishino (1992), and Yoshimi (2002).

13. This is, of course, not to say that all Japanese are indifferent to the situation of Koreans in Japan. For example, a letter to the *Asahi* editor from a housewife in Yamaguchi prefecture shows candid and sincere sympathy with the current difficulty faced by Koreans in Japan (Kitano 2005). Also, in light of a serious financial crisis imposed by the Tokyo metropolitan government on a Korean school in Kōtō ward, Tokyo, the oldest Korean school in Tokyo, Japanese neighbors and friends of the school, along with experts such as attorneys, came to its support in filing a lawsuit against the metropolitan government (Otake 2005). Such stories of local and individual support, solidarity, and empathy continue to be found, though diminishing in scale.

14. Defenders of Article Nine are also increasing. See "Grass-Roots Defenders of Article 9 on the Rise" (2006).

15. Informally, I have noticed lately that some readers of my work on Chongryun complain that I criticize the Japanese government but am silent about North Korean totalitarianism. Such comments reveal the unproblematic elision of Chongryun and North Korea, which is naïve to say the least, while also implying that one government's vice can be canceled out by another's equal vice, which is an obfuscation of justice.

16. For an example of one of the earliest Western reactions, see the Bush White House briefing, "Press Briefing on North Korea Missile Launch" (2006).

17. Interestingly, many reports erroneously identified non–South Korean nationality holders as "North Korean nationals" (for example "Japan Penalizing N. Korean Nationals" 2006).

CHAPTER 4

Acknowledgments: I would like to thank all my informants for sharing their experience, and the Toyota Foundation (2000–2001; Grant D00-A-509) and the Matsushita International Foundation (1999–2000; Grant 98–678) for generous funding that made my fieldtrips to Japan possible. I am grateful to Sonia Ryang and John Lie for organizing the 2005 conference on the Korean diaspora at UC Berkeley; to Stephen Steinberg, Robert Sauté, and the Korean diaspora conference participants; and to anonymous reviewers for commenting on earlier versions. Sonia Ryang's suggestions were of immense help in revising subsequent drafts. An earlier version was presented at the 2006 meeting of the American Sociological Association.

1. The names of interviewees have been changed to protect their privacy. Following their preferences, I have assigned them Korean- or Japanese-pronounced pseudonyms, where appropriate.

2. I use the slightly awkward expression "Japanese of colonial Korean descent" to refer to naturalized Koreans, as there is no better explanatory term. It also helps distinguish them from those Japanese whose family is of precolonial Korean origin, for example, the descendants of the Korean artisans brought to Japan by Toyotomi Hideyoshi in the sixteenth century.

3. Mika refers to a *zainichi* e-mail group, which she joined briefly.

4. In parallel, Koreans share an identical idea of authentic Koreanness. The responses to the influx of foreign workers in both Japan and South Korea are strikingly similar in that both governments privileged workers of Japanese and South Korean descent, respectively.

5. I shall describe six "rooted" individual cases in this chapter, adopting Paul Gilroy's use of roots and routes (1993)—"roots" meaning origins, lineage, or place, to which the imported Japanese word, *rūtsu*, refers. Canonical thinking on diaspora, epitomized in this catchy homonymic phrase, includes an unclear point of reference. For Clifford, "routes/roots" refers to an argument that "specific histories, tactics, everyday practices of dwelling and traveling: traveling-in-dwelling and dwelling-in-traveling" must be considered in comparative cultural studies (Clifford 1997: 36). Gilroy's use carries a slightly different meaning. The term "roots" for Gilroy means cultural and ethnic roots, or origin, while the notion of settling down, which is Clifford's roots as dwelling, is specified as "rootedness" (Gilroy 1993: 111–112). In Gilroy's writing, the term "roots" implies authentic and thus sufficient background and location (cf. Gilroy 1993: 116–117). However, "routes" implies travel, migration, displacement, and movement in general, and as such is the same use as Clifford's (Gilroy 1993: chs. 3, 4). A lack of roots, according to Gilroy, becomes a problem only after *national* consciousness emerges in the black diaspora (112). For Gilroy ethnicity is "an infinite process of identity construction" (223) and therefore a lack of roots need not entail negative consequences. Gilroy is skeptical of nationalist movements and their derivative desires for rootedness and meaningfulness attached to the search of authentic ethnic roots. Particular types of racism, which alienate blacks from collective history and culture, dangerously transform identity politics into a romanticized worship of authentic culture associated only with a place of origin traceable through lineage.

6. My use of the term "post-stateless" derives from an intention to question a notion of *zainichi* statelessness that is too closely associated with legal status. Simultaneously, I am skeptical of a rather celebrated stateless condition linked with the obscuring of national boundaries by globalization and transnationalism (see, for example, the critiques in Ang 2001 and 2003; Foner 2001; Friedman 2002; Lie 2005; and Waldinger and Fitzgerald 2004). Although naturalized Japanese of Korean descent are post-stateless in a legal sense, they are still within the confinement of the nation-state.

7. The annual figure has almost doubled since the 1990s, after *zainichi* legal status attained an unprecedented stability.

8. The Chinese characters constituting the term *kika* mean "return" and "transform." *Kika*'s etymology, adapted from ancient Chinese literature, conveys a notion of shift in moral allegiance; it is a de facto conversion.

9. Race and ethnicity are both socially constructed. Ethnicity—or "ethnicities," when expressing intragroup heterogeneity (Hall 1996 [1989]: 445)—is an increasingly preferred term because of the "biological unity" of human beings (Lie 2001: 2). In everyday language, race is mistaken for biological distinctions and ethnicity for culture, with individuals accepting both concepts

predominantly based on their parental lineage. In the United States, race is generally an imposed label attached to stigmatized lineages, whereas ethnicity is an expressive identification (Sanjek 1994; Song 2003; Waters 1999). Modern Japan provides a case where race can also be the basis of ideological supremacy (Yoshino 1992), even if it is often a residual category, materialized by the presence of allegedly inferior others (Weiner 1997).

10. Clifford defines the attributes of diaspora, following William Safran, as "a history of dispersal, myths/memories of the homeland, alienation in the host (bad host?) country, desire for eventual return, ongoing support of the homeland, and a collective identity importantly defined by this relationship" (Clifford 1997: 247). For Clifford, Safran's model is based on the strong identification with (the return to) the homeland (the classic/phylogeny model in Ryang's typology) and thus "centered" and teleological. See also Agnew (2005: 3–4) for the emphasis on shared history, both of displacement and suffering, and of adaptation and resistance.

11. Suzuki, in her study comparing the Korean diaspora in Japan and the United States, claims: "The focus on two diasporic groups, which are supposed to share a common cultural and ethnic origin, allows me to control the effect of culture, and to investigate how other factors, especially external factors affected their adaptation patterns" (2003: 309–310). I find the view to see "cultural and ethnic origin" as an essentialized component of diasporic groups, as does Suzuki, problematic. Sasaki (2003: ch. 8) has an interesting exploration of Chinese migrants to Japan via South Korea, although his conceptualization of diasporic seems overdependent on physical displacement.

12. See Asakawa (2003), Harajiri (1998), Kashiwazaki (2000a), Kuraishi (2000a), Sasaki (2003), Sugihara (1993), Takenoshita (2000) and Tai (2000, 2004).

13. Neither group currently exists. *Minzokumei o torimodosu kai* dissolved in 1994, and *Paramu no kai* discontinued their monthly meetings around 2000 (personal communication).

14. In Sagisawa Megumu's short story *Kokyō no haru* (Spring at home), the *zainichi* South Korean protagonist Kang-I-Sa describes his past as *nanchatte nihonjin* (pretended Japanese). Kang-I-Sa was formerly known as Kyōyama Eiji, his Japanese alias. However, the first character of his Japanese family name, Kyōyama, reveals Koreanness, and his family's pretended Japaneseness is thus dubious (Sagisawa 2004: 118). Kang-I-Sa's father, a native speaker of Japanese, named him based on the Japanese pronunciation of Chinese characters that resulted in a very unthinkable, strange Korean name, when the characters are pronounced in Korean. He then preferred his Korean name precisely because of this unusualness. His Korean name reflects his *zainichi*, neither Korean nor Japanese, identity. Although Mika had not read Sagisawa's work and her description of being a *nanchatte zainichi* is coincidental, her use of *nanchatte zainichi* and Sagisawa's protagonist's use of *nanchatte nihonjin* share a blurring but unbreakable gap between the authentic and the quotidian meanings attached to a group category.

15. Whether or not the employer prefers her Japanese name use is uncertain, for Fumiko never tried bringing up the issue at contract renewal meetings.

16. Doraemon is an animated character popular in Japan.

17. *Dōwa* is a bureaucratic euphemism referring to the issues of the Burakumin, Japan's outcaste minority.

18. Gilroy (2000: 6), in keeping with his vehement critique of "ethnic absolutism," proposes abandoning "race thinking." Racial categories are inadequate if too strong an association with phenotype or color persists. My concern with the race question is its invisibility when racial concepts are materialized in lineage.

19. Diaspora and diasporic identity formations have been critiqued along several dimensions in terms of, first, directions of migratory movement and political commitment, second, double-edged implications, and, finally, identity options. See Siu (2001), Ang (2001, 2003), and Song (2003) for each dimension.

CHAPTER 5

1. *Kinemajunpō* 1450 (Feb. 2006): 67.

2. *Kinemajunpō* 1350 (Feb. 2002): 38.

3. On the background of the 1994 nuclear crisis, see Kang (1995). For the influence of the 1998 missile issue on *zainichi* life, see, for example, Chōsenjin gakusei ni taisuru jinken shingai chōsai jinkai (1998).

4. The literature on the repatriation of *zainichi* to North Korea is very limited, but recently important contributions have begun to appear. See, for example, Kim and Takayanagi (1995), Ryang (1997a), Okonogi (2004), and Takasaki and Pak (2005). Tessa Morris-Suzuki has been especially energetic in researching the historical background on this issue in the 1950s. See Morris-Suzuki (2005) and chapter 2 in this volume.

5. Director: Izutsu Kazuyuki; script: Uhara Daisuke and Izutsu Kazuyuki; actors: Takaoka Sōsuke (An-Seong), Onoue Hiroyuki (Jaedeugi), Shioya Shun (Kōsuke), and Numajiri Erika (Kyeong-Ja); 119 minutes.

6. Director: Yukisada Isao; script: Kudō Kankurō; actors: Kubozuka Yōsuke (Sugihara), Shibasaki Kō (Sakurai), Hosoyamada Takahito (Jeong-Il); 122 minutes.

7. The author of *Go*, Kazuki Kaneshiro, born in 1968, said in an interview: "When I received the film offer for *Go*, I requested that they recruit a director in their thirties, just like me. Older generations would make a much too serious film when given the theme of *zainichi*" (Kudō 2003: 145). Eventually, Yukisada Isao, born in 1968, was recruited as the director.

CHAPTER 6

Acknowledgments: I wish to express my gratitude to Sonia Ryang for her detailed and constructive comments on earlier drafts. I would also like to thank Ken Haig and participants in the workshop at Berkeley in 2005, in particular Aihwa Ong, for their valuable comments and suggestions.

1. This phrase is found in the pamphlet issued by Gaikikyō (Gaitōhō mondai to torikumu zenkoku kirisutokyō renraku kyōgikai; the National Christian Conference for the Discussion of Problems of the Alien Registration Law) to call for the enactment of The Basic Law for Foreign Residents (Gaikikyō 1998). The same or similar slogans have been adopted by other organizations, too. Gaikikyō has worked for the advancement of the status of *zainichi* Koreans in Japanese society. See more in the text.

2. In this chapter the term *zainichi Koreans* refers to ethnic Koreans who, or whose family members, settled in Japan during or soon after the end of Japan's colonial rule of Korea. The term is fairly widely used in Japan, with some variations such as *zainichi Korian* and *zainichi kankoku chōsenjin*. See Sonia Ryang's introduction to this volume for more on the terminology surrounding *zainichi*.

3. Notable exceptions are the Ainu and Okinawans, to whom the *gaikokujin* category does not apply in the absence of *gaikoku* (foreign country) associated with them.

4. In everyday Japanese language, *gaijin* is frequently used to refer to Westerners (i.e., Europeans and North Americans), while *gaikokujin* tends to denote non-Western, non-Japanese persons from other parts of Asia, Africa, the Americas, and so on.

5. See, for example, John Lie's account of the reaction of the Japanese toward his foreign nationality (Lie 2001: 48).

6. A collection of interviews with *zainichi* Korean youth (Fukuoka 2000) includes a number of instances in which members of the majority population associate an ethnic Korean name with the person's foreigner status.

7. International law is understood as "a system of rules and principles that govern the international relations between sovereign states" (Dixon 1990: 2).

8. The Japanese translation of the term "citizen" can be either *kokumin* (literally "national-people") or *shimin* ("city-people"). In developing local incorporation programs, local governments in Japan have deliberately used the term *shimin* to include foreign nationals (Tegtmeyer Pak 2006: 85).

9. On the historical background of the codification of the law, see Kashiwazaki (1998).

10. This is not to say that Japan lacked a concept of foreigners before. In the early Meiji period, one's nationality status was determined and expressed in terms of *bungen*, or legal affiliation with a state (Kamoto 2001).

11. This means that they were treated as Japanese nationals by other countries when traveling abroad. For instance, Korean "picture brides" going to Hawai'i first had to obtain a Japanese passport before applying for a visa at the American consulate (Patterson 2000: 90)

12. In Manchuria, Chinese authorities encouraged naturalization by Koreans but in the 1920s introduced a stricter approach by making it conditional on cultural assimilation (Xu 2004; Park 2005: 112–116).

13. See Asano (2004) on the function of family registry in the overall legal system that governed colonial rule.

14. The majority of foreign nationals in prewar Japan were Chinese, who were more often called as such (*chūgokujin*) rather than the more general term *gaikokujin*. Though smaller in population, Westerners represented the image of "typical foreigners." Some of them served as advisers to the Meiji government, while others engaged in trade and commerce in port cities.

15. The "ethnocultural conception of nationhood" is an expression introduced by Brubaker to characterize the case of Germany (Brubaker 1992).

16. On the administrative practice of naturalization up to the 1970s, see Kim (1990).

17. On the role of censuses and maps in the formation of national identity, see Anderson (1991: Ch.10) and Kertzer and Arel (2002: 31–34).

18. "Nationality clause" [*kokusekijōkō*] refers to a clause in a law or an administrative rule that limits eligibility for a given program, position, and so on to Japanese nationals only.

19. Although the League of Koreans, the largest Korean organization, initially demanded voting rights for Koreans, by 1948 it withdrew the demand and turned to focus on civil rights for foreign nationals (Pak 1989: 129).

20. Nakayama (1995: 253), my translation. The Association was originally established in 1965 and then reorganized in 1972. Its membership consisted of teachers in Osaka city's public school system, with several principals filling the ranks of directors. This passage was in response to the criticism that to apply generic words like *gaikokujin* to Koreans would only dilute the past crime committed by imperial Japan and represents a lack of historical perspective.

21. However, Ōnuma was also one of the earliest intellectuals to question the validity of the axiom. He has suggested the need for *zainichi* Koreans to explore the option of obtaining Japanese nationality as of right (Ōnuma 1993).

22. As of 2007, approximately 430,000 Korean nationals held special permanent resident status that is given to colonial migrants and their descendants (Japan Ministry of Justice, and Japan Immigration Association 2008). Both aging in the community and the acquisition of Japanese nationality have contributed to the attrition of Koreans from this category.

23. After 1985, children who were born to an intermarried couple obtained Japanese nationality at birth if one parent was a Japanese national. By the mid-1980s, the proportion of Korean-Japanese intermarriages had risen to over 70 percent of the total number of registered marriages involving Korean nationals in Japan (Morita 1996: 179).

24. Nearly half of the respondents chose a term with the prefix *zainichi*, such as *zainichi kankokujin*. Being affiliated with an ethnic organization, the respondents were expected to have a stronger tie with the *zainichi* Korean community and hence stronger Korean ethnic identity compared with those who did not.

25. Tai (2006) discusses how these two groups have transformed and reoriented their activism with the arrival of newcomers.

26. Materials are published on Mindan's Web site: http://www.mindan.org/

sidemenu/sm_sansei27.php (accessed July 30, 2006). As of the early 1990s, the total number of local authorities was approximately 3,300, but in recent years the numbers of towns and villages have decreased due to annexations.

27. The network issued a "Communiqué of Citizens of a Multinational and Multi-Ethnic Society for the Suffrage of all Long-Term Foreign Residents in Japan" in February 2005.

28. On the basis of this and other proposals, a group of NGOs published a document entitled *Zainichi NGO teigen* (A policy proposal compiled by NGOs concerned with *zainichi* Korean issues) and called for the enactment of the basic law concerning *zainichi* Koreans (Tanaka 2002: 57–61).

29. Tei (2001), for example, makes a provocative suggestion that *zainichi* Koreans are heading toward extinction as they cling to foreign nationality.

30. Respondents consisted of 204 "old-timers" (mostly *zainichi* Koreans but also ethnic Chinese) and 762 newcomers. Responses from the former group turned out to be close to the average, with 25.4 percent answering that they had experienced discrimination in their housing search.

31. See Tegtmeyer Pak (2000) and Kashiwazaki (2003) on the relationship between the Japanese government's internationalization plan and the development of integration programs at the municipal level.

32. Examples include Osaka city's Basic Guidelines for Foreign Resident Policy (1998) and Toyonaka city's Basic Guidelines for Promoting Internationalization: living together and working together for local-level internationalization (2000). The latter, despite its title, mostly concerns settled resident foreigners.

33. Some local governments in the Kansai area (western Japan) had launched another type of consultative committee earlier, in the early 1990s. Members consist of both representatives of foreign residents and Japanese persons representing academics and local citizens' groups.

34. See Han (2004) for a critical evaluation of the assemblies in Kawasaki and Kanagawa.

35. Data on local referenda compiled by Mindan headquarters; see http://mindan.org/sidemenu/sm_sansei28.php (accessed July 30, 2006).

36. Japan Ministry of Internal Affairs and Communications (2006).

CHAPTER 7

Acknowledgments: The author thanks Tessa Morris-Suzuki, Aihwa Ong, Sonia Ryang, Mark Sawyer, and two anonymous reviewers for their comments and suggestions, and Kyle Choi for research assistance.

1. Japanese citizenship policies are based on the principle of citizenship by descent; therefore, native-born foreign residents do not automatically qualify for citizenship.

2. This number includes both foreign-born and native-born Korean Americans, as well as those who selected more than one race, and is thus not significantly higher than the total number of Koreans in Japan, which is roughly

one million if we include naturalized Koreans as well as recent immigrants from South Korea. The three largest Asian American groups were Chinese, Filipinos, and Asian Indians in 2000.

3. The proportion of naturalized citizens among the foreign population of Japan is about 19 percent. Only 1 percent of the total foreign population naturalized in 2000 (Japan Ministry of Justice 2000–2003, SOPEMI 2001–2002).

4. Both Japan and the United States require five years of continuous residence, but in the United States that requirement must be met as a permanent resident.

5. The official naturalization requirements do not betray the unofficial emphasis on cultural assimilation. Naturalization applicants must meet the following requirements: (1) five years of continuous residence; (2) a history of good behavior and conduct; (3) must never have attempted the overthrow of the Japanese Constitution or government, either individually or as a member of a group; (4) must be able to support him/herself financially; (5) must be willing to give up existing nationality or be without any nationality; and (6) must be at least 20 years of age.

6. Examples of these questions are: "What is your position on the statement that a wife should belong to her husband and that he can beat her if she isn't obedient?" "What do you think about parents forcibly marrying off their children?" "Do you think that such marriages are compatible with human dignity?" See Rothstein (2006).

7. Nevertheless, because these rights are not guaranteed, foreign residents are vulnerable to cutbacks based on the political climate.

8. There is little evidence to suggest that Japanese authorities heeded these directives. Given the fact that Jim Crow laws in the U.S. Army did not officially come to an end until 1951, the Occupation did not provide much of a blueprint for racial tolerance.

9. The Japanese imperial government classified colonial subjects, including those in Taiwan and Korea, as Japanese nationals and, in 1925, passed a universal manhood suffrage act that allowed male colonial subjects living on the mainland of Japan to vote in Japanese elections.

10. Korea was called *chōsen* by the Japanese until Korea's liberation from Japan.

11. This shift was also due in part to changes in the configuration of power in the United States. The Republicans established majorities in both the Senate and the House of Representatives in 1946 (despite Harry Truman's election to the presidency), which was shortly followed by the domination of McCarthyism in American politics.

12. The first large-scale wave of Korean immigration to the United States occurred between 1903 and 1905, during which time more than 7,200 Koreans arrived in Hawai'i to work on sugar plantations. Korean immigration came to an abrupt halt in 1905, when the Japanese government, having established a protectorate in Korea following the Russo-Japanese War (1904–5), pressured the Korean government to suspend Korean emigration to the United States.

Not only did Japanese authorities seek to protect the position of Japanese workers in Hawai'i, but they also aimed to avert the escalation of anti-Japanese sentiments on the mainland by preventing Japanese in Hawai'i from moving to California (Patterson 1984).

13. The Japanese government granted exit permits to young Korean women, so-called picture brides, in order to quell the political activities of overseas Koreans, most of whom were male. As a result, more than a thousand Korean women immigrated to Hawai'i and the U.S. mainland between 1910 and 1924 (Houchins and Houchins 1976: 140).

14. For example, in 1940, the total Korean-American population numbered only 8,568, compared to 106,334 Chinese Americans, 285,115 Japanese Americans, and 98,535 Filipino Americans (Hing 1993).

15. The Kundan was disbanded in 1917 because of financial difficulties. Pak Yeong-Man was assassinated during a visit to China by a fellow Korean in 1928. Pak's supporters accused Syngman Rhee of hiring an assassin to kill Pak in order to monopolize the financial network of the Korean communities in Hawai'i and the U.S. mainland (Lyu 1977a: 74).

16. Houchins and Houchins (1976: 149) maintain that the Heungsadan was not an active political organization, as most of its members belonged to the Korean National Association.

17. Rhee earned a Ph.D. in political science at Princeton University in 1910.

18. The United Korean Committee of America was formed eight months before the attack on Pearl Harbor as an umbrella organization representing nine major Korean-American organizations and chaired by Syngman Rhee.

19. For example, by 1969, 1,247 of the total 1,507 Koreans who immigrated to the United States in 1960, or 82.7 percent, had naturalized (H.-c. Kim 1977: table 5, p. 118). The high rates of naturalization by Korean immigrants from 1959 to 1971 were in part due to the large numbers of spouses and children of U.S. citizens who immigrated to the United States after the Korean War and who were thus eligible to naturalize using special provisions. In addition, half of all Koreans who naturalized between 1965 and 1981 were spouses of U.S. citizens (Barkan 1992, Abelmann and Lie 1995: 58).

20. In addition, Korean Americans had one of the highest interethnic marriage rates in Hawai'i in the 1960s: 80 percent for Koreans compared to 40 percent for Hawai'i's other ethnic groups (Kitano and Kawanishi 1994: 111, M. H. Jo 1999).

21. Neil Gotanda (2001: 80) refers to the process of "citizenship nullification" in reference to instances in which citizenship rights have been compromised as a result of the "implicit link between an Asiatic racial category and foreignness."

22. This is an argument that I develop further in another work (Chung 2009).

23. During this time, the total foreign population in Japan more than doubled, from about 850,000 in 1985 to 1.97 million in 2004.

References

"10 Women Hurt While Jostling for Glimpse of 'Yon-sama.'" 2004. *Japan Times*, November 27. http://search.japantimes.co.jp/print/news/nn11-2004/nn20041127a7.htm (accessed February 14, 2006).

Abelmann, Nancy, and John Lie. 1995. *Blue Dreams: Korean Americans and the Los Angeles Riots*. Cambridge, Mass.: Harvard University Press.

Abramson, Larry. 2006. "Q&A: The NSA's Domestic Eavesdropping Program." National Public Radio, May 17. http://www.npr.org/templates/story/story.php?storyId=5187738 (accessed August 12, 2006).

Ager, Alastair. 1999. "Perspectives on the Refugee Experience." In A. Ager (ed.), *Refugees: Perspectives on the Experience of Forced Migration*. London: Continuum.

Agnew, Vijay. 2005. "Introduction." In V. Agnew (ed.), *Diaspora, Memory, and Identity: A Search for Home*. Toronto: University of Toronto Press.

Alba, Richard, and Victor Nee. 2003. *Remaking the American Mainstream: Assimilation and Contemporary Immigration*. Cambridge, Mass.: Harvard University Press.

Alexander, Jeffrey C. 2001. "Theorizing the 'Modes of Incorporation': Assimilation, Hyphenation, and Multiculturalism as Varieties of Civil Participation." *Sociological Theory* 19 (3): 237–249.

Ancheta, Angelo N. 1998. *Race, Rights, and the Asian American Experience*. New Brunswick, N.J.: Rutgers University Press.

Anderson, Benedict. 1991. *Imagined Communities: Reflections on the Origin and Spread of Nationalism*. Rev. ed. London: Verso.

Ang, Ien. 2001. *On Not Speaking Chinese: Living Between Asia and the West*. London: Routledge.

———. 2003. "Together-in-Difference: Beyond Diaspora, into Hybridity." *Asian Studies Review* 27 (2): 141–154.

Anonymous. 1996. Letter to the Enemy Property Control Office from a Korean resident in a government-controlled apartment house, Pusan, July 10, 1947.

In *F. E. Gillette pogoseo* [F. E. Gillette written reports], vol. 1. Seoul: Institute of Asian Cultural Studies, Hallym University.

Arendt, Hannah. 1958. *The Origins of Totalitarianism*. New York: Harcourt & Brace.

Asakawa, Akihiro. 2003. *Zainichi gaikokujin to kikaseido* [Resident foreigners in Japan and the naturalization administration]. Tokyo: Shinkansha.

Asano, Toyomi. 2004. "Shokuminchi deno jōyakukaisei to nihonteikoku no hōtekikeisei: Zokujin tekini kiteisareta 'tan'i hōritsu kankei' to 'kyōtsūhō' no kinō o chūshin ni" [Revision of treaties in colonies and the legal formation of imperial Japan: Focusing on the application of the personal principle in "legislation units" and "coordinating law"]. In T. Asano and T. Matsuda (eds.), *Shokuminchi teikoku Nihon no hōteki kōzō* [The legal structure of Japan's colonial empire]. Tokyo: Shinzansha.

Ashida, Hitoshi. 1992. *Ashida Hitoshi nikki* [Ashida Hitoshi diary]. Vol. 6. Tokyo: Iwanami shoten.

Baldwin, Frank. 1969. "The March First Movement: Korean Challenge and Japanese Response." Ph.D. diss., Columbia University.

Banno, Junji. 2001. *Democracy in Pre-War Japan : Concepts of Government, 1871–1937: Collected Essays*. Andrew Fraser, trans. London: Routledge.

———. 2004. *Shōwashi no ketteiteki shunkan* [Decisive moments in Showa history]. Tokyo: Chikumashobō.

Barkan, Elliott Robert. 1992. *Asian and Pacific Islander Migration to the United States: A Model of New Global Patterns*. Westport, Conn.: Greenwood.

Benninghoff, H. Merrell. 1945. "Draft Statement Prepared for President Truman (15 September 1945)." In *Foreign Relations United States: Korea*, vol. 6. Washington, D.C.: U.S. Department of State.

Brown, Cecil. 1995. "Correspondence with Major General F. L. Parks, 19 May 1947." In *John R. Hodge munseojip* [John R. Hodge papers] *1945.6–1948.8*, vol. 2. Seoul: Institute of Asian Cultural Studies, Hallym University.

Brubaker, Rogers. 1992. *Citizenship and Nationhood in France and Germany*. Cambridge, Mass.: Harvard University Press.

———. 1997. Review of *Transnational Citizenship: Membership and Rights in International Migration*, by Rainer Baubock. *Ethnic and Racial Studies* 20 (2): 414–415.

Bruce, J. Campbell. 1955. "The Rusted Gate: Politics and Immigration." *The Nation*, November 26: 457–458.

Chan, Sucheng. 1991. *Asian Americans: An Interpretive History*. Boston: Twayne.

Chang, Iris. 1997. *The Rape of Nanking: The Forgotten Holocaust of World War II*. New York: BasicBooks.

Chang, Myeong-Su. 2003. *Bōryaku: Nihon sekijūji kitachōsen "kikokujigyō" no shinsō* [Conspiracy: The truth about the Japan Red Cross's North Korean "repatriation scheme"]. Tokyo: Itsukishobō.

Che, Sunny. 2000. *Forever Alien: A Korean Memoir, 1930–1951*. Jefferson, Mo.: McFarland.
Checkland, Olive. 1994. *Humanitarianism and the Emperor's Japan 1877–1977*. London: St. Martin's Press.
Cheong, Ki-Hae. 1997. *Kikokusen: Kitachōsen tōdo eno tabidachi* [Repatriation boat: A departure for the frozen land, North Korea]. Tokyo: Bungeishunjūsha.
Cheong, Sung-Hwa. 1991. *The Politics of Anti-Japanese Sentiment in Korea: Japanese-South Korean Relations under the American Occupation, 1945–1952*. Westport, Conn.: Greenwood Press.
Chi, Tong-Wook. 1997. *Zainichi o yamenasai*. Tokyo: Za Masada.
Chiba, Yoshihiro. 1989. "Kokusaikashakai ni okeru chihōgyōsei no arikata ni kansuru chōsakenkyū" [A survey on the role of local governance in globalizing society]. *Chihōjichi* 498: 25–41.
Choe, Seog-Ui. 2004. *Zainichi no genfūkei: Rekishi, bunka, hito* [Original landscapes of Japan-based Koreans: History, culture, people]. Tokyo: Akaishi shoten.
Choi, Chungmoo, ed. 1997. *The Comfort Women: Colonialism, War, and Sex. positions: east asia cultures critique* 5 (1) (special issue).
Chon, Wolson. 2006. *Kaikyō no aria* [Aria of the strait]. Tokyo: Shōgakkan.
Chōsenjin gakusei ni taisuru jinken shingai chōsai jinkai [A committee investigating infringements of Korean students' human rights in Japan]. 1998. *Futatabi nerawareta chima chogori* [Korean female school uniforms attacked again]. Tokyo: Zainihon chōsenjin jinkenkyōkai.
Choy, Bong-Yun. 1979. *Koreans in America*. Chicago: Nelson Hall.
Chung, Erin Aeran. 2009. *Citizenship and Immigration in Japan*. New York: Cambridge University Press.
Clifford, James. 1997. *Routes: Travel and Translation in the Late Twentieth Century*. Cambridge, Mass.: Harvard University Press.
Conde, David. 1947. "The Korean Minority in Japan." *Far Eastern Survey* 16 (4): 41–45.
"Court Axes Tax Cuts for Chongryun Hall." 2006. *Japan Times*, February 3. http://search.japantimes.co.jp/print/nn20060203a2.html (accessed April 1, 2006).
"Critical Refugee Situation (26 December 1945)." 1996. In *F. E. Gillette pogoseo* [F. E. Gillette written reports], vol. 1. Seoul: Institute of Asian Cultural Studies, Hallym University.
Cumings, Bruce. 1997. *Korea's Place in the Sun: A Modern History*. New York: Norton.
Curtin, J. Sean. 2004. "In Japan, the Crime Rate Also Rises." *Asia Times*, August 28. http://www.atimes.com/atimes/Japan/FH28Dh01.html (accessed April 2, 2006).
Dai, Suyung. 1996. "A Petition for Rescue of the Refugees, to the Military Governor of Kyong Sang Nam Do (17 December 1946)." In *F. E. Gillette*

pogoseo [F. E. Gillette written reports], vol. 1. Seoul: Institute of Asian Cultural Studies, Hallym University.

Darwish, Mahmoud. 1984. "We Travel Like Other People." In Samih Al-Qasim, Adonis, and Mahmoud Darwish, *Victims of a Map*. London: Al-Saqi Books.

Davis, Christopher. 1999. "Exchanging the African: Meetings at a Crossroads of the Diaspora." *South Atlantic Quarterly* 98 (1–2): 59–82.

Davis, Fred. 1979. *Yearning for Yesterday: A Sociology of Nostalgia*. New York: Free Press.

De Vos, George, and Daekyun Chung. 1981. "Community Life in a Korean Ghetto." In C. Lee and G. De Vos (eds.), *Koreans in Japan: Ethnic Conflict and Accommodation*. Berkeley: University of California Press.

De Vos, George, and Hiroshi Wagatsuma. 1966. *Japan's Invisible Race: Caste in Culture and Personality*. Berkeley: University of California Press.

Deverall, Richard L. G. 1952. *Red Star over Japan*. Calcutta: Temple Press.

Dixon, Martin. 1990. *Textbook on International Law*. London: Blackstone Press.

Du Bois, W. E. B. 1961 [1903]. *The Souls of Black Folk*. Greenwich: Fawcett Publications.

Ebashi, Takashi, ed. 1993. *Gaikokujin wa jūmindesu* [Foreigners are residents]. Tokyo: Gakuyōshobō.

Eckert, Carter. 1991. *Offspring of Empire: The Koch'ang Kims and the Colonial Origins of Korean Capitalism, 1876–1945*. Seattle: University of Washington Press.

Eggen, Dan, and Walter Pincus. 2006. "Varied Rationales Muddle Issue of NSA Eavesdropping." *Washington Post*, January 27. http://www.washingtonpost.com/wp-dyn/content/article/2006/01/26/AR2006012601990.html (accessed August 12, 2006).

Eltis, David. 2002. "Migration and Agency in Global History." In David Eltis (ed.), *Coerced and Free Migration: Global Perspectives*. Stanford, Calif.: Stanford University Press.

Epstein, Marc. 2005. "Diaspora coréenne: Les oubliés de Kim Il-sung." *L'Éxpress*, July 4. http://www.lexpress.fr/info/monde/dossier/japon/dossier.asp?ida=433872 (accessed February 14, 2006).

Feldblum, Miriam. 1999. *Reconstructing Citizenship: The Politics of Nationality Reform and Immigration in Contemporary France*. Albany: State University of New York Press.

Finn, Richard B. 1949. "Memorandum of Conversation: Koreans in Japan (February 3, 1949)." In *Records of the United States Department of State Relating to the Internal Affairs of Japan, 1945–1949*, reel 15. Tokyo: Japan National Diet Library.

———. 1992. *Winners in Peace: MacArthur, Yoshida, and Postwar Japan*. Berkeley: University of California Press.

Foner, Nancy. 2001. "Immigrant Commitment to America, Then and Now: Myths and Realities." *Citizenship Studies* 5 (1): 27–40.

Friedman, Jonathan. 2002. "From Roots to Routes: Tropes for Trippers." *Anthropological Theory* 2 (1): 21–36.

Fukuoka, Yasunori. 1991. *Dōka to ika no hazamade: Zainichi wakamonosedai no aidentitī kattō* [Between assimilation and dissimilation: Identity conflict among the younger generation Koreans in Japan]. Tokyo: Shinkansha.

———.1993. *Zainichi kankoku chōsenjin: Wakai sedai no aidentiti* [Koreans in Japan: Identity of younger generations]. Tokyo: Chūōkōronsha.

———.2000. *Lives of Young Koreans in Japan.* Tom Gill, trans. Melbourne: Trans Pacific Press.

Fukuoka, Yasunori, and Myungsoo Kim. 1997. *Zainichi kankokujin seinen no seikatsuto ishiki* [Life and consciousness of Korean youth in Japan]. Tokyo: Tokyo daigaku shuppankai.

Fukuoka, Yasunori, and Yukiko Tsujiyama. 1994. *Hontō no watashi o motomete* [In search of true self]. Tokyo: Shinkansha.

Gaikikyō (Gaitōhō mondai to torikumu zenkoku kirisutokyō renraku kyōgikai). 1998. *What Is the "Basic Law for Foreign Residents"?* Tokyo: Gaikikyō.

Gilroy, Paul. 1993. *The Black Atlantic: Modernity and Double Consciousness.* Cambridge, Mass.: Harvard University Press.

———. 2000. *Against Race: Imagining Political Culture Beyond the Color Line.* Cambridge, Mass.: Harvard University Press.

Ginsburg, Faye. 1995. "Production Values: Indigenous Media and the Rhetoric of Self-Determination." In D. Battaglia (ed.), *Rhetorics of Self-Making.* Berkeley: University of California Press.

Gotanda, Neil T. 2001. "Citizenship Nullification: The Impossibility of Asian American Politics." In G.H. Chang (ed.), *Asian Americans and Politics: Perspectives, Experiences, Prospects.* Washington, D.C.: Woodrow Wilson Center Press.

"Grass-Roots Defenders of Article 9 on the Rise." 2006. *Asahi.com.* http://www.asahi.com/english/Herald-asahi/TKY200605030112.html (accessed May 19, 2006).

Hall, Stuart. 1996 [1989]. "New Ethnicities." In D. Morley and K. Chen (eds.), *Stuart Hall: Critical Dialogues in Cultural Studies.* London: Routledge.

Hamamoto, Mariko. 1995. "Hitowa ikanishite mizukaraga umare sodatta basho de ihōjin tariuruka—Zainichi chōsenjin nanori no mondai" [How can a person be a foreigner in his birth place—The question of self-naming of Koreans in Japan]. In T. Nakauchi, N. Nagashima et al. (eds.), *Shakaikihan—tabū to hōshō* [Social norms—Taboo and reward]. Tokyo: Fujiwara shoten.

Han, Seung-Mi. 2004. "From the Communitarian Ideal to the Public Sphere: The Making of Foreigners' Assemblies in Kawasaki City and Kanagawa Prefecture." *Social Science Japan Journal* 7: 41–60.

Han, Tong-Hyeon. 2004a. "Chakui ni yoru esunikku aidentiti no hyōgen to jenda: 'Chima chogori seifuku' tanjō to joseitachi no eijenshi" [The expression of ethnic identity and gender through clothing: The birth of "Korean dress uniforms" and women's agency]. MA thesis, Rikkyō daigaku [Rikkyo University].

———. 2004b. "Chakui ni yoru esunikku aidentiti no hyōgen to jenda: Chima chogori seifuku tanjō o meguru eijenshi to koroniarizumu" [The expression of ethnic identity and gender through clothing: Examining agency and colonialism with reference to the birth of Korean dress uniforms]. In M. Itō (ed.), *Bunka no jissen, bunka no kenkyū* [Cultural practices, cultural studies]. Tokyo: Serikashobō.

———. 2006. *Chima chogori seifuku no minzokushi* [The ethnography of Korean school uniforms]. Tokyo: Sōfūsha.

Harajiri, Hideki. 1998. *"Zainichi" toshiteno korian* [Koreans as "zainichi"]. Tokyo: Kōdansha.

Hayano, Toru. 2004. "Rays of Reform, Shadows of War, Booms and Bashings Characterize the 'Koizumi Era.'" *Asahi.com*, December 29. http://www.asahi.com/column/hayano/eng/TKY200412290126.html (accessed April 1, 2006).

Hing, Bill Ong. 1993. *Making and Remaking Asian America through Immigration Policy, 1850–1990*. Stanford, Calif.: Stanford University Press.

Hodge, John R. 1995. "Conditions in Korea, 13 September 1945." In *John R. Hodge munseojip* [John R. Hodge papers] *1945.6–1948.8*, vol. 3. Seoul: Institute of Asian Cultural Studies, Hallym University.

Hogg, Chris. 2005. "Japan Racism 'Deep and Profound,'" *BBC News*, July 11. http://news.bbc.co.uk/1/hi/world/asia-pacific/4671687.stm (accessed April 2, 2006).

Holland, Suzanne. 2001. "Beyond the Embryo: A Feminist Appraisal of the Embryonic Stem Cell Debate." In S. Holland, K. Lebacqz, and L. Zoloth (eds.), *The Human Embryonic Stem Cell Debate: Science, Ethics, and Public Policy*, Cambridge, Mass.: MIT Press.

Honda, Katsuichi. 1981. *Chūgoku no tabi* [A journey to China]. Tokyo: Asahi shinbunsha.

Horsley, William. 2005. "Korean WWII Sex Slaves Fight On." *BBC News*, August 9. http://news.bbc.co.uk/2/hi/asia-pacific/4749467.stm (accessed February 14, 2006).

Houchins, Lee, and Chang-su Houchins. 1976. "The Korean Experience in America, 1903–1924." In N.J. Hundley (ed.), *The Asian American: The Historical Experience*. Oxford: Clio Books.

"I Grow Young." 1960. *Korea* 49: 32–33.

Ijūren (Ijū rōdōsha to rentai suru zenkoku nettowaku), ed. 2006. *Gaikouseki jūmin tono kyōsei ni mukete: NGO karano seisakuteigen* [Toward co-living with foreign residents: Policy proposals from NGOs]. Tokyo: Gendaijin bunsha.

"In Quest of a New Life." 1960. *Korea* 43: 34–35.

Inokuchi, Hiromitsu. 2000. "Korean Ethnic Schools in Occupied Japan, 1945–52." In S. Ryang (ed.), *Koreans in Japan: Critical Voices from the Margin*. London: Routledge.

International Crisis Group. 2005. "Japan and North Korea: Bones of Contention." *Asia Report* 100, June 27. http://www.crisisgroup.org/home/index.cfm?l=1&id=3533 (accessed February 14, 2006).
"Interview with Returnees from Japan." 1960. *Korea* 46: 7–9.
Io, ed. 2006. *Nihon no nakano gaikokujin gakkō* [Schools for foreigners in Japan]. Tokyo: Akashi shoten.
Ishimaru, Jirō. 2002. *Kitachōsen nanmin* [North Korean refugees]. Tokyo: Kōdansha.
Iwabuchi, Kōichi. 2000. "Political Correctness, Postcoloniality, and the Self-Representation of 'Koreanness' in Japan." In S. Ryang (ed.), *Koreans in Japan: Critical Voices from the Margin*. London: Routledge.
———. 2001. *Toransunashonaru japan: Ajia o tsunagu popyurā karuchā* [Transnational Japan: Popular culture bridging Asia]. Tokyo: Iwanami shoten.
———. 2004. "Hanryū ga zainichi kankokujin ni deautoki" [When Korean boom meets zainichi Koreans]. In T. Mōri (ed.), *Nisshiki hanryū* [Korean boom in Japanese mode]. Tokyo: Serikashobō.
James, Victoria. 2005. "Not Waving, but Suing." *New Statesman*, August 8. http://www.newstatesman.com/200508080012 (accessed April 1, 2006).
Japan Cabinet Office. 1997. "'Jinken kyōiku no tameno kokuren 10-nen' ni kansuru kokunai kōdō keikaku"[Domestic action plan for the UN decade for human rights education]. http://www.kantei.go.jp/jp/singi/jinken/kettei/970704keikaku.html (accessed July 30, 2006).
Japan Ministry of Internal Affairs and Communications. 2006. "A Report of a Study Group on the Promotion of *Tabunka kyōsei*." http://www.soumu.go.jp/s-news/2006/pdf/060307_2_bs1.pdf (accessed July 30, 2006).
Japan Ministry of Justice. [Annual.] *Hōmunenkan* [Ministry of Justice annual yearbook]. Tokyo: Hōmushō.
———. 2004. "Registration of Foreign Residents" *Immigration Bureau*. http://www.moj.gov.jp/ENGLISH/IB/ib-01.html (accessed March 1, 2007).
———. 2007. "Kokuseki-kankei: Kako 10-nenkan no kikakyoka shinseisha sū, kika kyokasha sū tō no suii" [Nationality-related matters: The trends of the annual total of naturalization applied and granted in the past decade]. http://www.moj.go.jp/TOUKEI/t_minjo3.html (accessed October 13, 2008).
———. 2008. "Kōhōshiryō: Heisei 19-nenmatsu genzai ni okeru gaikokujin tōrokusha tōkei ni tsuite" [Public-release reference: On the statistics of the alien registration as of December 31, 2007]. http://www.moj.go.jp/PRESS/080601-1.pdf (accessed October 15, 2008).
Japan Ministry of Justice, and Japan Immigration Association. [Annual.] *Zairyū gaikokujin tōkei* [Statistics on resident foreigners in Japan]. Tokyo: Hōmushō and Nyūkankyōkai.
"Japan Penalizing N. Korean Nationals." 2006. *KBS Global*, August 27. http://english.kbs.co.kr/news/news_print.php?key=2006082707 (accessed August 29, 2006).
"Japanese Marriages Falling Victim to 'Yongfluenza.'" 2004. *Crisscross News*

Japan, July 17. http://www.crisscross.com/jp/shukan/234 (accessed February 14, 2006).
"Japan's Crime Rate on Rise." 2002. *BBC News*, November 19. http://news.bbc.co.uk/1/hi/world/asia-pacific/2490993.stm (accessed April 1, 2006).
"Japan's Crime Rate Soars." 2001. *BBC News*, August 3. http://news.bbc.co.uk/2/hi/asia-pacific/1472175.stm (accessed April 1, 2006).
Jo, Moon H. 1999. *Korean Immigrants and the Challenge of Adjustment*. Westport, Conn.: Greenwood Press.
Johnston, Eric. 2002. "North Koreans Get Little Sympathy in Japan: Pyongyang's Abductions Spell Fallout for Chongryun." *Japan Times*, November 20. http://search.japantimes.co.jp/member/member.html?nn20021120c1.htm (accessed February 14, 2006).
Johnston, William. 2005. *Geisha, Harlot, Strangler, Star: A Woman, Sex, and Morality in Modern Japan*. New York: Columbia University Press.
Jung, Yeong-Hae. 1996. "Aidentitī o koete" [Beyond identity]. In S. Inoue et al. (eds.), *Sabetsu to kyosei no shakaigaku* [Sociology of discrimination and pluralism]. 1–33. Tokyo: Iwanami shoten.
Kaku, Y. 2005. "Senior Style: Going DVD for Yon-sama." *Asahi.com*, January 5. http://www.asahi.com/english/lifestyle/TKY200501150159.html (accessed February 14, 2006).
Kamoto, Itsuko. 2001. *"Kokusaikekkon" no tanjō* [The birth of the "international marriage"]. Tokyo: Shinyōsha.
Kanagawa jichitai no kokusaiseisaku kenkyūkai. 2001. *Kanagawaken gaikokuseki jūmin seikatsujittai chōsa hōkokusho* [A report of a research project on the lives of foreign residents in Kanagawa prefecture]. Yokohama: Kanagawa prefectural government.
Kang, Chol-Hwan. 2002. *The Aquariums of Pyongyang: Ten Years in the North Korean Gulag*. New York: Basic Books.
Kang, Sang-Jung. 1991a. "'Zainichi' no genzai to mirai no aida" [Between present and future of 'zainichi']. In J. Iinuma (ed.), *Zainichi kankoku chōsenjin sono nihonshakai ni okeru sonzaikachi* [Koreans in Japan: Their existential value in Japanese society]. Osaka: Kaifūsha.
———. 1991b. "Hōhō toshiteno 'zainichi'—Yang Tae-Ho shi no hanron ni kotaeru" ['Zainichi' as method—in response to Mr. Yang T'ae-Ho's critique]. In J. Iinuma (ed.), *Zainichi kankoku chōsenjin sono Nihon shakai ni okeru sonzai kachi* [Koreans in Japan: Their existential value in Japanese society]. Osaka: Kaifūsha.
———. 2003. *Nitchō kankei no kokufuku* [Surmounting Japan–North Korea relations]. Tokyo: Shūeisha.
———. 2004. *Zainichi*. Tokyo: Kōdansha.
Kang, Seong. 1995. *Pachinkoto heikito chima chongori: Enshutsusareta chōsenhantō kuraishisu* [Pachinko and weapon and Korean dress: Korean Peninsula crisis produced]. Tokyo: Gakuyūshobō.
Kashiwazaki, Chikako. 1998. "Jus Sanguinis in Japan: The Origin of Citizenship in a Comparative Perspective." *International Journal of Comparative Sociology* 39 (3): 278–300.

———. 2000a. "The Politics of Legal Status: The Equation of Nationality with Ethnonational Identity." In S. Ryang (ed.), *Koreans in Japan: Critical Voices from the Margin*. London: Routledge.

———. 2000b. "To Be Korean without Korean Nationality: Claim to Korean Identity by Japanese Nationality Holders," *Korean and Korean American Studies Bulletin* 11 (1): 48–70.

———. 2003. "Local Government and Resident Foreigners: A Changing Relationship." In S. Furukawa and T. Menju (eds.), *Japan's Road to Pluralism: Transforming Local Communities in the Global Era*. Tokyo: Japan Center for International Exchange.

Kawagoe, Michiko. 2000. "Zainichi no keiken: Hyōmeisareru koshōto keiken o megutte' [The experience of zainichi: On the names and experiences that are represented]. *Korian mainoriti kenkyū* 4: 88–102.

Kermode, D. W. 1946. "Enclosure for Dispatch No. 361 (29 August 1946)." In *Records of the U.S. Department of State Relating to the Internal Affairs of Korea*, vol. 1. Seoul: Areumchulpansa.

Kertzer, David I., and Dominique Arel, eds. 2002. *Census and Identity: The Politics of Race, Ethnicity, and Language in National Censuses*. Cambridge: Cambridge University Press.

Kim, Bu-Ja, and Ching-Ja Yang. 1995. *Motto shiritai "ianfu"mondai: Sei to minzoku no shiten kara* [Let's learn more about the "comfort women" issue: Seen from gender and nation]. Tokyo: Akashi shoten.

Kim, Chan-jung. 1997. *Zainichi korian hyakunenshi* [A hundred-year history of zainichi Koreans]. Tokyo: Sangokan.

Kim, Hyung-chan. 1977. "Some Aspects of Social Demography of Korean Americans." In H.-c. Kim (ed.), *The Korean Diaspora: Historical and Sociological Studies of Korean Immigration and Assimilation in North America*. Santa Barbara, Calif.: ABC-Clio, Inc.

Kim, Il-Myeon. 1978. *Chōsenjin ga naze "Nihon-mei" o nanorunoka: Minzoku ishiki to sabetsu* [Why Koreans use "Japanese names": Ethnic consciousness and discrimination]. Tokyo: Sanichishobō.

Kim, Jackie J. 2005. *Hidden Treasures: Lives of First Generation Korean Women in Japan*. Lanham, Md.: Rowman and Littlefield.

Kim, Lili Meeyoung. 2001. "The Pursuit of Imperfect Justice: The Predicament of Koreans and Korean Americans on the Homefront during World War II." Ph.D. diss., University of Rochester.

Kim, Tae-Gi. 1997. *Sengo Nihon seiji to zainichi chōsenjin mondai* [Postwar Japanese politics and the issue of Koreans in Japan]. Tokyo: Keisōshobō.

Kim, Tae-gyu. 2005. "New individual identification system sought." *The Korea Times*, Feb. 24. http://search.hankooki.com/times/times_view.php?term=new+individual+identification+system+sought++&path=hankooki3/times/lpage/tech/200502/kt2005022420180211800.htm&media=kt (accessed February 14, 2006).

Kim, Tae-Yeong. 1999. *Aidentiti oritikusu o koete* [Beyond identity politics]. Tokyo: Sekaishisōsha.

Kim, Yeong-Dal. 1990. *Zainichi chōsenjin no kika* [The naturalization of Korean residents in Japan]. Tokyo: Akashi shoten.

———. 1996. "Hoshō: Kaisetsu to tōkei no hosoku" [Supplement: Additional explanation and statistics]. In Y. Morita, *Sūji ga kataru zainichi kankoku chōsenjin no rekishi* [A history of Koreans in Japan seen from statistics]. Tokyo: Akashi shoten.

Kim, Yeong-Dal, and Toshio Takayanagi, eds. 1995. *Kitachōsen kikoku jigyō kankei shiryōshū* [Documents on North Korean repatriation]. Tokyo: Shinkansha.

Kim, Yung Gil. 1960. "My First Debut." *Korea* 45: 10–11.

Kitano, Harry H. L., and Yuko Kawanishi. 1994. "Peripheral Effects: Intermarriage." In G. O. I. Totten and H. E. Schockman (eds.), *Community in Crisis: The Korean American Community after the Los Angeles Civil Unrest of April 1992*. Los Angeles: Center for Multiethnic and Transnational Studies, University of Southern California.

Kitano, Keiko. 2005. "Minzoku no kokoro mamoru wakamono mitomeyō" [Let's recognize the young people who are trying to safeguard the nation's heart]. *Asahi shimbun*, February 1: 14.

Koh, Sun Hui. 1995. "'Shin kankokujin' no teijūka: Enerugisshuna gunzō" [Settlement pattern of new Koreans: An energetic image]. In H. Komai (ed.), *Teijūka suru gaikokujin* [Settling foreigners]. Tokyo: Akashi shoten.

Koike, Kiyohiko. 2006. "Point of View: SDF's Iraq Mission Tarnishes Japan's Image." *Asahi.com*, March 21. http://www.asahi.com/english/Herald-asahi/TKY200603210113.html (accessed April 1, 2006).

Kokot, Waltraud, Khachig Tölölyan, and Carolin Alfonso. 2004. "Introduction." In W. Kokot, K. Tölölyan, and C. Alfonso (eds.), *Diaspora, Identity and Religion: New Directions in Theory and Research*. London: Routledge.

Komai, Hiroshi, and Ichirō Watado, eds. 1997. *Jichitai no gaikokujin seisaku* [Foreign resident policy of local governments]. Tokyo: Akashi shoten.

Korean Returnees from Japan. 1960. Pyongyang: Foreign Languages Publishing House.

Koshiro, Yukiko. 1999. *Trans-Pacific Racisms and the U.S. Occupation of Japan*. New York: Columbia University Press.

Kurahashi, Masanao. 1994. *Jūgun ianfu mondai no rekishiteki kenkyū* [A historical study of the comfort women issue]. Tokyo: Kyōeishobō.

Kuraishi, Ichirō. 1996. "Rekishi no naka no 'zainichi chōsenjin aidentiti': Raifu histori kara no ichi kōsatsu" ["Korean identity in Japan" in history: An exploration using life history]. *Soshioroji* 41: 51–67.

———. 2000a. "Katari (naoshi) no jissen toshiteno ningen keisei: Nihon shakai no chōsenjin mainoritī ni okeru 'jiko' no kōsei o megutte" [Building characters through the practice of narrations: The construction of "self" among the Korean minority in Japan]. Ph.D. diss., Kyoto daigaku [Kyoto University].

———. 2000b. "Kyōiku jissen kiroku ni okeru shihaiteki katari no tassei kijo:

Zainichi chōsenjin kyōiku no jissen kiroku no tekisuto bunseki" [Order of the emergence of dominant discourse in the documentation in educational practice: The analysis of documents in educational practice of Koreans in Japan]. *Soshioroji* 45: 73–91.

Lankov, Andrei. 2004. *Crisis in North Korea: The Failure of De-Stalinization.* Honolulu: University of Hawaii Press.

Lee, Changsoo. 1981. "The Period of Repatriation, 1945–1949." In C. Lee and G. De Vos (eds.), *Koreans in Japan: Ethnic Conflict and Accommodation.* Berkeley: University of California Press.

Lee, Changsoo, and George De Vos, eds. 1981. *Koreans in Japan: Ethnic Conflict and Accommodation.* Berkeley: University of California Press.

Lee, Robert G. 1999. *Orientals: Asian Americans in Popular Culture.* Philadelphia: Temple University Press.

Li, Dong Kang. 1960. "They Are All Happy." *Korea* 44: 12–13.

Lie, John. 1995. "The Transformation of Sex Work in Twentieth-Century Korea." *Gender & Society* 9:310–327.

———. 2000. "Imaginary Homeland and Diasporic Realization: *Kikan Sanzenri*, 1975–1987." *Korean and Korean American Studies Bulletin* 11 (1): 11–26.

———. 2001. *Multiethnic Japan.* Cambridge, Mass.: Harvard University Press.

———. 2004. *Modern Peoplehood.* Cambridge, Mass.: Harvard University Press.

———. 2005. "Korean Diasporic Nationalism." Unpublished manuscript.

———. 2008. *Zainichi (Koreans in Japan): Diasporic Nationalism and Postcolonial Identity.* Global, Area, and International Archive, vol. 10. Berkeley: GAIA/University of California Press.

Littlefield, Heather. 2005. "Transgressing the Boundary of Self-Defense: Article 9 and the Evolution of the Japanese Self Defense Forces." *Perspectives* 6 (3). http://www.oycf.org/Perspectives/30_09302005/2d_Littlefield_SDFJapan.pdf (accessed April 1, 2006).

Lyu, Kingsley K. 1977a. "Korean Nationalist Activities in Hawaii and the Continental United States, 1900–1919 (Part I)." *Amerasia Journal* 4 (1): 23–90.

———. 1977b. "Korean Nationalist Activities in Hawaii and the Continental United States, 1919–1945 (Part II)." *Amerasia Journal* 4 (2): 53–100.

Massey, Douglas S., Joaquin Arango, Graeme Hugo, Ali Kouaouci, Adela Pellegrino, and J. Edward Taylor. 1998. *Worlds in Motion: Understanding International Migration at the End of the Millennium.* Oxford: Clarendon Press.

Matsuda, Toshihiko. 1995. *Senzenki no zainichi chōsenjin to sanseiken* [Koreans and voting rights in prewar Japan]. Tokyo: Akashi shoten.

McCarthy, Charles W., Alvin F. Richardson, and Raymond E. Cox. 1992. "State-War-Navy Coordination Committee: Utilization of Koreans in the War Effort (23 April 1945)." In K. Yi (ed.), *Haebang jeonhusa jaryojip* [Documents on pre-liberation and post-liberation history], vol. 1. Seoul: Wonjumunhwasa.

McCormack, Gavan. 2005. "Disputed Bones Fracture Japan-North Korea Relations." *OhmyNews*, April 20. http://english.ohmynews.com/articleview/article_view.asp?menu=c10400&no=221670&rel_no=1 (accessed February 14, 2006).

McNeill, David. 2005. "Japan's Enemy Within: The Shrinking North Korean Community Feels It Is under Siege." *Japan Times*, January 25. http://search.japantimes.co.jp/print/features/life2005/fl20050123zg.htm (accessed August 10, 2005).

———. 2006. "Enemy of the State." *Japan Times*, February 14. http://search.japantimes.co.jp/print/fl20060214zg.html (accessed April 1, 2006).

Minzokumei o torimodosu kai, ed. 1990. *Minzokumei o torimodoshita chōsenjin: Uri irumu* [Koreans who recovered their ethnic names: Our own names]. Tokyo: Akashi shoten.

Miyata Setsuko, Yeong-Dal Kim, and Tae-Ho Yang. 1992. *Sōshi kaimei* [Creating the last name and reforming the first name]. Tokyo: Akashi shoten.

Miyauchi, Hiroshi. 1999. "Watashiwa anatagata no koto o donoyō ni yobeba yoi no darōka? Zainichi kankoku chōsenjin? Zainichi chōsenjin? Zainichi korian? Soretomo?" [How do I address you? Koreans in Japan? *Zainichi* Koreans? Or else?]. *Korian mainoriti kenkyū* 3: 5–28.

Miyazaki, Akira. 1985. "Senryōshoki ni okeru beikoku no zainichi chōsenjin seisaku: Nihon seifu no taiō to tomoni" [The policy for Koreans during the early period of the U.S. occupation of Japan: In connection with the Japanese government's reactions]. *Shisō* 734: 122–139.

Mizuno, Naoki. 2001. "Kokuseki o meguru higashi ajia kankei (East Asian international relations concerning nationality)." In T. Furuya and S. Yamamuro (eds.), *Kindai Nihon ni okeru higashi ajia mondai* [The question of East Asia in modern Japan]. Tokyo: Yoshikawa kōbunkan.

Morita, Yoshio. 1996. *Sūjiga kataru zainichi kankoku chōsenjin no rekishi* [History of Koreans in Japan seen from statistics]. Tokyo: Akashi shoten.

Morris-Suzuki, Tessa. 1998. *Re-inventing Japan: Time, Space, Nation*. Armonk, N.Y.: M. E. Sharpe.

———. 2004. "An Act Prejudicial to the Occupation Forces: Migration Controls and Korean Residents in Post-Surrender Japan." *Japanese Studies* 24 (1): 5–28.

———. 2005. "A Dream Betrayed: Cold War Politics and the Repatriation of Koreans from Japan to North Korea." *Asian Studies Review* 29 (4): 357–380.

———. 2007. *Exodus to North Korea: Under the Shadow of Japan's Cold War*. Lanham, Md.: Rowman & Littlefield.

Murai, Naosaburō. 1945. "High Costs of Foodstuffs in Keijo (Seoul) (23 September 1945)." *Internal Affairs of Korea* 1: 75.

Nabeshima, Keizo. 2006. "The Year of Koizumi's Exit." *Japan Times*, January 1. http://search.japantimes.co.jp/print/eo20060101kn.html (accessed April 1, 2006).

Nakayama, Hideo. 1995. *Zainichi chōsenjin kyōiku kankei shiryō* [Reference materials concerning the education of zainichi Koreans]. Tokyo: Akashi shoten.
Nichibenren. 2004. "Declaration Seeking the Building of a Harmonious Multiethnic, Multicultural Society, and the Enactment of Legislation for the Basic Human Rights of Non-National and Ethnic Minorities." http://www.nichibenren.or.jp/en/activities/statements/20040808.html (accessed August 1, 2006).
Nishinarita, Yutaka. 1998. *Zainichi chōsenjin no "sekai" to "teikoku" kokka* [Japan-based Korean "world" and "imperial" states]. Tokyo: Tokyo daigaku shuppankai.
Nishino, Rumiko. 1992. *Jūgun ianfu: Moto heishitachi no shōgen* [Military comfort women: Testimonials of former soldiers]. Tokyo: Akashi shoten.
Oguma, Eiji. 1995. *Tan'istu minzoku shinwa no kigen* [The origin of the myth of mono-ethnic society]. Tokyo: Shinyōsha.
Okonogi, Masao, ed. 2004. *Zainichi chōsenjin wa naze kikoku shitanoka* [Why were Koreans in Japan repatriated?]. Tokyo: Gendai jinbunsha.
Ong, Aihwa. 1999. "Introduction: Flexible Citizenship: The Cultural Logics of Transnationality." In A. Ong, *Flexible Citizenship: The Cultural Logics of Transnationality*. Durham, N.C.: Duke University Press.
Onishi, Norimitsu. 2004. "Freed from Captivity in Iraq, Japanese Return to More Pain." *New York Times*, April 23. http://www.nytimes.com/2004/04/23/international/asia/23JAPA.html?pagewanted=2&ei=5007&en=7457902d6d26dbe2&ex=1398052800&partner=USERLAND (accessed on May 7, 2006).
Onishi, Norimitsu. 2007. "Abe Rejects Japan's Files on War Sex" *New York Times*, March 2. http://www.nytimes.com/2007/03/02/world/asia/02japan.html?ex=1330491600&en=46b8ee3c003bb079&ei=5088&partner=rssnyt&emc=rss (accessed on May 5, 2007).
Ōnuma, Yasuaki. 1983. "'Gaikokujin no jinken' ron saikōsei no kokoromi" [An attempt to reconstruct the theory of the human rights of foreign nationals]. In Hōgaku kyōkai (ed.), *Hōgaku kyōkai hyakushūnen kinen ronbunshū* [Collection of essays commemorating the one hundred years of the association of law scholars], vol. 2. Tokyo: Yūhikaku.
———. 1993. *Shimpan Tan'itsu minzoku shakai no shinwa o koete* [Beyond the myth of mono-ethnic society, new edition]. Tokyo: Tōshindō.
Osaka city. 1998. *Osaka-shi gaikokuseki jūmin shisaku kihon shishin* [Osaka city's basic guidelines for foreign resident policy]. Osaka: Osaka city.
Otake, Tomoko. 2005. "Korean School Strives to Keep its Homeland Culture Alive." *Japan Times*, December 11. http://search.japantimes.co.jp/print/fl20051211x2.html (accessed April 1, 2006).
Pak, Chong-Myeong. 1999. *Zainichi chōsenjin: Rekishi, genjō, tenbō* [Japan-based Koreans: History, contemporary situation, and outlook]. Tokyo: Akashi shoten.

Pak, Chul Soon. 1960. "My Wish Has Come True." *Korea* 44: 4–5.
Pak, Il. 1999. *"Zainichi" to iu ikikata* [A lifestyle called *"zainichi"*]. Tokyo: Kōdansha.
Pak, Kyeong-Sik. 1989. *Kaihōgo zainichi chōsenjin undōshi* [The history of political movements by resident Koreans in Japan after liberation]. Tokyo: Sanichishobō.
Park, Hyun Ok. 2005. *Two Dreams in One Bed: Empire, Social Life, and the Origins of the North Korean Revolution in Manchuria.* Durham, N.C.: Duke University Press.
Patterson, Wayne. 1984. "Japanese Imperialism in Korea: A Study of Immigration and Foreign Policy." In H. Conroy, S. T. W. Davis, and W. Patterson (eds.), *Japan in Transition: Thought and Action in the Meiji Era, 1868–1912.* Cranbury: Associated University Press.
———. 2000. *The Ilse: First-Generation Korean Immigrants in Hawai'i 1903–1973.* Honolulu: University of Hawai'i Press.
Petit, Jeanne Danielle. 2000. "Building Citizens: Women, Men and the Immigration Restriction Debates, 1890–1929." Ph.D. diss., University of Notre Dame.
Plotnicov, Leonard, and Myrna Silverman. 1978. "Jewish Ethnic Signalling: Social Bonding in Contemporary American Society." *Ethnology* 17 (4): 407–423.
"Police Raid N. Korea-Related Facilities." 2007. *Asahi.com*, April 26. http://www.asahi.com/english/Herald-asahi/TKY200704260115.html (accessed May 8, 2007).
"Police Search Chongryun Affiliate over '80 Abduction." 2006. *Japan Times*, March 24. http://search.japantimes.co.jp/print/nn20060324a4.html (accessed April 1, 2006).
"Press Briefing on North Korea Missile Launch." 2006. The White House, July 4. http://www.whitehouse.gov/news/releases/2006/07/20060704-1.html (accessed August 12, 2006).
"Pro-Pyongyang Group Searched." 2006. *Asahi.com*, March 23. http://www.asahi.com/english/Herald-asahi/TKY200603230402.html (accessed April 1, 2006).
Pyle, Kenneth. 1978. *The Making of Modern Japan.* Lexington, Mass.: D.C. Heath and Co.
Radhakrishnan, R. 1994. "Is the Ethnic 'Authentic' in the Diasopora?" In K. Aguilar-San Juan (ed.), *The State of Asian America: Activism and Resistance in the 1990s.* Boston: South End Press.
"Report on the Occupation Area of South Korea Since Termination of Hostilities, Part One: Political (September 1947)." 1992. In K. Yi (ed.), *Haebang jeonhusa jaryojip* [Documents on pre-liberation and post-liberation history], vol. 1. Seoul: Wonjumunhwasa.
Research Department, U.S. Foreign Office. 1992. "Korea's Capacity for Independence, Historical Background (31 January 1945)." In K. Yi (ed.), *Haebang*

jeonhusa jaryojip [Documents on pre-liberation and post-liberation history], vol. 1. Seoul: Wonjumunhwasa.

Rothstein, Edward. 2006. "Refining the Tests that Confer Citizenship." *New York Times,* January 23: B1–B2.

Ryang, Sonia. 1997a. "Japanese Travelers' Accounts of Korea." *East Asian History* 13 (Sept.): 133–152.

———. 1997b. *North Koreans in Japan: Language, Ideology, and Identity.* Boulder, Colo.: Westview Press.

———. 2000. "The North Korean Homeland of Koreans in Japan." In S. Ryang (ed.), *Koreans in Japan: Critical Voices from the Margin.* London: Routledge.

———. 2002. "A Long Loop: Transmigration of Korean Women in Japan." *International Migration Review* 36 (3): 894–911.

———. 2004. *Japan and National Anthropology: A Critique.* London: Routledge.

———. 2005a. "Introduction: On Korean Women in Japan, Past and Present." In J. Kim. *Hidden Treasures.* Lanham, Md.: Rowman & Littlefield.

———. 2005b. *Korian diasupora: Zainichi chōsenjin no aidentiti* [Korean Diaspora—Identity of Koreans in Japan]. Tokyo: Akashi shoten.

———. 2006a. *Love in Modern Japan: Its Estrangement from Self, Sex, and Society.* London: Routledge.

———. 2006b. "Does It Have to Be hESC? A Note on War, Embryo, and the Disabled." *Anthropological Quarterly* 79 (3): 509–530.

———. 2007. "The Tongue That Divided Life and Death: *Ichien gojissen.*" Paper presented in the workshop "Language and Colonial Modernity in Korea and Japan," Reischauer Center for Japanese Studies and Korea Institute, Harvard University, April 23, 2007.

———. 2008. *Writing Selves in Diaspora: Ethnography of Autobiographics of Korean Women in Japan and the United States.* Lanham, Md.: Lexington Books.

Safran, William. 2004. "Deconstructing and Comparing Diasporas." In W. Kokot, K. Tölölyan, and C. Alfonso (eds.), *Diaspora, Identity and Religion: New Directions in Theory and Research.* London: Routledge.

Sagisawa, Megumu. 2004. *Byūtifuru nēmu* [Beautiful name]. Tokyo: Shinchōsha.

Sanjek, Roger. 1994. "The Enduring Significance of Race." In S. Gregory and R. Sanjek (eds.), *Race.* New Brunswick, N.J.: Rutgers University Press.

Sasaki, Teru. 2003. "'Nihonjin ni naru' toiukoto: Nihon kokuseki shutokusha no kanten kara" [What it means to become Japanese: From the perspectives of naturalized Japanese]. Ph.D. diss., Tsukuba daigaku [University of Tsukuba].

———, ed. 2005. *Zainichi korian ni kenri toshiteno Nihon kokuseki o* [Give Japanese nationality to *zainichi* Koreans as of right]. Tokyo: Akashi shoten.

Satō, Bunmei. 1988. *Koseki uragaeshikō* [History of family registry analyzed from the back side]. Tokyo: Akashi shoten.
Seo, Geun-Sik. 1999. "Zainichi chōsenjin no rekishiteki keisei" [The historical formation of Japan-based Koreans]. In J. Pak (ed.), *Zainichi chōsenjin: Rekishi, genjō, tenbō* [Japan-based Koreans: History, contemporary situation, and outlook]. Tokyo: Akashi shoten.
Seo, Seung. 1994. *Gokuchū 19-nen: Kankoku seijihan no tatakai* [Nineteen years of imprisonment: Struggle of a South Korean political prisoner]. Tokyo: Iwanami shoten.
Shklar, Judith N. 1991. *American Citizenship: The Quest for Inclusion.* Cambridge, Mass.: Harvard University Press.
"Sin Guang Su's North Korean Spy Ring under Investigation." 2006. *Asahi. com,* March 24. http://www.asahi.com/english/Herald-asahi/TKY20060324 0377.html (accessed April 1, 2006).
Siu, Lok. 2001. "Diasporic Cultural Citizenship: Chineseness and Belonging in Central America and Panama." *Social Text* 69 [19 (4)]: 7–28.
Smith, Rogers. 1997. *Civic Ideals: Conflicting Visions of Citizenship in U.S. Public Law.* New Haven, Conn.: Yale University Press.
Snow, Jack. 1996. "Refugee Problem in Pusan and Kyongsang Namdo (15 July 1947)." In *F. E. Gillette pogoseo* [F. E. Gillette written reports], vol. 1. Seoul: Institute of Asian Cultural Studies, Hallym University.
Song, Miri. 2003. *Choosing Ethnic Identity.* Cambridge: Polity Press.
SOPEMI. 2001–2004. *Trends in International Migration: Continuous Reporting System on Migration.* Paris: OECD.
South Korean Interim Government. 1996. "Termination of Summer Grains Collection Program (22 October 1947)." In *F. E. Gillette pogoseo* [F. E. Gillette written reports], vol. 1. Seoul: Institute of Asian Cultural Studies, Hallym University.
Steinberg, Stephen. 1989. *The Ethnic Myth: Race, Ethnicity, and Class in America.* Boston: Beacon Press.
Sugihara, Mitsushi. 1993. "The Rights to Use Ethnic Names in Japan." *Journal of Intercultural Studies* 14 (2): 13–33.
Sugimoto, Yoshio. 1997. *An Introduction to Japanese Society.* Cambridge: Cambridge University Press.
"Survey: 62% Want SDF Acknowledged." 2006. *Asahi.com,* May 4. http:// www.asahi.com/english/Herald-asahi/TKY200605040088.html (accessed May 19, 2006).
Suzuki, Kazuko. 2003. "The State and Immigrant Adaptation: A Comparative Study of the Korean Diaspora in Japan and the United States." Ph.D. diss., Princeton University.
Suzuki, Yūko. 1993. *"Jūgunianfu" mondai to seibōryoku* [The "military comfort women" issue and sexual violence]. Tokyo: Miraisha.
———. 1996. *"Ianfu" mondai to sengo sekinin* [The "comfort women" issue and postwar responsibility]. Tokyo: Miraisha.

Tai, Eika. 1999. *Tabunkashugi to diasupora* [Multiculturalism and diaspora]: *Voices from San Francisco*. Tokyo: Akashi shoten.

———. 2004. "'Korean Japanese': A New Identity Option for Resident Koreans in Japan." *Critical Asian Studies* 36 (3): 355–382.

———. 2006. "Korean Activism and Ethnicity in the Changing Ethnic Landscape of Urban Japan." *Asian Studies Review* 30 (Mar.): 41–58.

Taira, Naoki, Hitomi Kawamoto, Yeong-geun Chin, and Toshiya Nakamura. 1995. "Zainichi chōsenjin seinen ni miru minzokuteki aidentiti no jōkyōni yoru shifuto ni tsuite" [On the situational shift of ethnic identity seen among the Korean youth in Japan]. *Japanese Journal of Educational Psychology* 43 (4): 380–391.

Takaki, Ronald. 1989. *Strangers from a Different Shore: A History of Asian Americans*. Boston: Little, Brown.

Takasaki, Sōji. 2004. "Kikoku undō towa nandattanoka [What was the repatriation movement?]," Part 1. *Ronza* (May): 114–143.

———. 2005a. "*Asahi shinbun to Sankei shinbun wa kikoku undō o dō hōdō shitanoka*" [How did *Asahi* and *Sankei* newspapers report the repatriation movement?]. In T. Sōji and C. Pak Cheong-Ji (eds.), *Kikoku undō towa nandattanoka* [What was the repatriation movement?]. Tokyo: Heibonsha.

———. 2005b. "Kikokumondai no keika to haikei" [Process and background of the repatriation]. In T. Sōji and C. Pak (eds.), *Kikokuundō towa nandattanoka* [What was the repatriation movement?]. Tokyo: Heibonsha.

Takasaki, Sōji, and Cheong-Jin Pak, eds. 2005. *Kikokuundō towa nandattanoka* [What was the repatriation movement?]. Tokyo: Heibonsha.

Takeda, Seiji. 1996. "Zainichi to taikōshugi" [Zainichi and confrontationalism]. In S. Inoue, C. Ueno, M. Ōsawa, S. Mita, & S. Yoshimi (eds.), *Iwanami kōza gendai shakaigaku 24: Minzoku, kokka, esunishiti* [Iwanami's contemporary sociology series 24; Nation, state ethnicity]. Tokyo: Iwanami shoten.

Takenaka, Akira. 1997. "'Nation' and Citizenship in Germany and Japan: A Comparative Study of Citizenship Policies toward Immigrants and Ethnic 'Others.'" Ph.D. diss., Columbia University.

Takenoshita, Hirohisa. 1995. "Tabunka kyōiku to esunishiti: Zainichi kankoku chōsenjin shūjūchiku o jireini" [Multicultural education and ethnicity: With the focus on Korean neighborhoods]. *Shakaigaku hyōron* 49 (4): 45–62.

———. 2000. "Intāmarijji kazoku no naka no esunishitī: Zainichi kankoku chōsenjin o meguru esunishitī hyōshō no poritikkusu" [Ethnicities practiced in interethnic families: Politics of ethnic representations about Koreanness in Japan]. *Kazoku kenkyū nenpō* [Annals of family studies] 25: 29–42.

Tamayo, William R. 1996. "Asian Americans and the McCarran-Walter Act." In H.-c. Kim (ed.), *Asian Americans and Congress: A Documentary History*. Westport, Conn.: Greenwood Press.

Tanaka, Hiroshi. 1995. *Zainichi gaikokujin* [Resident foreigners in Japan]. Tokyo: Iwanami shoten.

———, ed. 2002. *Zainichi korian kenri sengen* [*Zainichi* Koreans' declaration of rights]. Tokyo: Iwanami shoten.
Tegtmeyer Pak, Katherine. 2000. "Foreigners Are Local Citizens Too: Local Governments Respond to International Migration in Japan." In M. Douglas and G. S. Roberts (eds.), *Japan and Global Migration*. London: Routledge.
———. 2006. "Cities and Local Citizenship in Japan: Overcoming Nationality?" In T. Tsuda (ed.), *Local Citizenship in Recent Countries of Immigration: Japan in Comparative Perspective*. Oxford: Lexington Books.
Tei, Taikin. 2001. *Zainichi kankokujin no shūen* [The end of *zainichi* South Koreans]. Tokyo: Chūōkōronsha.
———. 2006. *Zainichi no taerarenai karusa*. Tokyo: Chūō Kōronsha.
Tölölyan, Khachig. 1996. "Rethinking Diaspora(s): Stateless Power in the Transnational Moment." *Diaspora* 5 (1): 3–34.
Tolstoy, Leo. 1978. *War and Peace*. Rosemary Edmonds, trans. Harmondsworth: Penguin.
Toyonaka city. 2000. *Toyonakashi kokusaika shisaku suishin kihon hōshin* [Toyonaka city's basic guidelines for promoting internationalization]. Toyonaka: Toyonaka city.
Tsuda, Takeyuki. 2003. *Strangers in the Ethnic Homeland*. New York: Columbia University Press.
Tsurushima, Setsure. 1984. "Humans Rights Issues and the Status of the Burakumin and Koreans in Japan." In G. De Vos (ed.), *Institutions for Change in Japanese Society*. Berkeley: Institute for East Asian Studies, University of California.
"Turning Rapanese." 2007. *Monocle* 1(3): 98–101.
United States Armed Forces in Korea. Headquarters. 1988. *G-2 Periodic Report* (1945.9.9 to 1946.7.12). 2 vols. Seoul: Institute of Asian Culture Studies, Hallym University.
United States Army, XXIV Corps. Headquarters. 1948. "Memorandum for Commanding General: Transmitting Report of Conversation with President, Korean Residents Union in Japan, on Koreans in Japan (18 August 1948)." In *Records of the U.S. Department of State Relating to the Internal Affairs of Korea*, vol. 9. Seoul: Areumchulpansa.
United States Bureau of the Census. 2007. *The American Community— Asians: 2004, American Community Survey Reports*. February. Washington, D.C.: U.S. Department of Commerce.
United States Department of State. Diplomatic Section GHQ SCAP. 1948. "Staff Study Concerning Koreans in Japan (16 August 1948)." In *Records of the United States Department of State Relating to the Internal Affairs of Japan, 1945–1949*, reel 3. Tokyo: Japan National Diet Library.
United States Joint Chiefs of Staff. 1945. "Basic Directive for Post-Surrender Military Government in Japan Proper (3 November 1945)." http://www.ndl.go.jp/constitution/shiryo/01/036/036_001l.html (accessed August 31, 2006).
United States Joint Intelligence Study Publishing Board. 1992. "Joint Army-

Navy Intelligence Study of Korea (Including Tsushima and Quelpart); People and Government (April 1945)." In K. Yi (ed.), *Haebang jeonhusa jaryojip* [Documents on pre-liberation and post-liberation history], vol. 1. Seoul: Wonjumunhwasa.

United States Military Government in Korea. Headquarters. 1996. "Press Releases, 10 December 1946." In *F. E. Gillette pogoseo* [F. E. Gillette written reports], vol. 1. Seoul: Institute of Asian Cultural Studies, Hallym University.

United States Military Intelligence Service. 1992. "Survey of Korea (15 June 1943)." In K. Yi (ed.), *Haebang jeonhusa jaryojip* [Documents on pre-liberation and post-liberation history], vol. 1. Seoul: Wonjumunhwasa.

United States Office of Strategic Services. 1945. "Aliens in Japan (29 June 1945)." In *Documents from Occupation of Japan, United States Planning Documents, 1942–1945*, reel 14 (3-C-11). Tokyo: Japan National Diet Library.

United States Political Adviser for Japan. 1949. "Status of Koreans in Japan (August 15, 1949)." In *Records of the United States Department of State Relating to the Internal Affairs of Japan, 1945–1949*, reel 15. Tokyo: Japan National Diet Library.

Utsumi, Aiko. 2001. "Korean 'Imperial Soldiers': Remembering Colonialism and Crimes against Allied POWs." In T. Fujitani, G. White, and L. Yoneyama (eds.), *Perilous Memories*. Durham, N.C.: Duke University Press.

Wagner, Edward. 1951. *The Korean Minority in Japan: 1904–1950*. New York: Institute of Pacific Relations.

Waldinger, Roger, and David Fitzgerald. 2004. "Transnationalism in Question." *American Journal of Sociology* 109 (5): 1177–1195.

Waters, Mary C. 1999. *Black Identities: West Indian Immigrant Dreams and American Realities*. Cambridge, Mass.: Harvard University Press.

"We Are So Happy." 1960. *Korea* 44: 31.

Weiner, Michael, ed. 1997. *Japan's Minorities: The Illusion of Homogeneity*. London: Routledge.

"Welcome to First Group of Repatriates from Japan!" 1960. *Korea* 42: 2–3.

Winant, Howard. 2001. *The World Is a Ghetto: Race and Democracy since World War II*. New York: Basic Books.

"Women Swarm Narita for Arrival of 'Yon-sama.'" 2004. *Japan Times*, November 26. http://search.japantimes.co.jp/print/news/nn11-2004/nn2004 1126a5.htm (accessed February 14, 2006).

Xu, Chun-hwa. 2004. "'Manshūjihen' izen no kando niokeru chōsenjin no kokusekimondai" [The issue of Koreans' nationality in Kando before the Manchurian incident]. *Chōsenshi kenkyūkai ronbunshū* 42: 133–158.

Yamada, Meiko. 1991. *Ianfutachi no taiheiyōsensō* [The Pacific War of the military comfort women]. Tokyo: Kōjinsha.

Yamaguchi, Jiro. 2006. "LDP Landslide Buries Two-Party System." *Japan Times*, January 3. http://search.japantimes.co.jp/print/eo20060103a2.html (accessed April 1, 2006).

Yang, Eun Sik, and Gary Wanki Park. 1992. *Korean Americans: An Annotated Bibliography of Korean and English Language Materials*. Los Angeles: UCLA Asian American Studies Center, Resource Development and Publications.

Yang, Tae-Ho. 1984. *Pusankō ni kaerenai: "kokusaika" no nakano zainichi chōsen kankokujin* [Can't go back to the Pusan Port: *Zainichi* Koreans in the age of "internationalization"]. Osaka: Daisanshokan.

———. 1991a. "Jijitsu toshiteno 'zainichi'—Kang Sang-Jung shi eno gimon" ['Zainichi' as a fact—questions for Mr. Kang Sang-Jung]. In J. Iinuma (ed.), *Zainichi kankoku chōsenjin sono Nihon shakai ni okeru sonzai kachi* [Koreans in Japan: Their existential value in Japanese society]. Osaka: Kaifūsha.

———. 1991b. "Kyōzon, kyōsei, kyōkan—Kang Sang-Jung shi eno gimon (II)" [Existing together, living together, feeling together—questions for Mr. Kang Sang-Jung, II]. In J. Iinuma (ed.), *Zainichi kankoku chōsenjin sono Nihon shakai ni okeru sonzai kachi* [Koreans in Japan: Their existential value in Japanese society]. Osaka: Kaifūsha.

Yau, Jennifer. 2004. "The Foreign Born from Korea in the United States." *Migration Information Source*. http://www.migrationinformation.org/feature/display.cfm?ID=273 (accessed February 2006).

Yi, Kil-Sang, ed. 1992. *Haebang jeonhusa jaryojip* [Documents on preliberation and post-liberation history], vol. 1. Seoul: Wonjumunhwasa.

Yi, Yang-Su. 1987–1988. "Honrōsareta jinsei ni shūshifu o utsu [I'll put a period to [my] life which has been manipulated]." Serialized in *Kurio* 5: 73–75; 6: 62–65; 7 43–47.

Yoshimi, Yoshiaki. 2002. *Comfort Women*. New York: Columbia University Press.

Yoshino, Kosaku. 1992. *Cultural Nationalism in Contemporary Japan: A Sociological Inquiry*. London: Routledge.

Yoshioka, Masuo. 1995. *Zainichi gaikokujin to shakai hoshō* [Resident foreigners and social security]. Tokyo: Shakaihyōronsha.

Zainichi chōsenjin no jinken o mamoru kai, ed. 1977. *Zainichi chōsenjin no kihonteki jinken* [The basic human rights of *zainichi* Koreans]. Tokyo: Nigatsusha.

Contributors

MARK E. CAPRIO, a professor in the Department of Intercultural Communication at Rikkyo University in Tokyo, earned his Ph.D. in Korean history at the University of Washington. He has written on issues regarding Japanese colonial history in Korea, the American occupations of Korea and Japan, and current U.S.–North Korean relations, He is currently completing a monograph titled *Japanese Assimilation Policies in Colonial Korea, 1910-1945*.

ERIN AERAN CHUNG is the Charles D. Miller Assistant Professor of East Asian Politics and co-director of the Racism, Immigration, and Citizenship Program in the Department of Political Science at The Johns Hopkins University. Her articles on citizenship, noncitizen political engagement, and racial politics have been published in the *Du Bois Review* and *Asian Perspective*. Her forthcoming book, *Citizenship and Immigration in Japan* (Cambridge University Press), examines how Japan's citizenship policies have shaped noncitizen political engagement in contemporary Japan through the lens of the Korean resident community.

ICHIRO KURAISHI is associate professor of education at Tokyo University of Foreign Studies, Japan. He received his Ph.D. from Kyoto University. His research interests include oral history, minority education in Japan, and media representations of Japanese minority issues. He is the author of *Empirical Sociology of Discrimination and Everyday Life: Research Notes of "I" as a Decoder* (in Japanese, Seikatsushoin, 2007), and he is currently completing a book titled *Educational Inclusion and Exclusion in Postwar Japan* (in Japanese).

CHIKAKO KASHIWAZAKI is associate professor in the Faculty of Economics, Keio University, Japan. She received her doctorate in sociology from Brown University. Her research interests include citizenship and nationality, ethnic relations, and immigration policy, with a primary focus on Japanese society.

JOHN LIE is Class of 1959 Professor of Sociology and Dean of International and Area Studies at the University of California, Berkeley. Among his books are *Modern Peoplehood* (Harvard University Press, 2004) and *Zainichi (Koreans in Japan): Diasporic Nationalism and Postcolonial Identity* (GAIA/ University of California Press, 2008).

YOUNGMI LIM is a Ph.D. candidate in sociology at the City University of New York Graduate Center. Her chapter in this volume is based on her dissertation, "Becoming Japanese: Contested Meanings of Race and Nationality in Contemporary Japan."

TESSA MORRIS-SUZUKI is professor of Japanese history in the Research School of Pacific and Asian Studies, Australian National University. Her research interests include frontiers, globalization, and the cross-border movement of people in East Asia. Among her recent publications are *Re-Inventing Japan: Time, Space, Nation* (M.E. Sharpe, 1998), *A View from the Frontier* (in Japanese, Misuzushobō, 2000), *The Past within Us: Media, Memory, History* (Iwanami shoten, 2004; Verso, 2005), and *Exodus to North Korea: Shadows from Japan's Cold War* (Rowman & Littlefield, 2007).

SONIA RYANG is associate professor of anthropology and international studies, C. Maxwell & Elizabeth M. Stanley Family and Korea Foundation scholar of Korean studies, and director of the Center for Asian and Pacific Studies, University of Iowa. Her recent books include *Writing Selves in Diaspora: Ethnography of Autobiographics of Korean Women in Japan and the United States* (Lexington, 2008); *North Korea: Toward a Better Understanding* (Lexington, 2008); and *Love in Modern Japan: Its Estrangement from Self, Sex, and Society* (Routledge, 2006).

YU JIA earned her Ph.D. in history at Rikkyo University. Her research interests focus on Korean and Japanese militarization during and immediately following the American Occupation of Korea and Japan. She is currently a postdoctoral fellow at Chung'an University in Seoul.

Index

Abe, Shinzo, 79, 80
Abe Sada, 78
Afterschool programs, 135
Aichi prefecture, 38
Ainu, 126
Akahata (journal), 156
Alien Land Law (California), 158
Alien Registration Laws, 38, 155
Alien Registration Order, 129
"Aliens in Japan," 27–28, 29
Allies: and Korean independence, 22–23
An Chang-Ho, 158, 160, 161
Ang, Ien, 101
Anti-communism: U.S., 162–63, 164
Anti-Japanese organizations, 160
Arrests: of Chongryun members, 76–77
Article Nine, 77–78, 79
Asakawa Akihiro, 175–76, 178
Ashida Hitoshi, 47
Assassinations, 160, 198n15
Assimilation: in Japan, 27, 33, 83–86, 104, 151, 173–76
Association for Establishing the "Rights for *Zainichi* Koreans to Obtain Japanese Nationality," 145
Association for Korean Residents. *See* Mindan
Association for Reclaiming Ethnic Names, 13, 87

Association for the Protection of the Human Rights of *Zainichi* Koreans, 131
Association of Cities with a Large Number of Foreign Residents, 143
Australia, 38

Baden-Württemberg region (Germany), 151
Bae Yong Joon, 63
Basic Law for Foreign Residents, 137, 194n1
Benninghoff, H. Merrell, 30
Black market, 26, 30, 33, 37
Boissier, Leopold, 47
Border politics, 39–40
Brazil: immigrants from, 135, 136, 143

Calcutta Accord, 55
California, 158, 159–60
California National Guard, 161
Censorship, 108
Che, Sunny, 22
Cheong Sung-Hwa, 34
China, 1, 22, 51, 52
Chinese, 29, 135, 195n14, 198n14
Chō Akio, 89, 93–94, 100, 104
Choe Seog-Ui, 28, 32–33, 35, 37
Choi, Mrs., 42–43, 59
Cho Ki-cheon, 15

221

Chongryun (Chōsensōren), 12, 45, 46, 64, 80, 130, 136, 157, 164, 188n2, 189nn4,9, 190n15; activities of, 65–69; and kidnapping of Japanese citizens, 62–63; raids on, 76–77; and repatriation, 48, 52–53, 54, 57, 166; schools, 69–75, 189n8
Chon Wolson, 76, 176
Chōsen, 8, 9
Chōsenjin, 5, 7, 9, 127
Citizenship, 16, 19, 34, 125, 198n21; Cold War and, 163–67; concepts and policies of, 149–52, 196n1; Japanese, 63, 81, 164–65, 194n8; McCarran-Walter act, 162–63; U.S., 148, 157–58
Clan genealogy, 6
Clothing: and ethnic identity, 70, 72–73, 74, 75
Cold War, 1, 10, 40, 151; and citizenship policies, 163–67; repatriation politics, 46–55
Colonialism, 1; Japanese, 4–5; and nationality, 16, 126–27, 197n9
"Comfort women," 79
Comic books, 168
Communism, communists: Japan-based Korean, 30–31, 66; and U.S. citizenship, 151, 162–63, 164
Concentration camps: in North Korea, 76
Concentration center: Kyushu, 34
"Confirmation of free will": and family power relationships, 58–59
Constitution, Japanese, 7; Article Nine, 77–78, 79
Consultation Center for Law and the Everyday Life of Compatriots, 136
Corps for the Advancement of Individuals (Heungsadan), 161, 198n16
Coursier, Henri, 57
Crime, 37, 189n11

Daedong bogukhoe, 159–60
Daisangokujin, 130
Dai Suyung, 36
Decade for Human Rights Education, 141–42

Democratic People's Republic of Korea (DPRK). *See* North Korea
Deportation: from United States, 162–63
Deverall, Richard L. G., 30
Diamond Kim (Kim Kang), 162
Diaspora, 119, 178, 192n10; identity and, 103–4; models of, 2–3, 85–86; racialization of, 105–6; visible and invisible, 86–88
Diene, Doudou, 79
Discrimination, 16, 67, 103, 138, 174, 196n30; against Japan-based Koreans, 38, 196n30; passing names and, 14, 192n14; in United States, 158–59
Dōho hōritsu seikatsu sentā, 136
Donghoe, 159
Dongnipdan (League of Korean Independence), 160–61
Doreamon, 98–99
DPRK. *See* North Korea
Dutch East Indies, 21

East Asian Co-Prosperity Sphere, 78
Education, 136; Chongryun, 66–67, 68, 70–71; Japanese public, 71–72
Election Laws (Japanese), 154
Electoral rights, 136–37
Employment, 90
Ethnic identity, 13, 18, 19, 32, 72, 86–88, 100–102, 155, 177–78, 192n11; female students and, 73–75; homeland and, 82–83; as Korean, 169–70; names and, 92–97, 192n14, 193, n15; options, 103–4
Ethnicity, 104, 191n5; in Japan, 123–24; nationality, 126, 128–29
Ethnic minorities, 138
Ethnic signaling: names and, 92–97
Exiles, 25, 60
Exoticism, 18
Ewha Women's College, 74

Family, 112; ethnic identification and, 101, 195n23; power relations within, 58–59
Family registry system, 154–55

Females: at Chongryun schools, 70–71, 75; ethnic identity of, 73–74
Filipinos, 135, 198n14
Films, 18; diaspora depicted in, 119–20; *zainichi* as focus of, 108–19
Fishery rights, 49
Food, 58; in occupied Korea, 36–37
Foreign Affairs Committee, 46–47
Foreignness: defining, 123–24; in Japan, 18–19; perceptions of, 86–87
Foreign residents, foreigners *(gaikokujin)*, 166, 194nn3, 4, 195n14; as category, 123–25, 194n10; coalition-building, 135–38; definitions of, 121–23; internationalization and human rights, 141–42; in Japan, 27–28, 166; legal nationality of, 125–26; local-level programs for, 139–40; multiculturalism and, 142–44; municipal policies on, 140–41; recently arrived/newcomer, 133–35; *zainichi* as, 129–33, 144–46
"Fourteen Points" speech (Wilson), 160
Free choice, 61; power relationships and, 58–60
Freedom: vs. determinism, 39
Fujiyama Aiichirō, 48–49
Fukuoka Yasunori: *Hontō no watashi o motomete*, 12
Fukuyama Masakichi, 25
Fund raising: for political action, 159–60

Gaikikyō (Gaitōhō mondai to torikumu zenkoku kirisutokyō renrakukyōgikai), 137
Gaikokujin shūjūtoshi kaigi, 143
Gender: and ethnic identity, 73–74
General Association of Korean Residents in Japan. *See* Chongryun
Gentleman's Agreement, 159
Germany, 151, 178
Girls: at Chongryun schools, 70–71; ethnic identity of, 73–75
Globalization, 134
Go (film), 18, 107, 108, 120, 193n7; themes in, 114–19

Government-General of Korea, 4
Great Britain, 22
Guidelines for the Local International Exchange Promotion Plan, 140
Guidelines for Promotion of *Tabunka Kyōsei*, 143

Haebang (journal), 156
Han Tonghyun, 74
Hate crimes: against Korean students, 62, 73, 75
Hawai'i, 194n11, 198n13; Koreans in, 159–60, 194n11, 198nn13, 20
Health care: national, 139–40
Heungsadan (Corps for the Advancement of Individuals), 161
H Japanese Elementary School, 75
Hodge, John R., 36, 37
Hokkaido, 76
Home, 3, 40
Homeland, 2, 3, 15, 101, 182n8, 192n10; ethnic, 82–83
Hong Kong, 21
Hontō no watashi o motomete (Fukuoka Yasunori), 12
Household registry *(koseki)*, 5, 6, 181n5
Housing: discrimination, 138, 196n30; for repatriated Koreans, 35–36, 57
Human rights, 16, 20, 107; for immigrants, 137–38, 141–42, 197n7
Hyogo prefecture, 38

ICRC. *See* International Committee for the Red Cross
Identity, 19, 165; in Japanese society, 72–73, 102–3; as Korean, 169–70, 191n4; options for, 103–4; politics of, 18, 19, 104, 170–78; *zainichi*, 82, 133–35
Ijūren (Ijū rōdōsha to rentai suru zenkoku nettowaku), 137
Immigrants, immigration, 56, 147–48; coalitions, 135–38; recent, 133–35; to United States, 158–59, 197–98nn12, 13, 19
Immigration Acts (U.S.), 159

Immigration Control Order, 129
Independence movement: Korean, 22–23, 25–26, 160–61
Indo-Chinese, 133
Inoue Masutarō: and Japanese Red Cross, 46, 54; on repatriation, 47, 48, 49, 50, 51, 57
Intellectuals: and identity politics, 19, 103, 170–73
International Committee for the Red Cross (ICRC), 17, 40; "confirmation of free will," 58–59; and Japanese Red Cross, 54–55; repatriation to North Korea, 42, 46, 47–51, 53–54, 57, 185n19
Internationalization, 140, 141
International Refugee Convention and Protocol, 66
Internment camps: World War II, 151–52, 161
Ishihara Shintarō, 75

Jaisohn, Philip (Seo Jae-Pil), 158
Jang In-Hwan, 159–60
Japan: colonial/imperial period, 4–5, 21; and Korean independence, 22–23; as monoethnic, 123–24, 148, 181n1; postwar, 6–8; residence rights in, 56–57; and South Korea, 50, 168–69; U.S. Occupation of, 16, 17, 29, 153–57
Japan Communist Party (JCP), 44, 65, 154, 156, 157
Japanese, 10; and anti-Korean attitudes, 48–49, 63–65, 168–69; kidnapping of, 17–18, 62–63, 76, 78–79, 107, 108; as nationality, 45, 81, 126–27, 134, 148, 182n14, 194n11, 195n23; naturalized, 13, 84–85, 87–92; in United States, 151–52, 158–59, 161, 198n14
Japanese Empire, 21
Japanese Nationality Law, 84
Japaneseness, 82, 87, 123
Japanese Red Cross (JRC), 52, 66; and Japanese government, 54–55; on repatriation, 42, 43, 46, 47–51, 53, 55–56, 185n19

Japan Federation of Bar Associations (Nichibenren), 137–38
Japanization, 164
Jeju Island uprising, 56
Joryeon (League of Koreans in Japan), 30, 65–66, 155–56, 164, 195n19; solidarity with North Korea, 156–57; suppression of, 7, 189n6
JRC. *See* Japanese Red Cross

Kanagawa Prefecture, 136, 138, 142
Kang Chol-hwan, 76
Kang Sang-jung: and identity politics, 173, 174, 176, 177, 178; *Zainichi*, 170–72
Kankoku, kankokujin, 8, 9
Kanryū (Hanryu; K-pop), 63, 78, 168
Kansai region, 132, 196n33
Kansas, 160
Kawasaki city, 142, 143
Kazakhstan, 1
Ken-Kanryu, 168
Khrushchev, Nikita, 52
Kidnapping: of Japanese citizens, 17–18, 62–63, 76, 78–79, 107, 108
Kim Chengnei, 24, 25
Kim Il Sung, 10, 52, 58, 64, 67, 68, 186n26
Kim Jong Il, 68, 168
Kim Kang (Diamond Kim), 162
Kim Koo, 159
Kimm v. Rosenberg, District Director, Immigration and Naturalization Service, 162–63
Kishi Nobusuke, 50, 53, 54, 55
KNA. *See* Korean National Association
Kobe: Korean uprising in, 30, 156, 189n7
Koizumi Junichiro, 62, 78
Korea, 31, 51, 183n1; independence of, 22–23; as Japanese colony, 4–5, 917n10; partitioning of, 9–10, 23, 30; post World War II, 6–7, 29, 184nn9, 12; repatriation to, 21, 34–38. *See also* North Korea; South Korea
Korea (journal), 53

Korean-American community, 196–97n2, 198n14; and Los Angeles riots, 149, 165; McCarran-Walter Act and, 163–64; during World War II, 161–62
Korean Association in Japan, 36
Korean language: study of, 70–71
Korean National Association (KNA; Kukminhoe), 160, 162
Korean National Revolutionary Party, 162
Korean Provisional Government (KPG), 26, 161; support for, 24–25
Korean Returnees from Japan, 53
Koreans: and Japaneseness, 82, 87; political visibility of, 165–66. *See also* Korean-American community; *Zainichi*
Korean War, 1, 4, 7, 17, 56, 162
Korean Workers' Party, 51
"Korea's Capacity for Independence, Historical Background," 25–26
Korea University, 68, 70, 71, 75
KPG. *See* Korean Provisional Government
K-pop. *See Kanryū*
Kukminhoe (Korean National Association; KNA), 160
Kundan, 160, 198n15
Kuremoto Nami, 91, 95, 101, 104; on Korean roots, 97–99, 101–2
Kyushu, 34

Labor, 17, 31, 38, 134, 159
Landlords: and Korean names, 93–95
LDP. *See* Liberal Democratic Party
League of Korean Independence (Dongnipdan), 160–61
League of Koreans in Japan (Joryeon), 30, 65–66, 155, 164, 195n19; and North Korea, 156–57; suppression of, 7, 189n6
Leftist organizations: and repatriation, 30–31
Liberal Democratic Party (LDP), 46–47
Lineage, 6, 82, 97

Livelihood Protection Benefits, 49
Los Angeles, 149, 161–62, 165

MacArthur, Douglas, 29, 31
MacArthur, Douglas, II, 54
McCarran-Walter Act, 151, 152, 157, 162, 163–64
McCarthyism, 158, 164, 197n11
Maihara city, 142
Male suffrage, 5, 127
Manchuria, 21, 38, 126–27, 194n12
Marriage, 6, 92, 95, 198n20; cross-national, 96–97; Japanese-Korean, 10, 27, 59, 81–82, 133, 147, 195n23
Medicine: in North Korea, 58
Meiji law, 155
Meiji Restoration, 5, 194n10
Michel, William: on repatriation, 48, 49, 52
Migrant workers, 10
Migration: border politics and, 39–40, 56; free, 40–41, 61
Mika, 81–82, 85
Military: Japanese, 29, 183n6; Koreans in U.S., 161–62
Mindan (Association for Korean Residents), 31–32, 92, 130, 134, 136–37, 157, 164, 166, 183n8, 195–96n26
Mindan International Cooperation Center, 136
Ministry of Education (Japan), 66, 68
Ministry of Health and Welfare (Japan), 49
Ministry of Home Affairs (Jichishō), 140
Ministry of Internal Affairs and Communications (Sōmushō), 140, 143
Mintōren (Minzoku sabetsu to tatakau renraku kyōgikai), 135, 136, 140
Minzokumei o torimodosu kai, 13, 87
Missile launches: by North Korea, 80
Miyo, 45
Monoethnicity: of Japan, 123–24, 148, 181n1
Mukuge, 135

Multiculturalism, 17; national policy and, 142–44
Multi-Ethnic Human Rights Education Center for Coexistence, 136
Municipalities: foreign resident policies in, 140–41, 142; multicultural policies, 143–44
Muslims: in Germany, 151
Mutual aid associations, 159
Mutual Security Treaty (U.S.-Japan), 54

Nakano Shigeharu, 72
Names, naming: Korean, 92–97, 100–101; naturalization and, 13–14, 89; real vs. passing, 12–13, 192n14, 193n15
Nanjing Massacre, 78
National affiliation, 7, 11–12
National belonging, 15–16
National Christian Conference for the Discussion of Problems of the Alien Registration Law (Gaikikyō), 137
Nationality, 8, 144, 195n18; of colonial subjects, 126–27, 197n9; Japanese, 45, 81, 134, 148, 182n14, 194n11, 195n23; of Japan-resident Koreans, 76, 182n14, 195n21; legal, 125–26; of postwar Koreans, 33–34, 49, 63–64, 127–33; South Korean, 16, 68–69, 182n9, 182–83n16; of *zainichi*, 129–33
Nationality Act (1950), 155
Nationality Law, 125
National Traitor Law, 31
Naturalization, 81, 84–85, 133, 190n2, 194n12, 197n5; identity and culture, 88–92, 104, 173–75; and Japanese nationality, 128, 184n14; and names, 13–14, 93, 95; process of, 150–51; in United States, 157–58, 198n19; U.S. vs. Japanese, 148–49
Naturalization Law (1790), 151, 158
Nebraska, 160
Network of Groups for Combatting Ethnic Discrimination. *See* Mintōren

Network of Japanese, Korean, and Foreign Residents in Japan to Realize the Suffrage of Long-Term Foreign Residents in Local Politics, 137
New Delhi Conference: Resolution 20, 50, 51, 187–88n36
New People's Association (Sinminhoe), 159
Nikkyōso, 132
9/17 crisis: impacts of, 62, 76, 79, 107–8
Normalization Treaty, 90
North Korea, 7, 8–9, 31, 186n26; Chongryun and, 66–67, 68, 69, 188n2, 190n15; Joryeon and, 156–57; kidnappings by, 17–18, 62–63, 76, 78–79; and League of Koreans in Japan, 65–66; in *Pacchigi!*, 112–14; political positioning of, 51–52; refugees from, 60–61; repatriation to, 40–47, 48–49, 52–55, 57–60
North Korean Red Cross, 53–54, 66, 185–86nn19, 20
North Koreans, 9, 12, 31, 64, 80, 108, 182nn10, 11; repatriation of, 17, 41–42; stereotypic views of, 116–17
North Korean Workers' Party, 44
Nuremberg Laws on Citizenship and Race, 151

Occupation: and Korean repatriation, 31–34; U.S., 16, 17, 22, 26, 28, 166, 184n9; of South Korea, 26, 30
Okazaki Katsuo, 46–47
Okinawans, 126
Ōmura Migrant Detention Center, 51
Osaka, 30, 38, 132, 155; immigrant organizations in, 135–36, 195n20, 196n32
Osaka City Association for Research on the Education of Foreign Children (Osaka-shi gaikokujin shitei kyōiku mondai kenkyū kyōgikai), 132, 195n20
Overseas Koreans, 9, 21, 25; political activities, 159–60

Pacchigi! (film), 18, 107, 119, 120; themes in, 108–14
Pak, Mrs., 41–42
Pak Fumiko, 89–90, 93, 94, 95, 104, 193n15
Pak Yeol, 31–32
Pak Yeong-Man, 158, 160, 198n15
Passports: for Koreans, 68–69, 194n11
Patriotism Association (Daedong bogukhoe), 60
People's Republic of China. *See* China
Persecution: 76–77
Peru: immigrants from, 135
Philippines, 21
Political activism: and citizenship, 163–64; visibility and, 165–66
POWs: Korean, 23–25, 183nn5, 6
Prejudice: against returnees, 16–17
Prejudice: Japanese, 16, 73; response to, 95–96
Prevention of Destruction Law, 7
Price controls: on food, 36–37
Propaganda: supporting repatriation, 53
Proposal for a Comprehensive Policy Plan on Foreigners, 137
Prostitution, 168
Public services, 140

Race, 23, 103, 191–92n9; and citizenship, 152, 158, 198n21; and diaspora, 105–6
Racial politics, 148
Racism, 85, 105, 197n8; ethnic identity and, 82–83, 102; Japanese, 79, 96
Raids: on Chongryun offices, 76–77
Rape of Nanjing, 78
Refugees, 3, 21, 56; from North Korea, 60–61
Registration, 33, 155
Reunification, 51
Remittances, 27
Repatriation, 65, 154, 166; Cold War politics and, 46–55; family power relations and, 58–59; film depictions of, 109, 112–14; housing, 35–36; of Koreans, 6–7, 17, 21, 25, 30, 31–38, 184n9; misinformation on, 57–58; to North Korea, 40–46, 67; voluntary, 55–56; after World War II, 22, 24
Representative Assembly for Foreign Residents, 142
Republic of Korea. *See* South Korea
Residence rights, 56–57, 68, 90, 195n22
Residency: permanent, 11, 148, 166, 195n22, 197n4. *See also* Foreign residents, foreigners; *Zainichi*
Residential registry, 5
Resident registration number 11–12
Resolution 20, 50, 51
Returnees, 35; to North Korea, 41–42, 76; prejudice against, 16–17, 67
Rhee, Syngman (Yi Seung-Man): ROK administration of, 10, 31, 33, 34, 156–57; in United States, 158, 160, 161, 162, 164, 198nn15, 17, 18
Rika Hiroshi (Yi Yang-Su), 44–46
ROK. *See* South Korea
Russian Far East, 21
Ryu Yong-gi, 176

Saitō Dae-Won (Kang Dae-Won), 90–91, 93, 94, 95, 102, 104
San Francisco Peace Treaty, 7, 45, 155
San Francisco School Board, 158
SCAP. *See* Supreme Commander for the Allied Powers
School Education Plan, 132
Schools: Chongryun, 66–67, 68, 69–71, 136, 189n8; government policies and, 75–76; Japanese public, 71–72, 130; closure of Korean, 30, 32, 190n13
Sebald, William J., 34
Selective Service System, 148
Self-Defense Force, 77, 79
Self-government: Korean independence and, 26
Self-victimization: kidnappings, 17–18
Senjin, 5, 7, 127
Seo Jae-Pil (Philip Jaisohn), 158
September 11, 2001: impacts on civil rights, 152

Sexual discrimination: in Chongryun schools, 70–71
Shiga Prefecture, 142
Shigemitsu Mamoru, 48
Shikuma Saburo, 154
Shimonoseki, 29
Sinminhoe, 159
Sino-Japanese War, 78
Slavery: sexual, 79
Snow, Jack, 36
Soap operas, 63, 78, 168
Social justice, 107
Society of Help Returnees to North Korea, 46
Sokuhō Ikkyō, 91–92, 95–96, 100, 102, 104
Son Masayoshi, 169
South Americans: in Japan, 133
South Korea, 3, 7, 8–9, 31, 42, 168, 182n9; Japanese relationships with, 52, 63, 66, 90, 136, 168–69; Joryeon and, 156–57; and repatriation to North Korea, 49, 50; U.S. occupation of, 16, 17, 26, 30, 51; visits to, 171–72
South Korean Information and Security Agency, 11
South Koreans, 9, 10, 90, 182–83n16; in Japan, 11–12, 68–69; returnees, 16–17
South Kyongsang Province, 35
South Pacific, 21, 38
Soviet Union, 30; Koreans in, 1, 21, 25; and North Korea, 51–52, 186n26
"Staff Study Concerning Koreans in Japan," 31, 33
Standard of living, 26, 58, 67–68
Statelessness, 84, 191n6
Stereotyping: of Koreans, 18, 27
Stevens, Durham, 160
Stimson, Henry, 161–62
Students: Chongryun, 66–67, 68; female, 64–65, 73–75
Subversive Activities Prevention Law, 66, 189n6
Supreme Commander for the Allied Powers (SCAP), 30, 33, 35; and Joryeon, 155–57; ethnic Korean schools, 129–30; and Koreans in Japan, 153–55, 184n9

Tabunka kyōsei, 142–44
Tachikawa city, 143
Taiwan, 21
Taiwanese: as Japanese nationals, 126, 197n9; in postwar Japan, 29, 30, 128
Takao Ozawa v. United States, 158
Takatsuki city, 135
Taminzoku kyōsei jinken kyōiku sentā, 136
Teachers, 132
Tei Taikin (Chung Daekyun), 177, 178; assimilation and naturalization, 173–74; *Zainichi kankokujin no shūen*, 174–75
Tejūgikokujin no chihōsanseiken o jitsugensaeru nichi, kan, zainichi nettowāku, 137
Television, 63, 78, 168
Tiger Brigade, 161
Tokkabi, 135
Tokyo, 38, 75–76, 136, 190n13
T-1 Korean School, 80; girls' uniforms, 69–71, 72; government policies, 75–76
Toru Hayano, 78
Tourism: to South Korea, 168
Toyoshi, 44–45

Unemployment, 37, 38
Uniforms: Chongryun student, 70, 72, 73, 74
United Korean Committee of America, 161, 198n18
United Nations, 182n8; Decade for Human Rights Education, 141–42; and Korean Peninsula, 51, 52
U.N. Universal Declaration of Human Rights, 45, 66, 187–88n36
United States, 8, 38, 51, 191–92n9, 197n11; citizenship in, 151–52, 162–63, 197n4; Korean citizenship, 157–58; Korean independence movement,

22, 25–26, 160–61; Koreans in, 1, 19, 21, 25, 147, 159–60, 197–98nn12, 13, 19; naturalization policies, 148–49; North Korean repatriation, 52, 54, 55; occupation of Japan, 28, 129, 166, 197n8; in occupied Korea, 23, 26, 30, 31–36, 184nn9, 12; postwar occupations, 16, 17, 29; World War II, 161–62
U.S. Citizenship and Immigration Service, 148
U.S. Enemy Property Central Office, 35
U.S. Military Government: in Korea, 26, 30, 35–36, 38
Uprisings: in Kobe and Osaka, 30, 189n7

Vietnamese, 135
Violence, 78; against Korean students, 62, 73, 75
Visas, 68
Voting rights, 136–37, 142; impairment of, 152, 154–55
Weck, Eugene de, 48
Welfare, 49, 57
Wilson, Woodrow: "Fourteen Points" speech, 160
Wind Society *(Paramu no kai)*, 13
Winter Sonata (Fuyu no sonata) (soap opera), 63, 78, 168
Women: comfort, 79; dress of Korean, 72–73

World War II, 1, 4, 6, 8, 21, 27; Japanese American internment, 151–52; Korean categorization during, 161–62
Wyoming, 160

Yamada, Mrs., 59
Yamagami Mika, 92, 95–96, 100–101, 104
Yao city, 135
Yi Seung-Man. *See* Rhee, Syngman
Yi Yang-Su, 44–46, 58, 59
Yobo, 4
Yoshida Shigeru, 31
Young Pioneers, 70
Youth: film depiction of *zainichi*, 108–14

Zainichi, 4, 11, 84, 107, 124, 194n2, 195n24; apolitical, 100–101, 104–5; coalition-building, 135–38, 196nn28, 33; criticism of, 175–76; ethnic signaling by, 92–97; film depictions of, 108–19; as foreign nationals, 129–33, 138–39, 144–46; identity politics for, 18, 19, 133–35, 169–78; Japanese treatment of, 56–57; marriage, 81–82, 92; national health care for, 139–40; repatriation of, 46–55; revealing, 97–100
Zainichi (Kang Sang-jung), 170–72
"Zainichi korian no kokuseki shutokuken" kakuritsu kyōgikai, 145

Printed in Great Britain
by Amazon